THE BEST OF
CRAZYHORSE

THE BEST OF

CRAZYHORSE

*Thirty Years of
Poetry and Fiction*

*Edited by
David Jauss*

The University of Arkansas Press
Fayetteville · London ·· 1990

Copyright © 1990 by
The Board of Trustees of the University of Arkansas
All rights reserved
Manufactured in the United States of America
94 93 92 91 90   5 4 3 2 1

DESIGNER: Chiquita Babb
TYPEFACE: Caledonia

The paper used in this publication meets the minimum requirements
of the American National Standard for Permanence of Paper for
Printed Library Materials Z39.48-1984. ∞

LIBRARY OF CONGRESS CATALOGING-IN-PUBLICATION DATA

The Best of Crazyhorse: thirty years of poetry and fiction / edited
by David Jauss.
     p.   cm.
   ISBN 1-55728-164-5 (alk. paper)—ISBN 1-55728-165-3 (pbk. :
   alk. paper)
     1. American literature—20th century.   I. Jauss, David.
II. Crazyhorse.   III. Title: Best of Crazyhorse.
PS536.2.B47   1990
810.8'0054—dc20   89-20642
                                                    CIP

To Tom McGrath,
who started it all,
and to Deb and Edith Wylder,
who kept it going

ACKNOWLEDGMENTS

Lee K. Abbott: "The Eldest of Things" is reprinted by permission of the author.

Agha Shahid Ali: "A Lost Memory of Delhi" copyright © 1987 by Agha Shahid Ali. Reprinted from *The Half-Inch Himalayas* by permission of Wesleyan University Press.

Barbara Anderson: "The Coat" from *Junk City* by Barbara Anderson, Persea Books, 1987. Reprinted by permission of the author.

Jack Anderson: "Phalaris and the Bull: A Story and an Examination" is reprinted by permission of the author.

Jon Anderson: "The Cypresses" and "Homage to Robert Bresson" are reprinted by permission of the author.

John Ashbery: "On Autumn Lake" copyright © 1974 by John Ashbery. Reprinted by permission of Georges Borchardt, Inc. and the author.

David Baker: "Call across the Years" is reprinted from *Haunts*, copyright © 1985 by David Baker, by permission of the author and Cleveland State University.

Marvin Bell: "In America" is reprinted by permission of the author. Copyright © 1987 by Marvin Bell.

Robert Bly: "Counting Small-Boned Bodies" and "Melancholia" from *The Light Around the Body* by Robert Bly. Copyright © 1967 by Robert Bly. Reprinted by permission of Harper & Row, Publishers, Inc. "Unrest in 1961" is reprinted by permission of the author.

Michael Dennis Browne: "Robert Bly Gets Up Early" from *The Sun Fetcher* by Michael Dennis Browne, Carnegie-Mellon University Press, 1978. Reprinted by permission of the author.

Christopher Buckley: "Kees at 70" from *Other Lives* by Christopher Buckley, Ithaca House, 1985. Reprinted by permission of the author.

Frederick Busch: "Greetings from a Far-Flung Place" from *Absent Friends* by

Frederick Busch, Alfred A. Knopf, Inc., 1989. Copyright © Frederick Busch. Reprinted by permission of the author.

Henry Carlile: "Four Variations on the Invisible Bittern" is reprinted by permission of the author.

Raymond Carver: "You Don't Know What Love Is" from *At Night the Salmon Move* by Raymond Carver, Capra Press, 1976. Reprinted by permission of the Estate of Raymond Carver. "Bonnard's Nudes" and "The Young Fire Eaters of Mexico City" from *Ultramarine* by Raymond Carver, Random House, Inc., 1986. Reprinted by permission of the Estate of Raymond Carver.

Richard Cecil: "The Interrupted Nap" from *Einstein's Brain* by Richard Cecil, University of Utah Press, copyright © 1986 by Richard Cecil. Reprinted by permission of the University of Utah Press.

Philip Dacey: "The Winter Thing" from *The Man with Red Suspenders* by Philip Dacey, Milkweed Editions, 1986. Reprinted by permission of the author.

Kate Daniels: "Elegy" is reprinted from *The White Wave* by Kate Daniels by permission of the University of Pittsburgh Press. Copyright © 1984 by Kate Daniels.

Deborah Digges: "Completing Some Medical Drawings" is reprinted by permission of the author.

Stephen Dobyns: "Beauty" is reprinted by permission of the author. Copyright © by Stephen Dobyns.

Susan Dodd: "Wild Men of Borneo" from *Old Wives' Tales* by Susan Dodd, The University of Iowa Press, copyright © 1984 by Susan Dodd. Reprinted by permission of The University of Iowa Press.

Mark Doty: "Turtle, Swan" is reprinted from *Turtle, Swan* by Mark Doty. Copyright © 1987 by Mark Doty. Reprinted by permission of David R. Godine, Publisher.

Norman Dubie: "La Pampa" is reprinted from *The Spring House* by Norman Dubie by permission of W. W. Norton & Co., Inc. Copyright © 1986 by Norman Dubie.

Andre Dubus: "Sorrowful Mysteries" is reprinted from *The Times are Never So Bad* by Andre Dubus. Copyright © 1983 by Andre Dubus. Reprinted by permission of David R. Godine, Publisher.

Stephen Dunn: "Tucson" is reprinted by permission of the author. "Letter About Myself to You" from *Work and Love* by Stephen Dunn, Carnegie-Mellon University Press, 1981. Reprinted by permission of the author.

Pam Durban: "In Darkness" is reprinted from *All Set About with Fever Trees* by Pam Durban. Copyright © 1985 by Pam Durban. Reprinted by permission of David R. Godine, Publisher.

Cornelius Eady: "Sherbet" is reprinted by permission of the author. Copyright © 1987 by Cornelius Eady.

Russell Edson: "The Meeting" and "Elephants" are reprinted by permission of the author.

John Engels: "I Dream of Roy Hanna" is reprinted by permission of the author. "In the Palais Royale Ballroom" from *Weather-Fear: New & Selected Poems 1958–1982* by John Engels, University of Georgia Press, 1983. Reprinted by permission of the author.

John Engman: "One Minute of Night Sky" from *Keeping Still, Mountain* by John Engman, Galileo Press, copyright © 1983 by John Engman. Reprinted by permission of the author.

Elizabeth Evans: "Americans" is reprinted by permission of the author.

Carolyn Forché: "This Need Not Have Been So" is reprinted by permission of the author. Copyright © 1978, 1979, 1980–1989 by Carolyn Forché.

H. E. Francis: "The Cleaning Woman" is reprinted by permission of the author.

James Galvin: "Almost Noon" and "Little Anthem" are reprinted by permission of the author.

Gary Gildner: "The Wake on Goose River, North Dakota" from *Nails* by Gary Gildner, University of Pittsburgh Press, copyright © 1975 by Gary Gildner. Reprinted by permission of the author.

Albert Goldbarth: "Camera Lucida" is reprinted by permission of the author.

Patricia Hampl: "Last Letter" from *Resort and Other Poems* by Patricia Hampl, Houghton Mifflin, Inc., 1983. Reprinted by permission of the author and Houghton Mifflin, Inc. "Mozart during a Snowstorm" is reprinted by permission of the author.

James Hannah: "Breaking and Entering" from *Desperate Measures* by James Hannah, Southern Methodist University Press, 1988. Reprinted by permission of the author.

William Hathaway: "Why That's Bob Hope" is reprinted by permission of the author.

Edward Hirsch: "Paul Celan: A Grave and Mysterious Sentence" from *Wild Gratitude* by Edward Hirsch, Alfred A. Knopf, Inc., copyright © 1986 by Edward Hirsch. Reprinted by permission of the author.

Tony Hoagland: "One Season" is reprinted by permission of the author.

Garrett Kaoru Hongo: "Mendocino Rose" copyright © 1988 by Garrett Kaoru Hongo. Reprinted from *The River of Heaven* by Garrett Kaoru Hongo by permission of Alfred A. Knopf, Inc.

Andrew Hudgins: "Rebuilding a Bird" is reprinted by permission of the author.

Richard Hugo: "Confederate Graves in Little Rock" from *Sea Lanes Out* by Richard Hugo, Dooryard Press, 1983, and *Making Certain It Goes On: Collected Poems of Richard Hugo*, W. W. Norton & Co., 1984. Reprinted by permission of the Estate of Richard Hugo.

Lynda Hull: "Arias, 1971" and "1933" from *Ghost Money* by Lynda Hull, University of Massachusetts Press, 1986. Reprinted by permission of the author.

Richard Jackson: "Shadows" is reprinted by permission of the author.

Mark Jarman: "Good Friday" and "Miss Urquhart's Tiara" are reprinted by permission of the author. Copyright © by Mark Jarman.

Louis Jenkins: "The Plagiarist" is reprinted by permission of the author.

David Michael Kaplan: "In the Realm of the Herons" copyright © 1987 by David Michael Kaplan. Reprinted from *Comfort* by David Michael Kaplan by permission of Viking Penguin, Inc., and Brandt & Brandt Literary Agents, Inc.

Richard Katrovas: "Alley Flower" copyright © 1986 by Richard Katrovas. Reprinted from *Snug Harbor* by permission of Wesleyan University Press.

W. P. Kinsella: "Pretend Dinners" copyright © W. P. Kinsella. Reprinted by permission of Oberon Press.

Maxine Kumin: "Brushing the Aunts" from *Our Ground Time Here Will Be Brief* by Maxine Kumin. Copyright © 1975 by Maxine Kumin. All rights reserved. Reprinted by permission of Viking Penguin, a division of Penguin Books USA, Inc. "Introducing the Fathers" from *The Long Approach* by Maxine Kumin. Copyright © 1983 by Maxine Kumin. All rights reserved. Reprinted by permission of Viking Penguin, a division of Penguin Books USA, Inc.

Robert Lacy: "The Natural Father" is reprinted by permission of the author. Copyright © 1987 by Robert Lacy.

Philip Levine: "North" is reprinted by permission of the author. Copyright © by Philip Levine.

Larry Levis: "The Blue Hatband" from *The Dollmaker's Ghost* by Larry Levis, E. P. Dutton, Inc., 1982. Reprinted by permission of the author. "For the Country" is reprinted from *Wrecking Crew* by Larry Levis by permission of the University of Pittsburgh Press. Copyright © 1972 by Larry Levis.

Gary Margolis: "Between Us" is reprinted by permission of the author.

Bobbie Ann Mason: "Murphey's Pond" is reprinted by permission of the author. Copyright © 1985 by Bobbie Ann Mason.

William Matthews: "Driving Alongside the Housatonic River Alone on a Rainy April Night" is reprinted by permission of the author. "Kingston" from *Rising and Falling* by William Matthews and "An Elegy for Bob Marley" from *A Happy Childhood* by William Matthews. Copyright © 1973, 1974, 1975, 1976, 1977, 1978, 1979, 1983 by William Matthews. Reprinted by permission of Little, Brown and Company.

Thomas McGrath: "Gone Away Blues" and "Proletarian in Abstract Light" are reprinted by permission of Martin H. McGrath.

Sandra McPherson: "Picketing our Anti-Choice Senator at Reed College, September 1982" is reprinted by permission of the author. Copyright © 1985 by Sandra McPherson.

David Mura: "Listening" is reprinted by permission of the author. "The Emergency Room" from *After We Lost Our Way* by David Mura. Copyright © 1989 by David Mura. Reprinted by permission of E. P. Dutton, Inc.

Jack Myers: "The Energy It Takes to Pass Through Solid Objects" is reprinted by permission of the author.

William Olsen: "The Unicorn Tapestries" from *The Hand of God and a Few Bright Flowers* by William Olsen, University of Illinois Press, 1988. Reprinted by permission of the University of Illinois Press.

Steve Orlen: "Bagatelles" is reprinted by permission of the author.

Stanley Plumly: "American Ash" and "With Stephen in Maine" are reprinted by permission of the author.

David Rivard: "The Venice of the North" is reprinted from *Torque* by David Rivard by permission of the University of Pittsburgh Press. Copyright © 1988 by David Rivard.

Vern Rutsala: "This Life, This Day" from *Ruined Cities* by Vern Rutsala, Carnegie-Mellon University Press, copyright © 1987 by Vern Rutsala. Reprinted by permission of the author.

Peter Sacks: "Valerie" is reprinted by permission of Macmillan Publishing Company from *In These Mountains* by Peter Sacks. Copyright © 1986 by Peter Sacks.

Ira Sadoff: "At the Half-Note Cafe" is reprinted from *Emotional Traffic* by Ira Sadoff. Copyright © 1989 by Ira Sadoff. Reprinted by permission of David R. Godine, Publisher.

Dennis Schmitz: "For Raymond Roseliep" is reprinted by permission of the author.

Sheila Schwartz: "Mutatis Mutandis" is reprinted by permission of the author.

Charles Simic: "Brooms" and "Gravity" are reprinted by permission of the author.

Louis Simpson: "Akhmatova's Husband" from *The Best Hour of the Night* by Louis Simpson. Copyright © 1983 by Louis Simpson. Reprinted by permission of Ticknor & Fields, a Houghton Mifflin company.

Arthur Smith: "A Little Death" is reprinted by permission of the author.

Dave Smith: "Sunday Morning: Celia's Father" from *In the House of the Judge,* Harper & Row, 1983. Reprinted by permission of the author.

Ken Smith: "The Nicest Man" is reprinted from *Decoys and Other Stories* by Ken Smith. Copyright © 1985 by Ken Smith. Reprinted by permission of Confluence Press.

Gary Soto: "Heaven" is reprinted from *Black Hair* by Gary Soto by permission of the University of Pittsburgh Press. Copyright © 1985 by Gary Soto.

William Stafford: "The Earth" from *Stories That Could Be True* by William Stafford. Copyright © 1971 by William Stafford. "The Color That Really Is" from *A Glass Face in the Rain* by William Stafford. Copyright © 1979 by William

Stafford. "By a River in the Osage Country" from *An Oregon Message* by William Stafford. Copyright © 1987 by William Stafford. All reprinted by permission of Harper & Row, Publishers, Inc.

Maura Stanton: "Good People" from *Tales of the Supernatural* by Maura Stanton. Copyright © 1988 by Maura Stanton. Reprinted by permission of David R. Godine, Publisher. "Oz" from *The Country I Come From* by Maura Stanton, Milkweed Editions, 1988. Reprinted by permission of Milkweed Editions.

Gerald Stern: "Souls from Emerson" and "Weeping and Wailing" from *Paradise Poems* by Gerald Stern. Copyright © 1984 by Gerald Stern. Reprinted by permission of Random House, Inc.

Leon Stokesbury: "Lauds" is reprinted by permission of the author.

Barton Sutter: "Telling Time in the Middle of Nowhere" is reprinted by permission of the author.

Jeanie Thompson: "Thinking of Kay in Grasmere" from *How to Enter the River* by Jeanie Thompson, Holy Cow! Press, 1985. Reprinted by permission of the author.

John Updike: "All the While" (from "Living with a Wife") copyright © 1972 by John Updike. Reprinted from *Tossing and Turning* by John Updike by permission of Alfred A. Knopf, Inc.

David Wagoner: "The Singing Lesson" is reprinted by permission of the author.

Michael Waters: "Bonwit Teller" from *Anniversary of the Air* by Michael Waters, Carnegie-Mellon University Press, 1985. Reprinted by permission of the author.

Mary Jane White: "Jane Austen, Privately, on Reading" from *The Work of the Icon Painter* by Mary Jane White, Osiers Press, 1979. Reprinted by permission of the author.

C. K. Williams: "Still Life" from *Poems 1963–1983* by C. K. Williams. Copyright © 1969, 1971, 1977, 1983, 1988 by C. K. Williams. Reprinted by permission of Farrar, Straus & Giroux, Inc.

Miller Williams: "For Victor Jara" from *The Boys on Their Bony Mules* by Miller Williams, Louisiana State University Press, copyright © 1983 by Miller Williams. Reprinted by permission of Louisiana State University Press.

David Wojahn: "Particular Words" and "Song of the Burning" are reprinted from *Glassworks* by David Wojahn by permission of the University of Pittsburgh Press. Copyright © 1987 by David Wojahn.

Susan Wood: "Witness" is reprinted by permission of the author.

Charles Wright: "Childhood's Body" from *The Southern Cross* by Charles Wright, Random House, Inc., 1981. Reprinted by permission of the author. "Grace" copyright © 1972 by Charles Wright. Reprinted from *Hard Freight* by permission of Wesleyan University Press.

James Wright: "Caprice" and "On Having My Pocket Picked in Rome" copy-

❖

The editor wishes to express his gratitude to the previous and current editors of *Crazyhorse*, without whose dedicated and talented work neither the magazine nor this anthology would exist: editors Tom McGrath, Eugenia McGrath, Philip Dacey, and Howard Mohr; poetry editors James Galvin, Jorie Graham, David Wojahn, Ralph Burns, Lynda Hull, and Dean Young; fiction editor Joe Ashby Porter; criticism editor Dennis Vannatta; and managing editors Tom McGrath, Eugenia McGrath, Delbert Wylder, Edith Wylder, Russell Murphy, and K. Z. D. Stodola. These editors were assisted in their work by associate poetry editors Larry Levis, Nanette Kondrit, Ralph D. Eberly, Alice Ann Munson, Johnye Strickland, Marck Beggs-Uema, Sascha Feinstein, Rick Madigan, and Christa Hein; associate fiction editors Pam Durban, John Stratton, Russell Murphy, K. Z. D. Stodola, Christie Stobaugh, and Lila Havens; and associate criticism editor Stephen Tatum.

The editor is also grateful to the University of Arkansas at Little Rock for its generous support of *Crazyhorse* and this anthology. In particular, he wishes to thank Chancellor James Young, Vice Chancellor and Provost Joel Anderson, Vice Chancellor John Shelby, Dean Lloyd Benjamin, Associate Dean John Miller, Director of Development Wayne Davenport, and Professors Cal Ledbetter and Barry Maid.

CONTENTS

Contents xvii

In compiling this anthology, I have tried to do three things: select the best works published during *Crazyhorse's* thirty-year history, represent as many of its finest contributors as space would allow, and reflect some of the major trends in our literature during the past three decades. Of these three aims, the first was most important to me, for I believe the chief responsibility of an anthologist is to call attention to excellence. "The excellent," Aristotle tells us, "becomes the permanent," and I hope *The Best of Crazyhorse* helps the excellent poems and stories published in the magazine achieve the permanence they deserve. I also hope it leads readers to discover the many excellent poems and stories that *aren't* included. There simply wasn't enough room to include all of the worthy works published in the past thirty years (this is especially true of three brilliant novellas, Andre Dubus' "Molly," Andre Dubus III's "The Cage Keeper," and Barton Sutter's "My Father's War"), and the reader who turns to back issues of the magazine will find there many other poems and stories that deserve to last.

The primary aim of the anthology, then, is to call attention to the finest work of its contributors. But I also hope it will call attention to the superb work done by the magazine's many editors. *Crazyhorse* would not have lasted three years, much less three decades, if it were not for their inspired work.

The magazine's first editor was the poet Tom McGrath. He founded *Crazy Horse* (as it was then spelled) in Los Angeles in 1960 and over the next ten years made it one of the sixties' most eloquent proponents for political change. Under his guidance, the magazine attacked American militarism and capitalism with the vehemence and daring with which its namesake, the great Sioux chief, attacked Custer at the battle of the Little Big Horn. And its approach to poetry was as revolutionary as its approach to politics. In the first issue's "Manifesto," McGrath states that *Crazy Horse* wasn't interested "in either the shrunken trophies of the academic head-hunters nor in those mammoth cod-pieces stuffed with falsies, the primitive inventions of the Nouveau Beat." Instead, he calls for "a poetry where the surrealist lions of Lorca and the classically magnetic lambs of Marvell and Crane fly up together" as well as for "satire, japery, extravagance, humor, Brecht, case histories, parody, practical jokes, Criticism"—in short, "everything to help blow up the system."

As Deb Wylder noted in his introduction to *Crazyhorse*'s spring 1979 issue, "Like the Oglala Sioux and their great chief for whom the magazine was named, *Crazyhorse* has been nomadic." By the end of the sixties, it, and McGrath, had moved from Los Angeles to New York, then to North Dakota State University and Moorhead State University in Moorhead, Minnesota. In 1970, it moved to Southwest State University in Marshall, Minnesota, where, after McGrath's resignation, Philip Dacey became editor. Although Dacey and subsequent editors continued to publish political poetry, in the seventies the emphasis shifted away from politics—and from surrealism, Deep Images, and "extravagance"—toward more mainstream literary values. By 1976, when Dacey resigned and Howard Mohr took over as editor, *Crazy Horse* had become one of the most respected little magazines of the early seventies.

In 1977, Deb and Edith Wylder, who had been instrumental in acquiring *Crazy Horse* for Southwest State University, moved to Kentucky, and in 1978, when the journal fell on hard times in Minnesota, they acquired it for Murray State University. There, they established the journal's independence from its past by changing the spelling of its name to *Crazyhorse* and by expanding the issues to include fiction and, occasionally, critical essays. Under their guidance, the magazine grew not only in size—from 40 to 110 pages—but in reputation. Thanks to the work of poetry editors Jorie Graham and James Galvin and fiction editor Joe Ashby Porter, by the end of the decade *Crazyhorse* was widely regarded as one of the country's premier journals.

In 1981, the magazine moved to Arkansas, where it has enjoyed the support of the citizens of the state, who contributed money for its purchase, and the University of Arkansas at Little Rock, which has generously supported its publication. For most of the eighties, David Wojahn served as poetry editor (he resigned in 1986 and was replaced by Ralph Burns, then returned to the post in 1988 and since then has selected the poetry with the help of co-editors Lynda Hull and Dean Young), and throughout the decade, Dennis Vannatta served as criticism editor, and I served as fiction editor. Under the direction of managing editors Russell Murphy (1983–87) and K. Z. D. Stodola (1987–present), *Crazyhorse* has expanded—a typical issue now contains 145 pages—and criticism has become a regular feature. What hasn't changed is the commitment to quality that is evident throughout the magazine's history. During the eighties, poems and stories originally published in *Crazyhorse* were reprinted in the annual *Pushcart Prize* and *Best American Short Stories* collections and in many other books and anthologies.

In 1987, *Library Journal* ranked *Crazyhorse* in the top twenty of the several thousand magazines that publish poetry in the United States and in 1990, after polling more than one hundred editors and agents, *Writer's Digest* named it one of the fifty most influential magazines publishing fiction today.

Few literary journals have been around for the past three decades, and fewer still tell us more about our literature, and ourselves, during that time. I hope *The Best of Crazyhorse* gives adequate testimony to the accomplishments of the writers and editors whose work has made the magazine, in the words of Raymond Carver, "an indispensable literary magazine of the first order." And I hope it inspires writers and readers to help the magazine not only survive but thrive for another thirty years.

THE BEST OF
CRAZYHORSE

LEE K. ABBOTT

Lee K. Abbott was born in the
Panama Canal Zone in 1947 and
raised in New Mexico. He has
published four collections of sto-
ries, most recently *Strangers in
Paradise* and *Dreams of Distant
Lives*. He teaches at Ohio State
University.

THE ELDEST OF THINGS

Mozer's first dealer was a Latino named Spoon who roared up Chester out of Hough each Thursday in a vintage black-over-white Mercury so sweetly tuned it seemed capable of speech—a thunder as throaty and pure, Spoon told him once, as sex itself. Spoon would park behind the Church of the Covenant, and Mozer would appear a little after noon, just before his class in the Romantics. The method was always the same: Spoon would say "Man!" and "Madre!" and "Don't be sneaking up like that, hombre!" and Mozer would slip himself into that auto slowly and with great ceremony, its interior so full of red plush and shiny leathers it could have been the giant steel shoe of Satan himself. Spoon always had the radio tuned to JMO, or another spade station, his head, with its fer-

3

tile hair-do, bobbing to a rhythm he often identified as equal parts funk and blood-stuff, the bass in the door speakers so heavy it seemed to pound on Mozer's leg, maybe make a bruise, leave a welt. Spoon always dealt primo toot, iced and crystal, white enough to be a starlet's thigh, which he presented to Mozer in a glassine packet, rolling his Juarez eyeballs heavenward, saying the blow in question was either Chilean or direct from the Golden Triangle, strong enough to bend iron or set off train noises in the deep, primitive corners of your brainpan. Mozer always did a sample, which was protocol, the first snort bitter and laden enough to send him in search of words like *churl* and *hunch*—a language of need and its fulfillment. Then he paid, in old bills, Spoon the superstitious sort who thought of new money the way the Huns thought of, say, achievement in bronze. They'd say adios, Spoon still caught up in the throes of thump and new music. "You be careful," Spoon would say. "Maybe one day you don't want no more nose, okay? Maybe you go loco, want to be a bird or flashy gangster."

The female came into Mozer's life during that one semester he was calling Coleridge and Keats "tangents of lust" and "the milk-spurned bards of indecent closure," a pair like Mutt and Jeff, one full of limp and midnight oil, the other a dingus on the upside of the perilous peak that was a wintry but heartening time of versifiers. It was the coke, he figured, that made him blabber that way: the several lines before class each Tuesday and Thursday that spun him into the lecture hall in a state which he accepted as wired and supreme, all about him afflicted and cast low. His lessons were exercises in wonder, breathless accounts of perfection and the mysteries which attend knowledge, which invariably ended with him throwing off his sportcoat, or climbing onto his chair, and shaking his fists as if he were leaving this life for fable and legend.

Elaine Winston was a Miltonist, a first-year assistant professor with an office on the first floor, and, as he learned happily, herself mad with learning. His hair slicked back, he went to her one day, followed her into her office after seeing in her face what he was convinced was portance and, well, theophany. "Miss Winston," he said, his voice full of his Louisiana upbringing, "lookee here." Yet, before she could sit, even before she could say "Hello," Mozer placed on her desk a vial of fluff Spoon said could launch you into Deity-ville by way of your own biles and ferments.

It was Colombian rock, Spoon had said, mayhaps as old as the earth itself, on account of it had evil in it, which led to an expanded view of the universe, which led in ultimate terms to a consideration of shit like Hierarchy and Ultimacy itself. Mondo heavy stuff. Made you wanna bark, perform a foulness with your fingers. Took the contemplation right out of daily business of finding and keeping.

Both of them agreed later that it was no surprise that immediately, her hands steady with purpose, she opened the vial and, with the patience of a DEA assassin, laid out two thin but exact lines. After all, she told Mozer, she'd read the literatures and had been at the movies; plus she'd watched TV and, in her UC-Santa Barbara days, had tried root and downers and something which a now-lost boyfriend had described as Laotian, a melted fungus which you waved before your lips and lugged with you into Old Night—which was what Mozer yearned to hear; so, as he locked the door and switched off the light and unzipped her teacher's skirt, he was saying the Lady—the toot, the snow—was, like themselves, the outmost work of Nature, much beyond havoc and spoil; and that they, Elaine Winston and himself, Richard E. Mozer (of Tulane and the University of Texas-Austin), would soon be passing beyond tumult and din for the uplifting horizons of organized beauties and that composite body in which incorruptible matter predominates, love.

For months after this, through a Cleveland winter frigid and piled with ice and into a glorious spring, Mozer's lectures were magic and biology both—hour sessions even the student newspaper, *The Observer*, in an unsigned editorial called bifurcated and multifarious and "the eldest of things." One period Dr. Mozer spent on Shelley's "Music, When Soft Voices Die," spotting in its eight lines neither the beloved nor the quick," but privation and deficiency—in his mind the vision of a serpent with hips leading a legion of duteous and knee-crooking knaves. When he grabbed the chalk and dashed to the board to scrawl figures of analysis, he looked like a caveman, his face beleaguered, as if he'd embraced all his rascally needs. He told Elaine Winston, and she him, that they were entering a time of gulf and effulgence and pouring forth—a time washed by the waters of Abana and Pharpar, a time of fawn, renegado and hapless wight! During another class period, when he was to be addressing the horned moon and Mr. E. K. Chamber's *A Sheaf of Studies*, he fixed his head against the bosom of Mindy Griffith, a South Philadelphia sophomore COSI major, and claimed to hear, through her sweater and blouse and brassiere, not the heart but the steady, fairyland tromp-tromp of Mister Wordsworth's footsteps in the Rydale woods. "No bramble," he whispered. "No evergreen, no palm." There, holding her by the shoulders, he said there was in her courage and outlawry, even the wonted face renewed.

That March, when he should have been concerned that Elaine Winston was speaking of warmth and beach fronts and sweat, he began telling his classes about his family—his mother, who'd once been institutionalized because of her affections for Bacardi and Teacher's but who was now living with his younger brother in a rainy place called, could you believe it, Astoria, Oregon, elevation six feet, and who wrote letters with the m's and n's upside down, in which she remarked upon the past as if it were a machine that made laughter; and his father, who'd died four years ago from everything that could tempt man, including neglect of the spiritual realms and a Puritan's belief in powers slash principalities, not to mention splintered veins and a life whose wholesome moments were all twenty million years gone. And one day, after taking a richness from Spoon that was said to have come from the very ash, honest, of the rood itself, he informed his class, while his organs beat like a Sousa drum corps, that he'd had no youth at all, that he had vaulted across the decades, from gamete to scholar, without benefit of the swerve and downwardness of adolescence; and that, were he to marry, it would be to a woman whose face had something in it of friskiness and of thorn.

That afternoon, drinking Pepsi under a young maple in front of Gund Hall, Mozer told Elaine Winston of the goody Spoon had promised him: a mixture likened to the tears of a lost people—the Goths, say—cocaine cut with the subsoil those NASA technicians at Lewis Research Center were bringing back from Uranus, stuff that made fire of water, earth of air, Lord, he said, it was itself love. Which was the gift, he told Professor Winston, he most wanted to give her, conveying this wish by licking her hands and mentioning conglobed atoms and seminal forms and female divinity. "No," she said. "I can't." He told her he imagined them on the flaming ramparts of the world, him craftly and gaunt, her light incarnate. "I'm sorry," she said. "It's impossible." He mentioned glimmer and heartbaking rays and splendor. "Please," she sobbed, "no more." It was love, he said, and were she coke, he would now be at her toes, she that blessed white rail that stretched to infinity, she that orbit of song and purity; he was ready, he insisted, for bliss.

It was then, while he kissed her cheeks and eyes and forehead, that she confessed she'd taken another job. In Florida. She would be leaving at the end of the term.

During April, Mozer got used to the idea she was leaving by rededicating himself to his work. It was, he would say later, his period of plucking up and casting out, a time of victual and wound. He scratched out a paper on "So We'll Go No More A-Roving" for the MMLA section on Byron for the St. Louis meeting, a paper he delivered with such a sorcerer's fury that it appeared to many in the Marriott suite that, at a mention of laurel and myrtle, he might burst into flame. He mumbled about "features of intelligent genera" and marched into class wearing a rag around his ears, saying he was pity and Dido's pyre, that heavy-headed carouser who was the sin of apotheosis given tendon and hackle. In one class, rolling on a circuit made smooth and gleaming by two lines of what Spoon claimed was crystal chipped from the planet's first tree, Dr. Mozer forged a lecture that linked, in a moment quiet enough to have come from death, the Ens, the hinder parts of God's essence, and the "houmoousian," the latter of which his pupils were not to conceive of as the Father and Son and the Holy Ghost, but as Larry, Curly, and Moe—the modern Wise Men of burley-que and pain. It was an insight, Mozer noticed, that left eager Mindy Griffith limp with hope.

The following Tuesday, in the parking lot of the Church of the Covenant, the sky dark with soot, Mozer told Spoon he wanted stuff that said smote and wither, that would his soul and bounteous fortune consecrate. "An ounce," he said; Spoon, in a yellow fedora that could have come from a Mickey Spillane book, nodded gravely. "You feeling low, Doc?" he wondered. Mozer said that he and Elaine—for old time's sake, really, one final fling—were taking a room in the Shoreway Holiday Inn during finals. He used the words *mode* and *issue*. "I can dig it," Spoon said in an instant, as if it had materialized from the next world. Spoon was placing on the seat between them a Baggie which contained a substance that, to Mozer's mind, seemed, apart from its glow and density, to be living. "No mas," Spoon was saying. "As of today, I am out of the business." He was going back to Mexico, he allowed, where an acquaintance, a big-hearted caballero like himself, was in league with an hombre who knew a figure who had contact with the so-called, which might develop, given ingenuity and gorge, into a future of *resplandor*, radiance. There was mucho dinero to be made, he added. A man in the grip of an idea, he said, could go anywhere in this life. Mozer felt the world tilt, the sky crumble into a hole at the horizon. "What about me?" he said. There was music in the car, of course, like metals and whines. "I thought we had an understanding," he said. "Amigos," Spoon was making smacking noises; he said not to worry, the Professor was muy especial, he was being turned over to a gent—"like a colleague, man"—who, in Mozer's moment of need, would appear, bringing some Lady that was virtually coeternal with the Father Himself.

As he would reveal to his next dealer, The Suit, and the one to follow him, and the one to follow him, his week with Elaine Winston, now departed assistant professor, was lived in a place unapproached through necessity and chance. It was part manifestation, he said, part similitude. A haven hewn from hardiment and hazard. "There were no hard feelings," he would say, "no guilt." The first two days, they lived off room service chicken and wine and that varlet's concoction, which, Elaine swore, made you use the terms "hath" and "ye." It turned thought to deed, and that to a thing which uttered. If anything, Mozer would declare for years, they both grew more luscious: she was the bringing forth and the shining unto; he, decree and ascent. He sprinkled lines on her breasts and thighs and once entered the whooshing, ornamented, fibrous, unnettled chambers of her heart, as she sang to him of the whip and the cradle, the prattling bush and the metabole. Later, he laid a trail which led over a dresser, across the floor, to a coffee table, climbed a chair, followed the curtain folds and ended, it seemed, at the mouth of a warm cave, the first principle of things—"the junction," he hollered, "of form and meaning!" In his joy, he became ape and first man, a being of lope and skinned knuckle and savage mien.

After the third day, and until they left for the airport, they didn't again use the phone or open the drapes. One time, after not speaking for an hour, he went to her as he imagined Keats had gone to his Grecian Urn, muttering of the dales of Arcady, plus pipes and timbrels. She was lamentation, he told her. He looked into her ear, discovering a spot to put everything: his smoking brainstem, the shame and prize of himself, that ragged wind in his chest. An hour later, he found himself yelling about the cataract and trodden weed. She—no, not she alone, but she who was Eve and Sweet Betsy from Pike and Mother Hubbard and Radio City Rockette—she was garland and seashore and silk. She was, he decided, swarm populus and writ itself—chaste, messy writ, like a message from the soul. "In me, there's the rose," Elaine Winston said. And ire. And compass. And kirtled Sovereign. Mozer, collapsed against the bathroom door, was applauding. He was seeing everything, from beginning to end—from bang in the dark, through swamp and savannah and bustling boulevard, to bang in the dark. And then she stood at the end of the bed, its sheets a snarl of white, her breasts heavy and dark, her head so far away it seemed she was scraping the ceiling. There was in her, she vowed, alimental recompense and humid exhalation. She was quoting, he knew. There was, she was saying, a progeny of light. And recess of miracle. And supernal expanse. And when she finally pitched back onto the bed, exhausted, she was talking about optic emanation and preparation and the all-embracing, without which there could never be any, yes, privilege.

In the next hour he knew, even without his watch, that it was time to go, that days five and six had passed. What had come to him, he decided, was understanding; and it came when, feeding from a line that seemed composed of socket and hook and perfect mortice, he looked up and saw that her flesh was gone and what remained—what he slurped and bit and sucked, and what shouted to him of void and fathom and nitre—was not Elaine Winston, Miltonist, but his own love, brawling damp and full of fear. He saw his love as gnash and twisted limb and lips of dew. He saw it as text and high estate and supped wonders—a clamor of sally and retreat: unsorted, turbid, clip-winged and no more noble than a donkey in ferkin and wig. He saw himself as Mongol, pounding across a cedarn cove—that land of S. T. Coleridge!—hot for the maid that was passion: a chase which would take, he realized, forever.

Mozer's second dealer, The Suit, was an insurance lawyer who toiled downtown and did not care, as Spoon had, about musics or shiny vehicles. He was a Yale grad who, as promised, wanted to discuss life and the meaning thereof, who would arrange a meet in the men's room on the eighth floor of the Statler Office Tower on Euclid; and who would, before laying on Mozer crystal the size of a heavyweight's fist, address the context of coke, its bewitching history and its humble provenance. One time it was Mao-informed stuff, advanced but cryptic, scrutable only to those who knew of the universal hubbub and the mutiny of spirit. Another time the toot came from a slyboot, Lucretian kingdom and had to it much blindness and folly. On another occasion, the stuff was Hebrew, tartareous and cold.

Then there was the meeting before the start of the fall term, when Elaine had been gone for almost three months. Quietly, The Suit locked the washroom door and plucked from his jacket pocket an envelope which held what The Suit said was sublimation itself, a true sublime rumored to have come from the soaked deltas of Mars, misrule made elemental. "Jesus," The Suit said, placing the item on the counter. It appeared to be vibrating, as if it had breath and muscle. They peered at it awhile. Mozer said something about awe—the scalloped rim of the universe. The Suit nodded. Mozer said something about firmaments—the quaint auguries of nightswains. The Suit nodded. Mozer said something about glories, and when The Suit wondered what the Professor was going to do with this modern miracle, a light flickered on in Mozer's memory. He felt his brain shiver and quake, its meat darkening. He had one idea, then a second— both electric and comely, as if he were a mathematician, a man versed in the joys of problem and its solution. There was, it seemed, a machine's click in his forehead, and he saw, The Suit still at his elbow, the crooked and croupy in himself limp away into blackness. He took a deep breath— the first in months, he believed—and he heard, as if with a castaway's ears, a shout and a call, human noise after eons of silence. He was thinking about Mindy Griffith, that sophomore from Philadelphia, that one whose major in communications science had taught her, doubtlessly, the subtle and potent differences between talk and speech; yes, that fetching, unsafe creature who'd nearly left her desk that noontime when he'd read from the *Biographia* of shag and rack and dim, wicked hunter. Oh, he knew what he would do, all right. And he knew, too, that while one might say he'd have to be a pretty slimy motherfuck, at thirty-five, to hustle the innocent, another might say he'd have to be one hell of a fine person, confident as a gambler, with the guts of a Columbus, to share, to shepherd someone into that new world of love—that enchanted province of paradise and dread.

AGHA SHAHID ALI

Born in New Delhi, India, Agha
Shahid Ali earned graduate
degrees from the University of
Delhi, the University of Arizona,
and Penn State. He currently
teaches at Hamilton College. He is
the author of *The Half-Inch Hima-
layas* and several chapbooks.

A LOST MEMORY OF DELHI

I am not born
it is 1948 and the bus turns
onto a road without name

There on his bicycle
my father
He is younger than I

At Okhla where I get off
I pass my parents
strolling by the Jamuna River

My mother is a recent bride
her sari a blaze of brocade
Silverdust parts her hair

She doesn't see me
The bells of her anklets are distant
like the sound of china from

teashops being lit up with lanterns
and the stars are coming out
ringing with tongues of glass

They go into the house
always faded in photographs
in the family album

but lit up now
with the oil-lamp
I saw broken in the attic

I want to tell them I am their son
older much older than they are
I knock keep knocking

but for them the night is quiet
this the night of my being
They don't they won't

hear me they won't hear
my knocking drowning out
the tongues of stars

BARBARA ANDERSON

Barbara Anderson was born in
Brooklyn in 1947 and earned an
M.F.A. from the University of Ari-
zona, where she currently teaches.
Her most recent book, *Junk City*,
was a National Poetry Series selec-
tion in 1987.

THE COAT

The first time I noticed the blue
on the white snow was the day
my mother found a twenty dollar bill
on the way to the subway
and cautioned me to walk always
with my head to the ground
if I ever expected to find anything
in this world for free.
It was the first day my father wore
the enormous brown overcoat,
all he had left of his dead brother,

the coat I was afraid of
because I believed my father
walked everywhere like a ventriloquist
wisecracking to his fat unfunny brother
like they always had
on Sundays around the kitchen table
while my mother basted the chicken
or peeled the potatoes.
It was New Year's Day, 1961,
the upside-down year I turned over
and over again on the cover of *Mad* magazine
while my father got drunk
on the subway and joked and cried
for his brother who he would
never see again, *not for Auld Lang Syne*,
not for all the coming emptiness
of 1961 which turns over and over
like my uncle's inscrutable riddle
about the weight of gold or feathers
that I had to answer
before he would give me a silver dollar
or a chocolate kiss.
On the first day of 1961
my father cried on the subway
and my mother took the whole family
to see Natalie Wood and Warren Beatty
fall in love in a small town in Kansas
in a time my mother said she could remember,
the brief good years before the Depression,
and she was my age then, thirteen, not bitter yet, not sad.
On January 1, 1961, it was so cold
on the balcony of the Loew's Valencia
my mother allowed my father
to give me a sip of the brown liquor
and then another and another
as Natalie Wood ran hysterical

from a classroom after losing her first love
and reading a passage
from "Intimations of Immortality,"
some words about loss and strength
that I memorized as the theatre went dark again
and we all rode home a little drunk
and silent in the artificial midnight
lighting of the IRT where I wrote my first poem
and my mother counted her change like feathers or gold
and my father fell asleep on her shoulder
snoring with his ghostly brown coat wrapped around them.

JACK ANDERSON

Jack Anderson is the dance critic
for the *New York Times*. Born in
Milwaukee in 1935, he has pub-
lished seven books of poetry, in-
cluding *Toward the Liberation of
the Left Hand* and *Selected Poems*,
and six books about dance, includ-
ing *Ballet and Modern Dance: A
Concise History*.

PHALARIS AND THE BULL:
A STORY AND AN EXAMINATION

The Story:

The tyrant Phalaris locked his prisoners inside a magnificently wrought
brazen bull and tortured them over a slow fire. So that nothing unseemly
might spoil his feasting, he commanded the royal artisans to design the
bull in such a way that its smoke rose in spicy clouds of incense. When the
screams of the dying reached the tyrant's ears, they had the sound of
sweet music. And when the bull was reopened, the victims' bones shone
like jewels and were made into bracelets.

The Examination:

1. This story appears to be allegorical. Of what is it an allegory?

2. Which person or persons do you consider most vile: the tyrant Phalaris, the artisans who carried out his orders, or the court ladies who wore the bone bracelets?

3. Do you think it right that your sympathy extends almost automatically to the victims? But do you know who the victims were or why they were condemned? What if the victims had been Hitler and your twelve least favorite contemporary political figures—would this knowledge affect your sympathies?

4. Do you not sometimes wish that certain people might die, do you not long for the deaths of prime ministers or dictators, do you not envision presidents dying of heart attacks, generals shooting themselves while cleaning their rifles, skinflint landlords pushed into wells by rebellious peasants, industrialists skidding on newly waxed floors and sailing through penthouse windows, War Department scientists exposed to radiation while goosing cute researchers in the lab, demagogues exploding with the leaky gas main, your mother-in-law scalded by a pot of boiling chicken soup—do you not wish any or all of these were dead?

5. If the death of one man could bring bliss to the world, would you order that one death? If the deaths of two men could do it, would you order those two deaths? Or five deaths? Or a hundred? Or twenty million? How many deaths would you order to bring bliss to the world?

6. If it required only one man's death, after all, to bring bliss to the world and you sanctioned such a death, how would you feel should you learn that that one man was to be you?

7. Do you think that the most monstrous thing about the story of Phalaris is not that a tyrant put prisoners to death—since that has happened throughout history—but the particularly gruesome way he went about it?

8. Yet do you never catch yourself wishing that once, only once, once only but definitely once, you could sit beside the tyrant just to satisfy your curiosity about what the bull looked like, what the music sounded like?

9. Would you consider Phalaris and his artisans more, or less, reprehensible if the screams of the dying had reached the ear undisguised? If you were one of the victims, would it make any difference to you?

10. Which do you consider the more truly good man: the victim who wishes his screams to be heard as screams, or he who wishes them to be

heard as music? Do you think your answer is relevant to the problem of why at executions we praise the victim who meets his death with stoic calm and witty epigrams, rather than he who must be dragged to the scaffold pissing in his pants? In your opinion, is it or is it not a good thing that we do so?

11. Learning at this point in the examination that the first victim of the bull was the chief artisan who designed it, do you (a) believe that the artisan deserved his fate, and (b) feel vaguely uncomfortable about your own occupation, job, profession, or calling? Why or why not?

12. Based upon your interpretation of the story of Phalaris and the bull, do you view yourself in the light of your present situation in life as metaphorically equivalent to tyrant, artisan, victim, or wearer of bone jewelry?

13. And which am I?

JON ANDERSON

Born in Somerville, Massachu-
setts, in 1940, Jon Anderson is the
author of five books, including *In
Sepia, Cypresses,* and *The Milky
Way.* In 1982 he received the
Shelley Memorial Award for Ca-
reer Achievement. He teaches in
the graduate writing program at
the University of Arizona.

THE CYPRESSES

Of the leaning cypresses,
Franconati says, *These
Feathers constitute an evidence
Or inclination of God's breath.*
Seeing them from my study window
They are a gesture I begin
To understand: as the raised
Open hand, in farewell,
Salutes a depth of feeling.
Now the great ocean of wind moves,
Again the cypresses lean

& whatever their meaning,
It is a dignification, a rational
Grace, because the weight
Of even the topmost parts moves
In its own time. The wind
Is an ocean. A great armada
Of ships, pennants awash, rushes
To the horizon. They are on
An important errand, but will return
Bearing men haggard with war &
Having lived too long with the quick,
Bright meaningless striking of oars.

So this story, or poetry, first told
Among savages who were kings
In a land of cypresses by a man
Who was blind, unwinds its
Thousands of cadences: the dead are
Risen & the imagined countenanced.
When the cypresses lean again
I notice their light, slow
Tracings upon a sky full of clouds
Assuming familiar shapes;
In time, upon all the possible
Faces of all possible things.

HOMAGE TO
ROBERT BRESSON

Spaces await their people.
An alabaster row of public urinals.
An empty theater. A table,
Chairs, an oak door, heavily grained,
Brass knob turning & who
Shall enter, already lost forever

In their lives? Now
Will a soul reveal its human face,
Secret luminous flesh,
& because the soul is speechless
There will be little talk,
Better revealed in this single plate

Set like a day-moon or
Lidless eye before its chair.
Who sits shall eat, because
It is important to stay alive, to
Bear the soul's countenance
Down into the streets, their traffic,

Its endless movement. Here
A young priest, shaken, prays to give
False solace to the dying;
A girl, too young, casually prepares
To drown. Why are these
Forsaken, too long in anguish?

Why does the tree bear leaves,
The water bear downward into the earth?
This is the law, the rest
A commentary. She takes off her clothes,
Folding them. He enters
A room. Though nothing can be done,

They are not resigned.

JOHN ASHBERY

John Ashbery was born in
Rochester, New York, in 1927. His
books include *Self-Portrait in a
Convex Mirror,* which won the
Pulitzer Prize, the National Book
Award, and the National Book
Critics Circle Award, *Selected
Poems* and *April Galleons.* He is
currently art critic for *Newsweek.*

ON AUTUMN LAKE

Leading liot act to foriage is activity
Of Chinese philosopher here on Autumn Lake thoughtfully inserted in
Plovince of Quebec—stop it! I will not. The edge hugs
The lake with ever-more-paternalistic insistence, whose effect
Is in the blue way up ahead. The distance

By air from other places to here isn't much, but
It doesn't count, at least not the way the
Shore distance—leaf, tree, stone; optional (fern, frog, skunk);
And then stone, tree, leaf; then another optional—counts.

It's like the "machines" of the 19th-century Academy.
Turns out you didn't need all that training
To do art—that it was even better not to have it. Look at
The Impressionists—some of 'em had it, too, but preferred to forget it
In vast composed canvases by turns riotous
And indigent in color, from which only the notion of space is lacking.

I do not think that this
Will be my last trip to Autumn Lake.
Have some friends among many severe heads
We all scholars sitting under tree
Waiting for nut to fall. Some of us studying
Persian and Aramaic, others the art of distilling
Weird fragrances out of nothing, from the ground up.
In each the potential is realized, the two wires
Are crossing.

DAVID BAKER

David Baker is the author of three
books: *Laws of the Land*, *Summer
Sleep*, and *Haunts*. He teaches at
Denison University and is a con-
sulting editor for the *Kenyon Re-
view*. He was born in Bangor,
Maine, in 1954.

CALL ACROSS THE YEARS

for Dave Smith

1

Those summers, sundowns came late but never late enough
to find us sleepy. My brother and I would sit
back to back in the cut field's cool grass and watch
the bats wheel and dip in the wind of their making.
Or walk to the dusk trees where fireflies
sprouted like berries and floated into our open hands.

When she called from the one room lit only
with the blue of the television, across whatever

distance there was, we were never ready
though our legs were heavy from play, our hands dusty
with the dozens of fluttering bodies we had held,
pulsing like the veins in our own thin wrists.

Sleep, she said, though sometimes later the wind rose
and touched us in our sheets. *Sleep*, though
sometimes the curtains wheezed and the trees clawed
the sideboards and shingles and the smokehouse
rattled in its tin. Those mornings, when we woke,
we found the world shiny with the pools of our dreams.

2

That was the land of sun and rain, of play and sleep,
nineteen sixty-something every year. But one night
the deep rumble that swept our field so often
with its wind, a distant sigh, came harder, farther.
We woke calling across the dark of our room

which was already thick with grit. Leaves flew
wild as bats above our beds. It was no dream
though we lay still as feigned sleep, though the curtains
whipped themselves white, though outside the trees
were breaking our toys: sling-shot, treehouse, swing . . .

3

She came to us like a wish out of the storm and led
us through a house we did not recognize,
through the wreckage and swirling dark of it, out
into the rain-driven night louder than a scream,
then down—the cellar, the very ground, the door shut
and locked, one bare bulb sputtering on its wire.

We checked the seals of years of jars, shelves of food
lined in the sour dark, counted them, dusted them
with our breath, anything to ignore the roar
and crash of the world above us. Later, too tired
to work, we sang. Huddled in the cellar,
we sang together until the sun was high.

4

Tonight the rain is falling gently in the dark, as if
through the wind and dim of my past. The windows
are still opened and the edges of the curtains
above my desk are damp and hanging heavy.
Whose voice do I hear, after all these years, calling

through the roar of my memory? And why, though
the rain and wind tonight are soft, do I still shudder
thinking how easily these walls could crack
and fall, this roof rise, how easily the trees, their
leaves and many toys, could come crashing down and stay?

I will not sleep again tonight. I want to find
that child and soothe him. I want to get up and go out
beneath the tree, and walk there until the morning.
I want to come to this house, open the door,
and find us all here singing in the spreading sun.

MARVIN BELL

Born in 1937 in New York City and
raised on Long Island, Marvin Bell
has taught at the University of
Iowa since 1965. He has written
ten books of poetry, including
A Probable Volume of Dreams,
which won the Lamont Prize, and
New and Selected Poems. He lives
in Iowa City, Iowa, and Port
Townsend, Washington.

IN AMERICA

these things happen: I am taken
to see a friend
who talks too fast and is now teaching *Moby Dick*
according to jui-jitsui,
or judo according to Melville:
He says Melville gets you leaning
and lets go, or gets you to pulling
and suddenly advances, retreats
when you respond, and so on. OK, I
accept that, but then he starts

in on the assassination of
John F. Kennedy as planned by our
government, and he has a collection of
strange deaths at handy times
bizarrely of people who know something.
I know nothing. I want to know
nothing whatsoever. It once
was enough to be standing
on a field of American baseball,
minding my ground balls and business,
when the infielder to my left
shot me the news of what is now known as
The Bay of Pigs, then in progress
but secretly, and certainly
doomed for stupidity, mis-timing,
marsh-landings, and JFK's resolve
to unaccomplish the Agency's *fait-accompli*
by refusing air cover. This would crackle
the air waves, but later. Tall tales,
I figured, wrongly,
putting my fist in my glove
for America.
Moby Dick, you damn whale,
I've seen whales.
America, though—
too big to be seen.

ROBERT BLY

Besides fourteen books of poems, including *The Light Around the Body*, which won the National Book Award, and *Selected Poems*, Robert Bly has published numerous books of translations and edited the influential magazine *The Eighties* (formerly *The Seventies*, *The Sixties*, and *The Fifties*). He was born in Madison, Minnesota, in 1926 and now lives in Moose Lake, Minnesota.

COUNTING SMALL-BONED BODIES

Let's count the bodies over again.

If we could only make the bodies smaller,
the size of skulls,
we could make a whole plain white with skulls in the moonlight.

If we could only make the bodies smaller,
maybe we could fit
a whole year's kill in front of us on a desk.

If we could only make the bodies smaller,
we could fit
a body into a finger ring, for a keepsake forever.

MELANCHOLIA

1

A light seen suddenly in the storm, snow
Coming from all sides, like flakes
Of sleep, and myself
On the road to the dark barn,
Halfway there, a black dog near me.

2

Light on the wooden rail.
Someone I knew and loved.
As we hear the dates of his marriage
And the years he moved,
A wreath of dark fir and shiny laurel
Slips off the coffin.

3

A cathedral: I see
Starving men, weakened, leaning
On their knees. But the bells ring anyway,
Sending out over the planted fields
A vegetation, sound waves with long leaves.

4

There is a wound on the trunk,
Where the branch was torn off.
A wind comes out of it,
Rising, swelling,
Swirling over everything alive.

UNREST IN 1961

A strange unrest hovers over the nation:
This is the last dance, the wild tossing of Morgan's seas,
The division of spoils. A lassitude
Enters into the diamonds of the body.
In the high school the explosion begins, the child is partly killed,
When the fight is over, and the land and the sea ruined,
Two shapes inside us rise, and move away.

But the baboon whistles on the shores of death—
Climbing and falling, tossing nuts and stones,
He gambols by the tree
Whose branches hold the expanses of cold,
The planets whirling and the black sun,
The cries of insects, and the tiny slaves
In the prisons of bark:
Charlemagne, we are approaching your islands!

We are returning now to the snowy trees,
And the depth of the darkness buried in snow, through which you rode
   all night
With stiff hands; now the darkness is falling
In which we sleep and awake—a darkness in which
Thieves shudder, and the insane have a hunger for snow,
In which bankers dream of being buried by black stones,
And businessmen fall on their knees in the dungeons of sleep.

MICHAEL DENNIS

BROWNE

Born in Walton-on-Thames, England, in 1940, Michael Dennis Browne lives in Minneapolis, where he is a professor of English at the University of Minnesota. Among his published collections are *The Wife of Winter*, *The Sun Fetcher*, and *Smoke from the Fires*.

ROBERT BLY GETS UP EARLY

At the ticket counter, Minneapolis Airport, 7:30 A.M., standing in line—a hand on my shoulder! It is Robert Bly! Risen like a silo from out of the dark earth for one last greeting.

He is flying to Boston to read. Flying to Boston with a satchel of red bees. "I have red bees in my bag. I will have no hesitation in releasing them into your unconscious."

Robert Bly! Organic Foods! White Poncho! Vitamin E!

I get on my plane, sit down with *Esquire, The New Yorker,* and *Greek Lyric Poetry.* I reach for my notebook to write down a few bad lines about Robert Bly unexpectedly putting his hand on my shoulder so early in the morning at the airport—when a man sits down beside me—it is Robert Bly!

This plane goes to Pittsburgh but he has charmed his way harshly past the stewardesses. He flies simultaneously to so many places in his head, why should he not think that the Pittsburgh plane will take him also to his reading in Boston—perhaps even directly to the podium!

What does this manic Son of Norway want of me? He shoves a small blue book into my hands. It is by a young Norwegian poet who is traveling around the country in a Greyhound Bus with his girlfriend.

Do we have money for him, he asks? His eyes crackle with the lustre of Vitamin E.

O Robert Bly, you are on this earth only briefly, like an angel with a hangover. I see you striding, wings folded, across the main lobby of the Minneapolis International Airport, pushing a vast plow. From the shattered floor foams a tide of soldier ants, Latvian attorneys, centurions, phantoms, admirals, minor poets with half-opened parachutes. They flow out of the airport and into the landscape, determined to turn the country around.

O Robert Bly, get off my plane! I have two readings of my own to do in Pittsburgh!

Robert Bly hurtles to gate 7a with his satchel of bees. He gets on his plane—at last! He needs no charm now—he has a ticket! From deep in the poncho he releases a bee. The bee makes his way forward into the cabin, crawls up onto the pilot's shoulder, and croaks into his ear: "Take this plane to 4th-century Tibet."

CHRISTOPHER

BUCKLEY

Christopher Buckley has pub-
lished five collections of poetry,
most recently *Blossom & Bones:
On the Life and Work of Georgia
O'Keefe* and *Blue Autumn*. He
was born in Arcata, California, in
1948 and teaches at West Chester
University.

KEES AT 70

A refuge, permanent, with trees that shade
When all the other cities die and fade.

I grew tired
finally, even of clouds,
the last things
we could ever affect—
then something
about the bay,
the wordless clouds there
rolling off, and off,
suggesting that
perhaps there is
some quiet city in the mind
beyond jazz and summer beaches.

And for all appearances,
at the end of my modern rope,
I let go into those waves . . .
Here, the amusements
are shade-colored lizards
commanding their thin hearts
among the undersides of rock—
they blink into the sun
and never dream . . .

There were the years
of Alma, her white blouses
and direct, dark eyes,
who brought oranges
and Lucky Strikes from Oaxaca
and who had no idea . . .
There was the writing
in another name
for money, for magazines
flourishing in barbershops
Omaha to Iowa City . . .
                    Now,
there's only the saguaro
blossom and Spanish bayonet
to take the eye above
this earth's acquiescence
to the winds . . .
                    And yes,
I had daughters
named for exotic flowers
who went into the world
surrendering their light
like all precious things—
involved with a Manhattan parvenu,
the art scene on Nob Hill,
there was nothing,
no reservoir of will,

to keep them
from the stark advances
of the age, the atomic despair . . .

I am an emblem of my time—
the blank and unmarked page,
the man who isn't there,
now more prepared than most
to shade my mind
amid the long blue heat
and burning air . . .

for Glover Davis

FREDERICK BUSCH

Frederick Busch was born in
Brooklyn in 1941 and is the author
of sixteen books, among them
Invisible Mending, which won
the Jewish National Book Award,
Absent Friends, War Babies, and
Harry and Catherine. He is the
Fairchild Professor of Literature at
Colgate University.

GREETINGS FROM A FAR-FLUNG PLACE

for Eric Busch

She'd been working for an hour on her voice. The letter had begun,
"'Well, nuts,' I said. 'Get yourself another girl.'" She had read that in the
dialogue of a minor character in a forgotten murder mystery. It didn't
matter. She wouldn't mail the letter to her sister or call her on the phone
or in any other way open the communications between them which had
recently shut down like the factories she'd seen from the van as they raced
against some world's land speed record through a small industrial city on
the verge of death. They weren't estranged, she and her sister. It was
more like distance. They had the same widowed mother, and they had
distance.

There were three sheets of motel stationery. She had filled one side of one sheet, in her smallest and neatest hand, with beginnings aimed at helping her to locate a voice in which to address her sister. There was no stranger sleeping on the bed after tepid sex. There wasn't a cigarette burning in the shallow plastic ashtray. No liquor, tears or perspiration stained the cheap letterhead. The room was neat, though overheated, and it smelled of bathroom cleanser. She didn't weep or shake. She sat, in her white terrycloth bathrobe, and she worked at her trade: the voice.

Sister, beloved, here are greetings from a far-flung place.

That was all right. That was not bad. And Scranton had surely been flung, by history and currency and industry and plain use, about as far as it was possible for a city to be moved. The band had played a civic center's winter bash after a dance at Lehigh, in Bethlehem, Pa. Two engagements that close meant a satisfactory take, though not riches. She had gotten away with a Peggy Lee imitation in the boonies. She had nearly gotten away. She had stood absolutely still except for a tiny tick of the tummy and had sung very low—too low for her register, but they hadn't known, they'd thought her a throaty jazz singer—and the band had done the brassy *ooo-wa*, with a cymbal burnish on the end. Provincials like the horns that way. To her it sounded as cheap as their wages, as worn-out as her vocal cords, and as derivative as each of their other sets had been.

Sister, beloved. Far-flung place. All right. Mom of course always calls the places I go "far-flung" when she talks to you. *If* I'm the Good Sister when she talks. If I'm not, it's your turn, and I'm called "restless" and you're simply "darling" or "considerate." At which time the places I go are simply called "away." It reminds me of the bad books I read in these places we play. I spend most of my time on my back, as you and Danny doubtless have said to one another, but I have to disappoint you by saying that it's time spent reading. Most of these gigs—you were waiting for that word—consist of waiting for Ellis to see that the luggage and instruments get into the vans, and waiting for us to get stuffed and molded buttock to buttock into the vans, and waiting for the damned vans to get to wherever we're playing—Manny's Casa Roma, or a cement-block palace named The Poseidon Club—and then I wait to get dressed and I wait to be introduced by Ellis as "our girl singer," because, in spite of my being thirty-eight and in spite of its not being 1938, Ellis keeps trying to sound like a big band leader with slicked-down hair and brown skin. He can't forgive himself for being white and more or less untalented, and he's probably right.

So I wait. I read mystery books in paperback and I leave them in the room when I go. I have learned from them that death means as much in the mystery business as it does in mine, and that death after a hundred thousand words or so is usually meaningless, and that a favorite trick of the police is the Good Cop–Bad Cop routine. During the interrogation, one cop rages at the suspect and threatens a long prison term, immediate harm, and the prospect of jail-cell rape. The other restrains the Bad Cop and finally gets him out of the room. He offers the suspect cigarettes, which every suspect smokes, I've learned, and soft advice. Between them, the Bad Cop and the Good Cop break the suspect down. The poor bastard finally signs a confession.

Can a mother be two cops? When she's tough on one of us—when she intimates quite clearly how much the Bad Sister has hurt her in one of a thousand awful ways—then she makes the other into a Good Sister. And what sister does not strive to be good in the eyes of the law? She does her cops, we does our rob-hers.

She had one side of the paper left. She drank from a can of sugar-free soft drink and she stood to remove the bathrobe. Though she didn't look in the wide mirror, she did suck her stomach in and pull her shoulders back, as if the mirror looked with someone's eyes. She walked toward the bathroom, away from the gaze. But there was another mirror, over the sink. She said to it, "Not bad for forty-one. I mean thirty-eight. On the other hand, not that good either." She squeezed her belly and although there wasn't a lot to get hold of, a grip was not impossible.

Gripping herself was preferable, this moment, to being gripped by Henry, their sad drummer. He called like a cat when he made love, and he often was apologizing for something. Which explained, to her satisfaction at least, why the band could never, ever, swing: nobody was there to drive it. She had tried talking to Henry about Basie's rhythm section, but he never wanted to talk about Basie or the free-fall let's-not-stop-and-anyway-we-can't pouring onward that musicians and even their girl singers experienced a few times in a career. She liked Henry, and he used marvelous cologne, and though he was fifty his body was hard, like a younger man's, and his skin was exactly the light brown of the pottery made in Bybee, Kentucky, which her sister had brought home from college as the start of her dowry. His only drawbacks were occasional whining, and a need to be comforted that equalled his need to make trouble or cause excitement. He was not a topnotch drummer and, because of him, by the end of a long set they always swam in molasses. But he worried about her. And he was a chum. And when you don't have husband, children, dogs, cats, canaries or the real sense of having done too much to write home about, you keep hold of your chums.

It was really called The Hotel Meridian, and it truly was in Altoona, Pa. All the way from New York in the van, she'd realized when they arrived, she had been expecting the city *not* to be Altoona—because she didn't want to be the singer in the kind of band that played Altoona for the kind of money they'd make. It was a very large motel with a parking lot you could fly a jumbo jet from. *Plenty of Free Parking*, she figured their ads would say. Hail fell, and she stood and watched the little granules bounce and roll on the hood of the van. Henry came up beside her, square-shouldered and tall with a short strong neck, elegant with his scarf so white against his black coat, and he took her right hand. He brought it up to her face. "Look," he said, and she saw that her cold pale hand was a fist.

"I'm keeping my fingers warm," she said.

"You're turning into a knot," Henry told her.

He picked her fist up and kissed it. She felt about six years old for as long as the kiss lasted. Then she felt cold and stiff. And when Henry saw that she wasn't going to open her hand, he walked around to the back of the van, and she heard his deep voice take on a bantering tone with the others: men unpacking luggage at motels after driving. The girl singer went to the desk and then to her room. This was on another trip, another time. There were plenty of other times.

Her sister, Cindy, was pale and big-eyed, thirty-six years old, married to Danny, and living in a 1969 Mediterranean Villa house not quite as important to her as breath or her only child, Bud. The shower was a little too hot at first but she kept it that way to open her throat. She was about to begin her voice exercises, she even had her jaws open and was projecting against her palate, when she decided instead to sit on the floor of the tub beneath the almost-scalding water, and weep. She did it with her eyes open, and she watched her legs go from their winter whiteness to red.

This, dear sister, is what they mean by seeing red. And greetings from a far-flung place. Or am I, this time, merely "away"?

She crawled into the scald and then stood up beneath it and called, in a rugged harsh voice. The water against her ears and skull rumbled and she called again. That was enough. She turned the water off and stood, dripping, trying to pant. But she hadn't run, she hated jogging, even, and she could no more tolerate her own hysterics than she could tolerate Henry's or those of anyone else. There was wisdom and cunning distilled from mistreated generations behind the words, good ones to try to live by, that were the unsurprising credo of a shabby band of serious and only so-so jazz musicians: Be cool.

She turned the cold water on. She winced when it hit her shoulders and thighs, but she stood beneath it until she really was gasping. Then she turned it off and sang, softly and pretty well, and with the self-mockery of actual blues. God bless the child, she sang.

Not bad for a woman of thirty-eight.

So, Cindy, I've been thinking about the last time we were together for forty-seven hours and change. I'd been in Michigan City, Indiana, with the band, if you remember. That's where Scranton or Bethlehem will go to get their brain death confirmed, Michigan City, Indiana. Ellis had been down so far, he'd begun to do his little red medications, and the bus we'd chartered out of Chicago was run essentially by joint power. They were passing so many up and down the aisles and around, the bus driver began to giggle—he wasn't toking, mind you—because there's apparently a sign near Chicago that directs traffic to Nashville which, you'll remember, is not near Illinois. You'll also remember my visit, I think. I was wiped out. I hadn't wanted to come. But I'd been talking on the phone to Mom and she'd mentioned how confining your life with Danny was. And how, sometimes, you weren't "considerate," which meant I hadn't merely been "away," but had been out in the far-flung places while you were pinned at home. Which meant that you were the Bad Sister, I was the Good one, and if I wanted to stay that way I would do what our mother said. Can a sister be a stool pigeon? Can a mother be two cops?

The time of which I'm thinking is memorialized by the fact that I possessed slightly longer hair, a slightly slimmer waist, and slightly more voice. It was spring, and we were sitting in the Mediterranean Villa on the edge, the good edge to be sure, of Mamaroneck, NY, waiting for Danny to come home from another day spent adjusting insurance claims. I always think of him using screwdrivers and hydraulic jacks and metal cutters. Bud was fourteen, I think. He was ripe. We were drinking Danny's Scotch, as you seemed to enjoy calling it, and Bud was sitting with us and watching us drink. Alicia Brooks née Bernstein, girl singer, was sitting there with her long and, let's admit it, pretty damned good legs, propped up on the coffee table. My Liberty's print skirt was hanging around my thighs and I knew it. I was wearing a sheer tank top and poor

Bud was getting plenty of nipple. He was also looking right along my big black boots and partway up my crotch. I sat there and I moved my legs apart. Just the slightest bit. I did. And I was doing a joint. I hadn't wanted it. I hadn't remembered I carried the damned thing. I looked into my bag for a tissue and I found a scrawny joint that a music-lover had sent me. "Dear Ms. Brooks: Tonight I am going to get high and dream of washing your entire body in cognac while you sing *Love for Sale.* I hope you will accept the enclosed. I would like to think of you getting stoned and dreaming of me as my washcloth slides down the etceteras and into your usuals." And Cindy, babe: something made me light it up while you glared and stared and were too polite to throw me the hell out. And something made me shift my legs just a little, so the kid I used to feed when he was a baby could do a visual pelvic on me. His face was so serious and red! And what it was, of course, was Mom. I was there because of her, I knew it, I despised us all, and I did the number on your baby's bones instead of Mom's or yours or my own.

We were on the phone, and I had just finished telling her about Michigan City, Indiana, and for some reason I stitched on the fact that Benny Goodman played there once.

"A Jew," Mom said. "It's so hard to think of Jews playing jazz music."

"He dated Billie Holiday."

"She was the one took the drugs?"

"She was the genius who was black, Mom. Benny Goodman dated her for a while."

"If I am not mistaken, a famous composer composed for Mister Goodman—"

"A clarinet concerto. Goodman hired Teddy Wilson for his piano man. It was Bartok."

"Also a black?"

"Billie was black, Teddy was black, Bartok was white, Mom. Who did you have in mind?"

"Excuse me." I could hear it coming, Cindy. "Pardon me for not giving you a reason to make fun of me earlier. A mother—I forgot this in my pleasure at hearing your voice on the telephone—a mother has to take abuse no matter what age or the child's age."

"Mom. Don't fight."

"It takes two to make a fight, Allie. And with you, it only takes one."

"Don't cry."

"I cry when you talk to me that way. It's simple. Excuse me: isn't that why you do it?"

"Mom. How's Cindy? Tell me about Cindy. Don't fight. Don't cry. Talk to me about Cindy. How is she?"

She did the long shuddery sigh. Then she said, "Cindy. Oh, Allie, she is so inconsiderate sometimes. She doesn't mean to be. She's a nice child. But she has her problems. I understand this. I don't meddle and I don't pry. I wouldn't do that. But she has a lot of problems and sometimes they don't permit her to—to *see* us, you and me and the other people in her life. Well, on the edge of her life, if you know what I mean. Allie, it isn't as if she's traveling the way you are. You know, with a career that takes her so far. She isn't what you'd call *busy*. I mean, how many times can you vacuum-clean the house? She's at home, the child goes to school and then with friends, she stays home and Danny is there at night to eat and sleep and believe me, take it as truth, not a lot more. So I can understand why she can't get in touch. It's sadness. It makes you stand still in the middle of the room sometimes, you couldn't move if you wanted to. And sometimes you just don't want to. But there *you* are, every far-flung place I have ever heard of except Alaska, and believe me, I wouldn't be surprised to hear you calling me from *there*. That's the point. You would call me from there. Cindy can't call from Westchester County. She's unhappy. She is so unhappy that she doesn't have time. I know about depression, believe me. That is a depressed girl. So, Allie—would you call her? You'll call her tonight or tomorrow? Maybe visit her one of these days? Tell her the furniture's nice. I don't know. Let her talk to the big sister a while. Darling, you remember Cloris, the maid who is colored? How's your friend in the orchestra, I forget his name, it escapes me."

You know?

Greetings, babe, from a far-flung place. Did I tell you that the folks in Bethlehem were more depressed than the folks in Scranton? The *air* in Bethlehem felt brown. Only the college boys smiled any more than they had to. Scranton's okay. Bethlehem's okay. You're okay. I am too. We're all okay and we're all ofay, except for Henry and eight other guys in the band. Did I tell you about the one who plays sax and clarinet for us? He thinks he's Gerry Mulligan because he's white and plays baritone.

She was in her white terrycloth bathrobe and the motel stationery from the night before was next to the motel stationery from tonight. There wasn't any liquor in a glass and there wasn't a cigarette burning in the plastic ashtray and the TV set wasn't on. No man was sprawled in his shoes atop the cheap coverlet of her motel bed. She was clean from tonight's shower and her feet were in her snug furry slippers. She held the ballpoint pen against her lips and did not write.

The boys in their tuxedos were mostly handsome because very healthy and very young. The girls in their open-backed gowns were mostly ditto because ditto. You could have gotten away with some of those numbers because you're so scrawny, Cindy. Scrawn is in. It sounds like some kind of New England chowder: scrawn. Listen, I could tell you New England stories, complete with chowder, chowderheads, and heavy items with actual guns in their suits. I mean it. But this is a Pennsylvania number, and the items I have in mind were wearing rented midnight blue tuxedos without guns. Ellis looked so classy in his dinner jacket. Henry was particularly gorgeous. Most of the boys looked like their shirts hurt their necks. After a while they didn't. That was because they got so drunk. It was loud. The kids were pretending to be classy. We played swing numbers and they tried to jitterbug and Lindy. They mostly ended up doing sloppy Charlestons and falling either prone on the floor or into breakdancing.

There I was, our girl singer, doing *I'll Never Smile Again* and of course smiling. The bass sax does a solo riff, a little one, just before the end. Our guy had his cheeks out like Mulligan. I thought his face would explode. Ellis was laughing so hard, his hairpiece shifted. Then we broke, the guys drifted out to smoke on the front lawn and the kids got loaded some more.

I went outside the fraternity house onto the back lawn. That was where they'd put a lot of their furniture to make room for the dance. It was cold, but I was hot, and I sat on one of those big old leather easy chairs with my feet on an ottoman. I was sitting there with my eyes closed and my feet up, cooling off and worrying because in the middle of *A Fine Romance* I'd forgotten the name of the town we were in. I was also worrying because I was a lot older than these boys and girls, and in the middle of *A Fine Romance* it had struck me that I couldn't remember a good deal of how I'd got that way.

Nobody was out there. Then some boys showed up, four of them, and one of them had his tie off and his studs out and he had a neck on him you'd need a roadmap to drive around. He had that blond-red hair that Bud had when he was a baby. Except this guy was about six foot two and he weighed a lot more than two of me. Well, two of you. He was red down to his collar, and sweaty. The steam was coming off him. He looked so much like a big white horse. He was smiling at me with teeth and skin and eyes, except he was steaming like an animal and he was going to jump all over me. I could tell. He had watched my little Peggy Lee number and he and the other ones, big, all of them, were going to take a few turns with me. I rose up above myself as if I'd died. I became my own ghost. I looked down. I saw myself in the white satin-lookalike floor-length gown with the cleavage above it. I saw my legs, up on the ottoman, fully extended and a little apart. All propped up for rape, and no place to go, and they were going to split me open and pass me around. I saw myself in my Liberty's print and my black boots and my legs apart and your little boy Bud in front of me, staring.

It was big boys now. They were very drunk. They were *all* giving off a kind of smoke in the cold air. The one with the neck was unzipping and then zipping his fly, up and down, up and down. They were looking at me and waiting for the one with the neck to move. The way they were looking at me and looking forward to me reminded me of how Bud hadn't.

Henry said, "Go away."

The one with the neck said, "You work for me, or what?"

Henry said to me, "Come inside now. It's cold. All right? Come in."

I did not cry. I thought about higher education. I said, "Good of you to join me, Henry."

"Good of you to join *me*," he said. He turned back to the boys and said, "Go away now. Go to bed. Go home."

"You're *in* my home, man," Neck told him. Then he said to his friends, "I'm just like calling a spade a spade. You know?"

I turned around and I was going to announce to them what they were and who they were and why they were. Henry put the gentlest pressure on my elbow. He cupped it and guided me around and up the back stairs and in. I was angriest, just then, because on their faces I had read their utterly faithful reliance on the fact that sooner, or perhaps regrettably later, I was going to be willing to do, or have done, what they'd have forced me to—although it was just beyond their comprehension, those wide healthy faces had told me, that a girl singer in a second-class band would not want to shudder underneath a truckful of them. I thought about Bud, looking along my legs. I thought about you and I thought about Mom. I mostly thought about me. Henry lit a cigarette and put it in my lips. I dragged on it. He called a cab and sent me back to the motel in it. I bathed.

She moved the pen against her lips and looked at the pages she had written two days before. God bless the child. She tore the letterhead up and she put the pen on the dressing table. She swiveled in her chair and leaned back to put her crossed ankles on the edge of the bed. Her bathrobe fell open and she looked at her legs. She closed the bathrobe and put her legs together. Her hand lay on her lap. It was in a fist. She looked at it and waited for the fist to open up.

This is to remind you about Bud and how he sat and looked at me because of what I did. This is to remind you about how you didn't do anything about it.

This is also a reminder to Mom that I will not sign the confession.

This will serve as a reminder to me that I already have.

And now, here in the Members' Room of the Hotel Imperial in Red Bank, New Jersey, and on behalf of the fellas in the band, ladies and gentlemen, I'd like to invite you to join us in giving a big welcome to our girl singer, Alicia Brooks, who tells us *I've Got the World on a String*.

Sister, babe.

Far out.

HENRY CARLILE

Henry Carlile's first book, *The Rough-Hewn Table*, was the Dev ins Award winner in 1971. *Running Lights*, his second book, appeared in 1981. Since 1967 he has taught at Portland State University. He was born in San Francisco in 1934.

FOUR VARIATIONS ON THE INVISIBLE BITTERN

All morning I searched for the right decoy,
wanting a bittern in its reedlike pose,
but found only mallards, wood ducks, teal,
canvasbacks, old squaws, scaups,
a lovely ruddy duck already spoken for,
whistling swans, Canada geese
and one magnificent, unaffordable loon.
Always we settle for less.

Instead I bought you a pied-billed grebe,
recalling its mating song
heard on the walks we used to take

53

by Reed College pond
where we saw the green heron
but no bittern.

❖

Unlikely now together we will ever see one.
Before we married, the bitterns I observed
and later wrote about were seldom paired.
Before one flushed from cover I might see
only an eye reflective and wary.

Sixteen and curious as Audubon to know
how rushes gathered into something
birdlike and flew away,
I'm ashamed to admit I shot one.
It fell like a spent bag of change.

Its outraged yellow eye seemed to accuse me.
But why exaggerate? It was a dead bird.
Audubon had killed his share to better purpose:
dead models stiffly painted live.

❖

And carefully you wrote of what you had seen only
in photographs, in taxidermed and dusty glass-eyed
specimens, habitats of unnatural history museums.
More stately and serious, years later and older,
the ghost bird lived from your lines and flew.

Though not as I had seen it through swamp vapors,
over the water-ferned and cattailed green margins
of hidden ponds, Venetian scenery of spring meadows,
unlikely in flight as one of those post da-Vincian
manned contraptions that always crashed.

The bittern somehow airborne, dipping and weaving,
gathered straight down into a stillness,
in semblance of rushes, matched their swaying,
betrayed only by its eye's flavescent yellow.

❖

You wrote once of how you could go blindly on
loving a life from which something is missing.
I never read those lines and believed
it was the bittern you referred to.

Say bitterns appear like grace to the fallen and
bitter, the solitary souls who step through loss
without hope of discovery, without leaving a trace.

Say now your life is singular (even if it's not)
that you find those rarely observed features,
that starry pupil refined into a tangible self
hood, a temperature several degrees above human.

I want that bird to show itself to you.
Eighteen years you were my best and wisest friend.
I never wanted to be what is missing.

RAYMOND CARVER

Raymond Carver was born in
Clatskanie, Oregon, in 1938. Be-
sides his five collections of fiction,
which include *Will You Please Be
Quiet Please?*, *Cathedral*, and
Where I'm Calling From, he pub-
lished five volumes of poetry, most
recently *A New Path to the Water-
fall.* He died in 1988.

YOU DON'T KNOW WHAT LOVE IS
(an evening with Charles Bukowski)

You don't know what love is Bukowski said
I'm 51 years old look at me
I'm in love with this young broad
I got it bad but she's hung up too
so it's all right man that's the way it should be
I get in their blood and they can't get me out
They try everything to get away from me
but they all come back in the end
They all came back to me except
the one I planted

I cried over that one
but I cried easy in those days
Don't let me get onto the hard stuff man
I get mean then
I could sit here and drink beer
with you hippies all night
I could drink ten quarts of this beer
and nothing it's like water
But let me get onto the hard stuff
and I'll start throwing people out windows
I'll throw anybody out the window
I've done it
But you don't know what love is
You don't know because you've never
been in love it's that simple
I got this young broad see she's beautiful
She calls me Bukowski
Bukowski she says in this little voice
and I say What
But you don't know what love is
I'm telling you what it is
but you aren't listening
There isn't one of you in this room
would recognize love if it stepped up
and buggered you in the ass
I used to think poetry readings were a copout
Look I'm 51 years old and I've been around
I *know* they're a copout
but I said to myself Bukowski
starving is even more of a copout
So there you are and nothing is like it should be
That fellow what's his name Galway Kinnell
I saw his picture in a magazine
He has a handsome mug on him
but he's a *teacher*
Christ can you imagine
But then you're teachers too
here I am insulting you already

No I haven't heard of him
or him either
They're all termites
Maybe it's ego I don't read much anymore
but these people who build
reputations on five or six books
termites
Bukowski she says
Why do you listen to classical music all day
Can't you hear her saying that
Bukowski why do you listen to classical music all day
That surprises you doesn't it
You wouldn't think a crude bastard like me
could listen to classical music all day
Brahms Rachmaninoff Bartok Telemann
Shit I couldn't write up here
Too quiet up here too many trees
I like the city that's the place for me
I put on my classical music each morning
and sit down in front of my typewriter
I light a cigar and I smoke it like this see
and I say Bukowski you're a lucky man
Bukowski you've gone through it all
and you're a lucky man
and the blue smoke drifts across the table
and I look out the window onto Delongpre Avenue
and I see people walking up and down the sidewalk
and I puff on the cigar like this
and then I lay the cigar in the ashtray like this
and take a deep breath
and I begin to write
Bukowski this is the life I say
it's good to be poor it's good to have hemorrhoids
it's good to be in love
But you don't know what it's like
You don't know what it's like to be in love
If you could see her you'd know what I mean
She thought I'd come up here and get laid

She just knew it
She told me she knew it
Shit I'm 51 years old and she's 25
and we're in love and she's jealous
Jesus it's beautiful
she said she'd claw my eyes out if I came up here and got laid
Now that's love for you
What do any of you know about it
Let me tell you something
I've met men in jail who had more style
than the people who hang around colleges
and go to poetry readings
They're bloodsuckers who come to see
if the poet's socks are dirty
or if he smells under the arms
Believe me I won't disappoint em
But I want you to remember this
there's only one poet in this room tonight
only one poet in this town tonight
maybe only one real poet in this country tonight
and that's me
What do any of you know about life
What do any of you know about anything
Which of you here has been fired from a job
or else has beaten up your broad
or else has been beaten up by your broad
I was fired from Sears and Roebuck five times
They'd fire me then hire me back again
I was a stockboy for them when I was 35
and then got canned for stealing cookies
I know what's it like I've been there
I'm 51 years old now and I'm in love
This little broad she says
Bukowski
and I say What and she says
I think you're full of shit
and I say baby you understand me
She's the only broad in the world

man or woman
I'd take that from
But you don't know what love is
They all came back to me in the end too
every one of em came back
except that one I told you about
the one I planted
We were together seven years
We used to drink a lot
I see a couple of typers in this room but
I don't see any poets
I'm not surprised
You have to have been in love to write poetry
and you don't know what it is to be in love
that's your trouble
Give me some of that stuff
That's right no ice good
That's good that's just fine
So let's get this show on the road
I know what I said but I'll have just one
That tastes good
Okay then let's go let's get this over with
only afterwards don't anyone stand close
to an open window

BONNARD'S NUDES

His wife. Forty years he painted her.
Again and again. The nude in the last painting
the same young nude as the first. His wife.

As he remembered her young. As she was young.
His wife in her bath. At her dressing table
in front of the mirror. Undressed.

His wife with her hands under her breasts
looking out on the garden.
The sun bestowing warmth and color.

Every living thing in bloom there.
She young and tremulous and most desirable.
When she died, he painted a while longer.

A few landscapes. Then died.
And was put down next to her.
His young wife.

THE YOUNG FIRE EATERS
OF MEXICO CITY

They fill their mouths with alcohol
and blow it over a lighted candle
at traffic signs. Anyplace, really,
where cars line up and the drivers
are angry and frustrated and looking
for distraction—there you'll find
the young fire eaters. Doing what they do
for a few pesos. If they're lucky.
But in a year their lips
are scorched and their throats raw.
They have no voice within a year.
They can't talk or cry out—
these silent children who hunt
through the streets with a candle
and a beer can filled with alcohol.
They are called *milusos*. Which translates
into "a thousand uses."

RICHARD CECIL

Richard Cecil was born in Baltimore in 1944 and educated at the University of Maryland, the University of Iowa, and Indiana University, where he currently teaches. He is the author of *Einstein's Brain*.

THE INTERRUPTED NAP

Central air recirculates the room
raising little hairs along my arms
exactly as they rise when, almost asleep,
alone, I stroke them with my fingertips.
I'm so accustomed to touching you at night
that in this dark I've made at noon with drapes
drawn against the terrible August sun,
I automatically reach for something smooth,
skinlike: the velvet chairback, the cat, my wrist.

I run my nails along the lines of veins
as lightly as the manufactured wind
runs along the surfaces of this room,
cooling them. I close my eyes. I shiver.
I sink down into the sofa's cushions
like a diver in a deep-sea bell:
outside, savage atmospheres; inside,
the delicate networks of blood and nerves; between,
thin walls of steel, of glass, of skin.

I remember almost drowning. In early evening,
blinding sunset reflected in the pool,
I dove incautiously into the shallow end
and dashed my head against the concrete rim.
I could have breached the surface with my hand,
but so cool and dark and absolutely quiet
the bottom seemed, I knew that I was miles
below my playmates' faces peering down.
When the lifeguard fished me with her hook,

I rose by the stretched elastic of my trunks
into the noise and heat and light, amazed,
for I thought that I had slipped all nets.
When she firmly pressed her lips to mine
to force her breath into my emptied chest,
I fought. I clamped my teeth so desperately
she had to prize them open with a stick.
Oxygen burned like acid in my lungs.
Next day, I bragged about my first French kiss.

At six, I didn't want to owe my life.
But thirty years later, waiting for you
in the artificial dark, I forgive her
harsh resuscitation. She couldn't know
how pleasantly my shroud of water wrapped me,
how snug my coffin of endless sleep, how often,
abandoned for an afternoon, nothing
half as pleasant as almost drowning happens,
until you shove the door against its jamb,

pouring heat and light and noise inside.
And I don't criticize your rough embrace.
We lucky divers always wake to violence,
tons of gravity hurled down on us, furious
congratulations shouted in our ears.
Silence is the consolation of the lost.
Self-sufficiency. They've cut the line by which
anyone could haul them in. I envy them.
Then I envy no one, waking in your arms.

PHILIP DACEY

Philip Dacey, the editor of *Crazy-
horse* from 1971 to 1975, was born
in St. Louis in 1939. His four
books of poems include *The Boy
under the Bed* and *The Man with
Red Suspenders*. He teaches at
Southwest State University in
Marshall, Minnesota.

THE WINTER THING

We were going to
but the storm came.
It would have been the first time
for either of us.
The place and the hour were set.
Everything was ready.
The storm said no.

The storm poured out of us,
white denial,
white reticence.

We filled the road between us
with that whiteness.
No cars could move,
they wondered so
at the elaborate system
of beautiful roadblocks
people are as good
as wind at creating,
drifts this high
from shoulder to shoulder.

So we left our homes
and went out into it,
the Thing we had made
our environment, she there,
I here, and made
snow-angels, touching,
at all points,
one on top of another,
you couldn't tell them apart.

KATE DANIELS

Kate Daniels is the author of two
books of poetry, *The White Wave*
and *The Niobe Poems*. The co-
editor, since 1979, of *Poetry East*,
she teaches at Louisiana State Uni-
versity. She was born in Rich
mond, Virginia, in 1953.

ELEGY

Not to be born is the best for man.
W. H. AUDEN

I'm sorry: I don't think much
about you anymore.
The children I'm planning to have
with my new husband
take up all my time these days.
Did I tell you we painted the extra
bedroom blue and pasted stars on the ceiling?
At night, waking from a dream,
a child could believe it's the real thing.

I never let you mean much to me
anyway, because I was afraid of you.
The field outside town
where I lay down and made you
is gone now, grown into a whole town
of condominiums and ugly stores.

I've never been able to write you
even one decent letter.
You think I don't care.
There were workmen eating sandwiches
on a brick wall the day you died.
We stepped through the thick, red dust.
Remember that song I used to sing you?
Tell me: I don't.

DEBORAH DIGGES

Deborah Digges was born in Jefferson City, Missouri, in 1950 and is the author of *Vesper Sparrows* and *Late in the Millenium*. The recipient of the Delmore Schwartz Memorial Poetry Prize, she is on the English faculty at Tufts.

COMPLETING SOME MEDICAL DRAWINGS

The summer I collaborate the body with *Gray's Anatomy*,
I learn anger is a kind of praise.
I drive in the heat to show you the sketches,
cross a river, only to watch you
shake your head and go upstairs,
move deeper into the house I was born in.
I start over these evenings
when the dark smokes off the water.
In the drift and cool, my sons can sleep,
their breathing a thin cacophony,

as I draft, cross-hatch, pull from the page
that which purifies the blood, this time more
carefully: *inferior vena cava, left auricle, left
ventricle, aorta,* until the white space recedes
like the horizon at first sight of land,
sand and sky in focus where the heart blooms
in context. I used to say, like love,
you had no sense of irony, who beat your daughters
then broke your arm mending a tree.
Who did the autopsy on Pretty Boy Floyd the day
you were married. You even opened up your mother,
gave her another twenty years.

                          The trick of the artist
is implication, revealed, imagined.
The trick of the body is its true connections, flesh
of the flesh of the flesh invented, literally,
from nothing. In the map work of these arteries
the blood remembers who you are.
I can trace you back from Holland to Ellis Island,
back to those gutted New Jersey beaches
where the sea is a sadness whose rivers empty
near the emergency entrance of Bellevue and St. Vincent's.
I can even follow the history of the long drive
to the middle of the country.
Now you imagine your death, head-on, at each hillcrest.
There is no recovery.
The line, moved from its center, crosses
and doubles back, takes form.
Look closely. See how shadows are really
the failure of light in smaller and smaller measures.
Inevitable, perfect, they complete themselves and disappear
here in the heart, the landlocked heart.

STEPHEN DOBYNS

Born in Orange, New Jersey, in
1941, Stephen Dobyns has pub-
lished seven books of poems, in-
cluding *Cemetery Nights and
Body Traffic*, and twelve novels.
He teaches at Syracuse University.

BEAUTY

The father gets a bullet in the eye, killing him
instantly. His daughter raises an arm to say stop
and gets shot in the hand. He's a grocer from Baghdad
and at that time lots of Iraqis are moving to Detroit
to open small markets in the ghetto. In a month,
three have been murdered and since it is becoming
old news your editor says only to pick up a photo
unless you can find someone half decent to talk to.

Jammed into the living room are twenty men in black,
weeping, and thirty women wailing and pulling their hair—
something not prepared for by your Episcopal upbringing.

The grocer had already given the black junkie his money
and the junkie was already out the door when he fired,
for no apparent reason, the cops said. The other daughter,
who gives you the picture, has olive skin, great dark eyes
and is so beautiful you force yourself to stare only

at the passport photo in order not to offend her.
The photo shows you a young man with a thin face cheerfully
expecting to make his fortune in the black ghetto.
As you listen to the girl, the wailing surrounds you
like bits of flying glass. It was a cousin who was shot
the week before, then a good friend two weeks before that.
Who can believe it? During the riots, he told people
to take what they needed, pay when they were able.

Although the girl has little to do with your story,
she is, in a sense, the entire story. She is young,
beautiful and her father has just been shot. As you
accept the picture, her mother grabs it, presses it
to her lips. The girl gently pries her mother's fingers
from the picture and returns it. Then her sister with
the wounded hand snatches the picture and you want to
unwrap the bandages, touch your fingers to the bullet hole.

Again the girl retrieves the picture, but before she
can give it back, a third woman in black grabs it,
begins kissing it and crushing it to her bosom. You think
of the unflappable photographers on the fourth floor
unfolding the picture and trying to erase the creases,
but when the picture appears in the paper it still bears
the wrinkles of the fat woman's heart, and you feel caught
between the picture grabbing which is comic and the wailing

which is like an animal gnawing your stomach. The girl
touches your arm, asks if anything is wrong and you say,
no, you only want to get out of there; and once back
at the paper you tell your editor of this room with fifty
screaming people, how they kept snatching the picture.

So he tells you about a kid getting drowned when he was
a reporter, but that's not the point, nor is the screaming,
nor the fact that none of this will appear in a news story

about an Iraqi grocer shot by a black drug addict,
and see, here is his picture as he looked when he first
came to our country eight years ago, so glad to get
out of Baghdad. What could be worse than Baghdad?
The point is the 16-year-old daughter giving back
the picture, asking you to put it in your pocket, then
touching your arm, asking if you are all right and
would you like a glass of water? The point is she hardly

belongs to that room or any reality found in newspapers,
that she's one of the few reasons you get up in the morning,
pursue your life all day and why you soon quit the paper
to find her: beautiful Iraqi girl last seen surrounded by
wailing for the death of her father. For Christ's sake,
those fools at the paper thought you wanted to fuck her,
as if that's all you can do with something beautiful,
as if that's what it means to govern your life by it.

SUSAN DODD

Susan Dodd received the Iowa
School of Letters Award for Short
Fiction for her first book, *Old
Wives' Tales*. Her other books are
No Earthly Notion, *Mamaw*, and
Hell-Bent Men and Their Cities.
She was born in Chicago in 1946
and is currently Briggs-Copeland
Lecturer on Fiction at Harvard.

WILD MEN OF BORNEO

My father, seventy-nine, squats in a square of morning light. His hands, removing snails from a jade plant, look naked, shamed in the glare of the California sun. These hands never meant to live so long, their fingers pared down to nothing. Yet they move rapidly, plucking the snails with surgical steadiness. The family fortune: my father's hands.

"You're looking good, Pa," I say.

He doesn't look up from the cluster of deep green leaves, cushy as the pads of children's thumbs. "So you said. Last night."

He picked me up at the airport himself, crawling through Los Angeles at rush hour, locked behind tinted windows in the Buick's conditioned air.

He was an hour early for my arrival. I, his son, didn't take my eyes off my watch during landing. The flight was already twenty minutes late as we started our descent: I was keeping the old man waiting. Even in retirement, he remains a surgeon. I imagined him in the airport's sordid men's room, scrubbing up, watching the clock.

"Guess the climate agrees with you," I say. Lame: the physician's son.

He looks up. "*I* agree with *it*," he tells me smoothly. "Why fight it?"

My father turns from me and raises his eyes to the piercingly clear sky. The light is like that in a hospital amphitheater, uncomplaisant and antiseptic. He smiles grimly, a man perfectly accustomed to prolonging life beyond the point of diminishing marginal returns.

My father and I have much in common. We lack for nothing but wives. We are both in positions to see to our own comforts. We admire, on strictly timed visits, one another's amenities, for we are men who appreciate comfortable lives. Born to a tradition of tact, we delete references to the wives who abandoned us. My father managed to keep his for thirty-three years. I could hold onto mine for only five.

We speak of "my mother," of course. But somehow, in death, she has divided like an amoeba. "My mother" is another woman, not my father's wife. When she died of cancer of the colon, my father, saviour of lives, could not help but take it as a personal affront. Her death humiliated him. Now when he speaks of "your mother," his tones of sorrow are tokens of affection for me. His wife is another case entirely, a strictly forbidden topic, a buried mistake.

My father told me a year or so ago of a predatory, gabby widow he met at a cocktail party. She plied him with questions about his past and prospects. "What about your late wife?" she said.

"My wife," my father told her, "has never been late."

Now I do not believe my father actually said this. He is a helplessly courteous man. But he *wanted* to say it, which is more to the point. I suspect him of secretly worshipping a recollection of a dim creature who was always on time. However, he does not speak of her, nor have her in mind, when he says to me, "your mother."

He knows I am about to leave him. He understands that I have come to California to tell him so. My last visit is not long enough past to justify this one. Besides, it is April, and my usual journeys are dictated by the fiscal year. My father knows I have come to take my leave.

He will not deign to inquire. He will not permit me to wedge the announcement easily into our conversation if he can help it. But he is waiting for me to hammer it home, I can tell.

He takes me out to lunch. We sit at a chrome and oak table, separated from Balboa Bay by a wall of amber glass. My father eats a club sandwich, impressing me still with his capable hands, his own teeth. He wears his gardening clothes—a yellow porkpie hat, plaid pants, a red cardigan. I admire the jauntiness he has acquired in retirement, a bold adaptation to this unnatural habitat. Perhaps he has cultivated brazen visibility as a means of survival. Now that he can no longer play golf, he seems to take pains to look as if he does.

"Your mother loved it here," he says.

"The Yacht Club?"

"California. She said it made her think the world wasn't so old, after all."

I smile.

"She couldn't get over the fruits and vegetables in winter. I thought avocados and kiwi fruit would start sprouting from my ears. And she'd bring the damnedest-looking squash home from the Safeway . . ."

I see my opening. "You miss her, Pa," I say.

My father sets the mangled triangle of his sandwich firmly on the edge of his plate. When he looks at me, his light gray eyes are steely. I imagine this is the expression he used to buck up patients who must be made to accept bad news. "Your mother had a great deal of . . . zest," he says.

He is not about to brook a second opinion.

The fact is, my mother was frail. In her opinions, more than her person. She fell in love with my father the year she lost her own. I, by the time I was twelve, could convince her of anything, provided my father left me to my own devices. My mother, my father's wife, was a woman weakened by respect for men. She laid her fragile doubts to rest in a warm cradle of affection and regard and bridled her own enthusiasms. My father and I could come and go as we pleased. She always waited for us.

Sometimes my mother cried in the afternoons. But she always swore she didn't. The days must have been long for her. Waiting. Some days I would come home late from school to find her sitting in the darkened living room, on the edge of the piano bench, at the bass end of the key-board. There would be no sheet music in sight, and my mother never could play from memory. I would switch on the old brass floor lamp, and the silk shade would cast a false golden glow over her face, her auburn hair, her narrow shoulders.

"You're home," she'd say, as if I'd done something miraculous. The lids of her eyes would be rosy and swollen.

At a certain age, I was not too cautious to ask if she'd been crying. She always denied it with a girlish laugh. In time, perhaps to forestall my indelicate question, she moved from the piano bench to the crewel-work wingback chair beside the fireplace. She would hold a book in her lap, and listen for the door to open so she could switch on a lamp before I reached the room.

"Have you been crying, Mom?"

"A sad book, lovey. I'm a silly old sob-sister." I permitted her laugh to convince me. She became an admirer of Anne Morrow Lindbergh and other brave lady writers who had outlived their children.

I never told my father that his wife, my mother, wept behind his back. I expected him to know it, just as she expected me to guard her secret. My father was a brilliant doctor, with a gift for diagnostics. At the very least, he should have seen the days were bound to be long for her.

Two and a half years ago, at my mother's burial, I did not look at her husband to see if he cried when her cushioned, polished casket was cradled in the sandy California ground. I was afraid for a moment I might hate him either way, despise his strength or his weakness. I edged closer to him and kept my eyes on my ex-wife, Linda, who stood with the minor mourners on the opposite side of the grave. Linda and my mother had been very fond of each other. I distracted myself from my father by wondering if my wife had ever been reduced to tears by the unbearable weight of a long afternoon.

Although they had courted me for several years, I accepted a position with the World Bank only after my father and I had lost our wives. I could not leave my whereabouts to chance, knowing women waited for me. Linda might have come along wherever I went, of course, and we had no children. But each time I considered the prospect of a foreign post, there arose a pathetic picture of my wife languishing in a hammock in Karachi or Calcutta with the sun still high in the sky. I heard her soft, desperate voice struggling to confide in some Swahili-speaking houseboy, or haggling over a piece of stringy meat at a stall in the Casbah. I toyed with such scraps of imagination until I froze fast to them, like a child's tongue stuck to a metal fencepost in winter. I tore myself away from exotic ambitions, claimed the World Bank was a poor risk: some parts of the world are not fit to be seen by a man with dependants.

I neglected, however, to extrapolate my theories to Maclean, Virginia. I hastened to my office at the Brookings Institution each morning and never paused to ask how my wife spent her days. She mistook my conscientiousness for passion, my confidence for disregard. When she left me, I found her, for the first time, stunning. Not long ago she married a linguist from Georgetown and moved to Peru without batting an eye. Like my mother, Linda was sadly underestimated.

When the World Bank tendered what I felt would be its final offer, I discussed it with my father. I could not calculate the precise effect my whereabouts might have on him.

"They could send me to some pretty out-of-the-way places," I said.

"You're young," he told me, as if that answered everything.

"For two- or three-year hitches," I said.

"It's your decision, son."

"But what about you?"

He gazed past my shoulder toward an oil portrait of my mother, the oddly incongruous gift his colleagues had commissioned to mark his retirement from the staff of Sloan-Kettering. "I always wanted to see Borneo when I was a boy," he said. "Borneo. Imagine."

"Why Borneo?"

"'The Wild Men of Borneo.' In those days, all the circuses and carnivals had them." He seemed to study me speculatively for a moment, taking my measure. "Before your time," he said.

I waited for him to continue, but he didn't. "I guess that settles it, then," I said foolishly.

My father nodded, his expression solemn and innocent, sealing a bargain without logic. The lack of irony in his eyes aged him in mine.

That was two years ago. I have yet to see Borneo, but I have traveled to South America, Africa, the Far East. I have explored the economic ruins of world powers, the fiscal jungles of developing nations. I have kept a sharp eye on deficits, gross national products, and per capita incomes while governments toppled. At the World Bank, as at Brookings, I have earned a reputation as a "troubleshooter," a cool correspondent of currency wars. I, however, prefer to regard myself as merely a chip off the old block—a man with a gift for diagnostics.

Now I am to be rewarded for the slim margin of error in my second guesses: Tokyo. The assignment is something of a plum. I have been promised a host of benefits: administrative autonomy, car with driver, the opportunity to sway world markets. My flight departs from Dulles one week from tomorrow. I have come to take leave of my father. He knows, without being told. He waits through the long afternoon.

"What time is your plane on Sunday?" It is Friday.

"Early. Seven-thirty."

He nods. "No traffic problems, then."

"Why don't I just get a limousine?"

I am dismissed with a gesture, a wave of his still-competent hand. "How about some Mexican food tonight?" he says. "There's this place Nixon loved in San Juan Capistrano . . ."

I give the old man credit: he has managed to work the evils of politics and the perils of foreign travel into a single proposition. He is a master of the suggestive remark.

"Sure. I could go for some chiles rellenos."

"And margaritas. We'll make a night of it."

He is waiting.

"Pa—"

"So, where's it going to be?"

"The place in San Juan Capistrano sounds fine," I say.

His laugh is brutally abbreviated, like the bark of a dog with a choke chain clutching its throat. I remember him telling me once, long ago, "The first incision's always the hardest to make . . . but it shouldn't be. That's rarely the one a patient dies from."

"Tokyo, Pa. Next week."

"For how long?"

My fingers curl, tighten, as if I am holding a scalpel. I relax them, force my own hand to hold firm. "For a couple of years, anyway."

"Tokyo . . . sounds like you're moving up pretty fast, boy."

I shrug. It wouldn't do, now, to tell him about the living allowance, influence on exchange rates, a waiting driver, the balance of trade.

"Tokyo." He shakes his head. "Not exactly Borneo, is it?"

The restaurant is crowded. Even with a reservation, we have to wait twenty minutes for a table. My father and I, two independent men, stand side by side at the blue and white tiled bar, drinking margaritas. A swag of plastic peppers festoons a mirrored arch, the bartender's proscenium. Absurdly young and beautiful, he performs with the staccato precision of a picador among the lustrous glasses and whirring chrome machines.

The old man plays host, drawing me out about world gold prices, the Federal Reserve. He has put on a navy blue blazer, a vague nautical insignia on its breast pocket. His handkerchief is paisley silk. Coarse salt glimmers at the corners of his mouth.

I catch myself stumbling, losing the strength of my convictions under my father's merciless charm. Then there is the inevitable lull. He lets me off the hook.

"Sorry about the wait, son."

"Friday nights," I say.

"Funny . . . time always seems so much longer when you're waiting for something." He sets his thick-lipped greenish glass on the bar and spreads his hands on either side of it. He stares in mild astonishment at how they betray him. "I'm beginning to understand what your mother . . . what Claire . . . meant."

Speechless, I touch my father's sleeve.

"She'd use that expression, 'Time hangs heavy on your hands.' I never understood her."

Beneath my fingers, my father's bent elbow twitches, once, as if he is trying to shake me off. "She was always waiting for something, your mother."

"We all are, Pa."

"I suppose so."

In the next room, a mariachi band is playing "Vaya con Dios."

"Don't get me wrong," my father says, "but I wish sometimes you'd been a girl."

Indescribable pain fills my chest, suffocating me. My father observes, making a swift, sure diagnosis.

"It just might be easier, son."

"How?"

"If you were a daughter, maybe I could ask you not to go."

"What if I went anyway?"

My father looks away, through the archway into the crowded, noisy dining room. He tilts his head to one side, seems to be listening to the music, inhaling the overspiced air. There is a twisted smile on his salty lips.

"Tonight I'd dance with you," he says.

A waitress in an embroidered blouse approaches us. There is a string of veined turquoise beads around her neck. She has the coarse-grained, unfinished look of a primitive madonna. "Your table is ready, sir." She addresses me, not my father.

My old man lifts his glass. "To Tokyo," he says.

"To Borneo," I correct him, gently touching my glass to his.

He takes my arm and allows me to lead him into the next room.

MARK DOTY

Mark Doty, who was born in
Maryville, Tennessee, in 1953,
has published two volumes of
poems, *Turtle, Swan* and *Beth-
lehem in Broad Daylight*. He
teaches at Goddard College and in
the M.F.A. program at Vermont
College.

TURTLE, SWAN

Because the road to our house
is a back road, meadowlands punctuated
by gravel quarry and lumberyard,
there are unexpected travelers
some nights on our way home from work.
Once, on the lawn of the Tool

and Die Company, a swan;
the word doesn't convey the shock
of the thing, white architecture
rippling like a pond's rain-pocked skin,

beak lifting to hiss at my approach.
Magisterial, set down in elegant authority,

he let us know exactly how close we might come.
After a week of long rains
that filled the marsh until it poured
across the road to make in low woods
a new heaven for toads,
a snapping turtle lumbered down the center

of the asphalt like an ambulatory helmet.
His long tail dragged, blunt head jutting out
of the lapidary prehistoric sleep of shell.
We'd have lifted him from the road
but thought he might bend his long neck back
to snap. I tried herding him; he rushed,

though we didn't think those blocky legs
could hurry—then ambled back
to the center of the road, a target
for kids who'd delight in the crush
of something slow with the look
of primeval invulnerability. He turned

the blunt spear point of his jaws,
puffing his undermouth like a bullfrog,
and snapped at your shoe,
vising a beakful of—thank God—
leather. You had to shake him loose. We left him
to his own devices, talked on the way home

of what must lead him to new marsh
or old home ground. The next day you saw,
one town over, remains of shell
in front of the little liquor store. I argued
it was too far from where we'd seen him,
too small to be his . . . though who could tell

what the day's heat might have taken
from his body. For days he became a stain,
a blotch that could have been merely
oil. I did not want to believe that
was what we saw alive in the firm center
of his authority and right

to walk the center of the road,
head up like a missionary moving certainly
into the country of his hopes.
In the movies in this small town
I stopped for popcorn while you went ahead
to claim seats. When I entered the cool dark

I saw straight couples everywhere,
no single silhouette who might be you.
I walked those two aisles too small
to lose anyone and thought of a book
I read in seventh grade, *Stranger than Science*,
in which a man simply walked away,

at a picnic, and was,
in the act of striding forward
to examine a flower, gone.
By the time the previews ended
I was nearly in tears—then realized
the head of one-half the couple in the first row

was only your leather jacket propped in the seat
that would be mine. I don't think I remember
anything of the first half of the movie.
I don't know what happened to the swan. I read
every week of some man's lover showing
the first symptoms, the night sweat

or casual flu, and then the wasting begins
and the disappearance a day at a time.
I don't know what happened to the swan;

I don't know if the stain on the street
was our turtle or some other. I don't know
where these things we meet and know briefly,

as well as we can or they will let us,
go. I only know that I do not want you
—you with your white and muscular wings
that rise and ripple beneath or above me,
your magnificent neck, eyes the deep mottled autumnal colors
of polished tortoise—I do not want you ever to die.

NORMAN DUBIE

Norman Dubie is the author of
fourteen books of poetry, includ-
ing *Selected & New Poems*, *The
Springhouse*, and *Groom Falconer*.
Born in Barre, Vermont, in 1945,
he teaches at Arizona State
University.

LA PAMPA

The dead truck sits in the shimmering wheat.
The vegetables on the sill were meant to go
To seed. Looking past them there is a tomb.
Beyond the tomb, in the heat, two boys
Enter a grove they were told not to: in the branches
Is the drying skin of a dead bull
Slaughtered that noon, the boys' father
Sits on the ground in the dripping shadow of the skin.
He is eating plums. Last night, their newborn sister

Slept beside the paraffin stove, their mother
Had left some of her milk in a cup
In the icebox, it was blue, sticky
And too sweet they thought. Their grandfather
In fever spoke of the judges of the dead,
Of words of necessity: *a young librarian*
Went straight in the chair, a tooth lost
In her upper lip. They were so silent
While they knelt there in the grove—they felt
It was just their luck that at the moment
Their father stood to dust himself off
The younger brother was seized, it seemed, by hiccups.
The next winter he fell into the well. Past midnight
The older brother remembers while the sergeant
Tortures the young librarian
In white pajamas and turquoise slippers.

ANDRE DUBUS

The recipient of a MacArthur
Fellowship and numerous other
awards, Andre Dubus has pub-
lished ten works of fiction, most
recently *We Don't Live Here Any-
more, Voices from the Moon, The
Last Worthless Evening*, and *Se-
lected Stories*. He was born in
Lake Charles, Louisiana, in 1936
and now lives and writes in Haver-
hill, Massachusetts.

SORROWFUL MYSTERIES

When Gerry Fontenot is five, six, and seven years old, he likes to ride in the car with his parents. It is a grey 1938 Chevrolet and it has a ration stamp on the windshield. Since the war started when Gerry was five, his father has gone to work on a bicycle, and rarely drives the car except to Sunday Mass, and to go hunting and fishing. Gerry fishes with him, from the bank of the bayou. They fish with bamboo poles, corks, sinkers, and worms, and catch perch and catfish. His father wears a .22 revolver at his side, for cottonmouths. In the fall Gerry goes hunting with him, crouches beside him in ditches bordering fields, and when the doves fly, his father

93

stands and fires the twelve-gauge pump, and Gerry marks where the birds fall, then runs out into the field where they lie, and gathers them. They are soft and warm as he runs with them, back to his father. This is in southern Louisiana, and twice he and his father see an open truck filled with German prisoners, going to work in the sugar cane fields.

He goes on errands with his mother. He goes to grocery stores, dime stores, drugstores, and shopping for school clothes in the fall, and Easter clothes in the spring, and to the beauty parlor, where he likes to sit and watch the women. Twice a week he goes with her to the colored section, where they leave and pick up the week's washing and ironing. His mother washes at home too: the bedclothes, socks, underwear, towels, and whatever else does not have to be ironed. She washes these in a wringer washing machine; he likes watching her feed the clothes into the wringer, and the way they come out flattened and drop into the basket. She hangs them on the clothesline in the backyard, and Gerry stands at the basket and hands them to her so she will not have to stoop. On rainy days she dries them inside on racks, which in winter she places in front of space heaters. She listens to the weather forecasts on the radio, and most of the time is able to wash on clear days.

The Negro woman washes the clothes that must be ironed, or starched and ironed. In front of the woman's unpainted wooden house, Gerry's mother presses the horn, and the large woman comes out and takes the basket from the back seat. Next day, at the sound of the horn, she brings out the basket. It is filled with ironed, folded skirts and blouses, and across its top lie dresses and shirts on hangers. Gerry opens the window his mother has told him to close as they approached the colored section with its dusty roads. He smells the clean, ironed clothes, pastels and prints, and his father's white and pale blue, and he looks at the rutted dirt road, the unpainted wood and rusted screens of the houses, old cars in front of them and tire swings hanging from trees over the worn and packed dirt yards, dozens of barefoot, dusty children stopping their play to watch him and his mother in the car, and the old slippers and dress the Negro woman wears, and he breathes her smell of sweat, looks at her black and brown hand crossing him to take the dollar from his mother's fingers.

On Fridays in spring and summer, Leonard comes to mow the lawn. He is a Negro, and has eight children, and Gerry sees him only once between fall and spring, when he comes on Christmas Eve, and Gerry's father and mother give him toys and clothes that Gerry and his three older sisters have outgrown, a bottle of bourbon, one of the fruitcakes Gerry's mother makes at Christmas, and five dollars. Leonard receives these at the back door, where on Fridays, in spring and summer, he is paid and fed. The Fontenots eat dinner at noon, and Gerry's mother serves Leonard a plate and a glass of iced tea with leaves from the mint she grows under the faucet behind the house. She calls him from the back steps, and he comes, wiping his brow with a bandanna, and takes his dinner to the shade of a sycamore tree. From his place at the dining room table, Gerry watches him sit on the grass and take off his straw hat; he eats, then rolls a cigarette. When he has smoked, he brings his plate and glass to the back door, knocks, and hands them to whoever answers. His glass is a jelly glass, his plate blue china, and his knife and fork stainless steel. From Friday to Friday the knife and fork lie at one side of a drawer, beside the compartments that hold silver; the glass is nearly out of reach, at the back of the second shelf in the cupboard for glasses; the plate rests under serving bowls in the china cupboard. Gerry's mother has told him and his sisters not to use them, they are Leonard's, and from Friday to Friday, they sit, and from fall to spring, and finally forever when one year Gerry is strong enough to push the lawn mower for his allowance, and Leonard comes only when Gerry's father calls him every Christmas Eve.

Before that, when he is eight, Gerry has stopped going on errands with his mother. On Saturday afternoons he walks or, on rainy days, rides the bus to town with neighborhood boys, to the movie theater where they watch westerns and the weekly chapter of a serial. He stands in line on the sidewalk, holding his quarter that will buy a ticket, a bag of popcorn, and, on the way home, an ice-cream soda. Opposite his line, to the right of the theater as you face it, are the Negro boys. Gerry does not look at them. Or not directly: he glances, he listens, as a few years later he will do with girls when he goes to movies that draw them. The Negroes enter through the door marked *Colored*, where he supposes a Negro woman sells tickets, then climb the stairs to the balcony, and Gerry wonders whether someone sells them popcorn and candy and drinks up there, or imagines them smelling all the bags of popcorn in the dark beneath them. Then he watches the cartoon and previews of next Saturday's movie, and he likes them but is waiting for the chapter of the serial whose characters he and his friends have played in their yards all week; they have worked out several escapes for the trapped hero and, as always, they are wrong.

He has eaten his popcorn when the credits for the movie appear, then a tall man rides a beautiful black or white palomino horse across the screen. The movie is black and white, but a palomino looks as golden and lovely as the ones he has seen in parades. Sitting in the dark, he is aware of his friends on both sides of him only as feelings coincident with his own: the excitement of becoming the Cisco Kid, Durango Kid, Red Ryder, the strongest and best-looking, the most courageous and good, the fastest with horse and fists and gun. Then it is over, the lights are on, he turns to his friends, flesh again, stands to leave, then remembers the Negroes. He blinks up at them standing at the balcony wall, looking down at the white boys pressed together in the aisle, moving slowly out of the theater. Sometimes his eyes meet those of a Negro boy, and Gerry smiles; only one ever smiles back.

In summer he and his friends go to town on weekday afternoons to see war movies, or to buy toy guns or baseballs, and when he meets Negroes on the sidewalk, he averts his eyes; but he watches them in department stores, bending over the water fountains marked *Colored*, and when they enter the city buses and walk past him to the rear, he watches them, and during the ride he glances, and listens to their talk and laughter. One hot afternoon when he is twelve, he goes with a friend to deliver the local newspaper in the colored section. He has not been there since riding with his mother, who has not gone for years either; now the city buses stop near his neighborhood, and a Negro woman comes on it and irons the family's clothes in their kitchen. He goes that afternoon because his friend has challenged him. They have argued: they both have paper routes, and when his friend complained about his, Gerry said it was easy work. Sure, his friend said, you don't have to hold your breath. You mean when you collect? No, man, when I just ride through. So Gerry finishes his route, then goes with his friend: a bicycle ride of several miles ending, or beginning, at a neighborhood of poor whites, their houses painted but peeling, their screened front porches facing lawns so narrow that only small children can play catch in them; the older boys and girls play tapeball on the blacktop street. Gerry and his friends play that, making a ball of tape around a sock, and hitting with a baseball bat, but they have lawns big enough to contain them. Gerry's father teaches history at the public high school, and in summer is a recreation director for children in the city park, and some nights in his bed Gerry hears his father and mother worry about money; their voices are weary, and frighten him. But riding down this street, he feels shamefully rich, wants the boys and girls pausing in their game to know he only has a new Schwinn because he saved his money to buy it.

He and his friend jolt over the railroad tracks, and the blacktop ends. Dust is deep in the road. They ride past fields of tall grass and decaying things: broken furniture, space heaters, stoves, cars. Negro children are in the fields. Then they come to the streets of houses, turn onto the first one, a rutted and dusty road, and breathe the smell. It is as tangible as the dust a car raises to Gerry's face as it bounces past him, its unmuffled exhaust pipe sounding like gunfire, and Gerry feels that he enters the smell, as you enter a cloud of dust; and a hard summer rain, with lightning and thunder, would settle it, and the air would smell of grass and trees. Its base is sour, as though in the heat of summer someone has half-filled a garbage can with milk, then dropped in citrus fruit and cooked rice and vegetables and meat and fish, mattress ticking and a pillow, covered it, and left it for a week in the July sun. In this smell children play in the street and on the lawns that are dirt too, dust, save for strips of crisp-looking yellowish grass in the narrow spaces between houses, and scattered patches near the porches. He remembers the roads and houses and yards from riding with his mother, but not the smell, for even in summer they had rolled up the windows. Or maybe her perfume and cigarettes had fortified the car against the moment the laundry woman would open the back door, or reach through the window for her dollar; but he wonders now if his mother wanted the windows closed only to keep out dust. Women and men sit on the front porches, as Gerry and his friend slowly ride up the road, and his friend throws triangular-folded papers onto the yards, where they skip in rising dust.

It is late afternoon, and he can smell cooking too: hot grease and meat, turnip or mustard greens, and he hears talk and laughter from the shaded porches. Everything seems to be dying: cars and houses and tar paper roofs in the weather, grass in the sun; sparse oaks and pines and weeping willows draw children and women with babies to their shade; beneath the hanging tent of a willow, an old man sits with two crawling children wearing diapers, and Gerry remembers Leonard eating in the shade of the sycamore. Gerry's father still phones Leonard on Christmas Eve, and last year he went home with the electric train Gerry has outgrown, along with toy soldiers and cap pistols and Saturday serials and westerns, a growth that sometimes troubles him: when he was nine and ten and saw that other neighborhood boys stopped going to the Saturday movies when they were twelve or thirteen, he could not understand why something so exciting was suddenly not, and he promised himself that he would always go on Saturdays, although he knew he would not, for the only teenaged boy who did was odd and frightening: he was about eighteen, and in his voice and eyes was the desperation of a boy lying to a teacher, and he tried to sit betwen Gerry and his friends, and once he did before they could close the gap, and all through the movie he tried to rub Gerry's thigh, and Gerry whispered *Stop it*, and pushed at the wrist, the fingers. So he knew a time would come when he would no longer love his heroes and their horses, and it saddened him to know that such love could not survive mere time. It did not, and that is what troubles him, when he wonders if his love of baseball and football and hunting and fishing and bicycles will die too, and wonders what he will love then.

He looks for Leonard as he rides down the road, where some yards are bordered with colored and clear bottles, half-buried with bottoms up to the sun. In others a small rectangle of flowers grows near the porch, and the smell seems to come from the flowers too, and the trees. He wants to enter one of those houses kept darkened with shades drawn against the heat, wants to trace and define that smell, press his nose to beds and sofas and floor and walls, the bosom of a woman, the chest of a man, the hair of a child. Breathing through his mouth, swallowing his nausea, he looks at his friend and sees what he knows is on his face as well: an expression of sustained and pallid horror.

On summer mornings the neighborhood boys play baseball. One of the fathers owns a field behind his house; he has mowed it with a tractor and built a backstop of two-by-fours and screen, laid out an infield with a pitcher's mound, and put up foul poles at the edge of the tall weeds that surround the outfield. The boys play every rainless morning except Sunday, when all but the two Protestants go to Mass. They pitch slowly so they can hit the ball, and so the catcher, with only a mask, will not get hurt. But they pitch from a windup, and try to throw curves and knuckleballs, and sometimes they play other neighborhood teams who loan their catcher shin guards and chest protector, then the pitchers throw hard.

One morning a Negro boy rides his bicycle past the field, on the dirt road behind the backstop; he holds a fishing pole across the handlebars and is going toward the woods beyond left field, and the bayou that runs wide and muddy through the trees. A few long innings later, he comes back without fish, and stops to watch the game. Standing, holding his bicycle, he watches two innings. Then, as Gerry's team is trotting in to bat, someone calls to the boy: Do you want to play? In the infield and outfield, and near home plate, voices stop. The boy looks at the pause, the silence, then nods, lowers his kickstand, and slowly walks onto the field.

'You're with us,' someone says. 'What do you play?'

'I like first.'

That summer, with eight dollars of his paper route money, Gerry has bought a first-baseman's glove: a Rawlings Trapper, because he liked the way it looked, and felt on his hand, but he is not a good first baseman: he turns his head away from throws that hit the dirt in front of his reaching glove and bounce toward his body, his face. He hands the glove to the boy.

'Use this. I ought to play second anyway.'

The boy puts his hand in the Trapper, thumps its pocket, turns his wrist back and forth, looking at the leather that is still a new reddish brown. Boys speak their names to him. His is Clay. They give him a place in the batting order, point to the boy he follows.

He is tall, and at the plate he takes a high stride and a long, hard swing. After his first hit, the outfield plays him deeply, at the edge of the weeds that are the boys' fence, and the infielders back up. At first base he is often clumsy, kneeling for ground balls, stretching before an infielder has thrown so that some balls nearly go past or above him; he is fearless, though, and none of the bouncing throws from third and deep short go past his body. He does not talk to any one boy, but from first he calls to the pitcher: *Come babe, come boy;* calls to infielders bent for ground balls: *Plenty time, plenty time, we got him;* and, to hitters when Gerry's team is at bat: *Good eye, good eye.* The game ends when the twelve o'clock whistle blows.

'That it?' Clay says as the fielders run in while he is swinging two bats on deck.

'We have to go eat,' the catcher says, taking off his mask, and with a dirt-smeared forearm wiping sweat from his brow.

'Me too,' he says, and drops the bats, picks up the Trapper, and hands it to Gerry. Gerry looks at it, lying across Clay's palm, looks at Clay's thumb on the leather.

'I'm a crappy first baseman,' he says. 'Keep it.'

'You kidding?'

'No. Go on.'

'What you going to play with?'

'My fielder's glove.'

Some of the boys are watching now; others are mounting bicycles on the road, riding away with gloves hanging from the handlebars, bats held across them.

'You don't want to play first no more?'

'No. Really.'

'Man, that's some *glove*. What's your name again?'

'Gerry,' he says, and extends his right hand. Clay takes it, and Gerry squeezes the big, limp hand; releases it.

'Gerry,' Clay says, looking down at his face as though to memorize it, or discern its features from among the twenty white faces of his morning.

'Good man,' he says, and turning, and calling goodbyes, he goes to his bicycle, places his fishing pole across the handlebars, hangs the Trapper from one, and rides quickly up the dirt road. Where the road turns to blacktop, boys are bicycling in a cluster, and Gerry watches Clay pass them with a wave. Then he is in the distance, among white houses with lawns and trees; is gone, leaving Gerry with the respectful voices of his friends, and peace and pride in his heart. He has attended a Catholic school since the first grade, so knows he must despise those feelings. He jokes about his play at first base, and goes with his Marty Marion glove and Ted Williams Louisville Slugger to his bicycle. But riding home, he nestles with his proud peace. At dinner he says nothing of Clay. The Christian Brothers have taught him that an act of charity can be canceled by the telling of it. Also, he suspects his family would think he is a fool.

A year later, a Negro man in a neighboring town is convicted of raping a young white woman, and is sentenced to die in the electric chair. His story is the front-page headline of the paper Gerry delivers, but at home, because the crime was rape, his mother tells the family she does not want any talk about it. Gerry's father mutters enough, from time to time, for Gerry to know he is angry and sad because if the woman had been a Negro, and the man white, there would have been neither execution nor conviction. But on his friends' lawns, while he plays catch or pepper or sits on the grass, whittling branches down to sticks, he listens to voluptuous voices from the porches, where men and women drink bourbon and talk of niggers and rape and the electric chair. The Negro's name is Sonny Broussard, and every night Gerry prays for his soul.

On the March night Sonny Broussard will die, Gerry lies in bed and says a rosary. It is a Thursday, a day for the Joyful Mysteries, but looking out past the mimosa, at the corner streetlight, he prays with the Sorrowful Mysteries, remembers the newspaper photographs of Sonny Broussard, tries to imagine his terror as midnight draws near—why midnight? and how could he live that day in his cell?—and sees Sonny Broussard on his knees in the Garden of Olives; he wears khakis, his arms rest on a large stone, and his face is lifted to the sky. Tied to a pillar and shirtless, he is silent under the whip; thorns pierce his head, and the fathers of Gerry's friends strike his face, their wives watch as he climbs the long hill, cross on his shoulder, then he is lying on it, the men with hammers are carpenters in khakis, squatting above him, sweat running down their faces to drip on cigarettes between their lips, heads cocked away from smoke; they swing the hammers in unison, and drive nails through wrists and crossed feet. Then Calvary fades and Gerry sees instead a narrow corridor between cells with a door at the end; two guards are leading Sonny Broussard to it, and Gerry watches them from the rear. They open the door to a room filled with people, save for a space in the center of their circle, where the electric chair waits. They have been talking when the guard opens the door, and they do not stop. They are smoking and drinking and knitting; they watch Sonny Broussard between the guards, look from him to each other, and back to him, talking, clapping a hand on a neighbor's shoulder, a thigh. The guards buckle Sonny Broussard into the chair. Gerry shuts his eyes, and tries to feel the chair, the straps, Sonny Broussard's fear; to feel so hated that the people who surround him wait for the very throes and stench of his death. Then he feels it, he is in the electric chair, and he opens his eyes and holds his breath against the scream in his throat.

Gerry attends the state college in town, and lives at home. He majors in history, and is in the Naval ROTC, and is grateful that he will spend three years in the Navy after college. He does not want to do anything with history but learn it, and he believes the Navy will give him time to know what he will do with the rest of his life. He also wants to go to sea.

He thinks more about the sea than history; by Christmas he is in love, and thinks more about the girl than either of them. Near the end of the year, the college president calls an assembly and tells the students that, in the fall, colored boys and girls will be coming to the school. The president is a politician and will later be lieutenant-governor. There will be no trouble at this college, he says. I do not want troops or federal marshals on my campus. If any one of you starts trouble, or even joins in on it if one of them starts it, I will have you in my office, and you'd best bring your luggage with you.

The day after his last examinations, Gerry starts working with a construction crew. In the long heat he carries hundred-pound bags of cement, shovels gravel and sand, pushes wheelbarrows of wet concrete, digs trenches for foundations, holes for septic tanks, has more money than he has ever owned, spends most of it on his girl in restaurants and movies and nightclubs and bars, and by late August has gained fifteen pounds, much of it above his waist, though beneath that is enough for his girl to pinch, and call his Budweiser belt. Then he hears of Emmett Till. He is a Negro boy, and in the night two white men have taken him from his great-uncle's house in Mississippi. Gerry and his girl wait. Three days later, while Gerry sits in the living room with his family before supper, the news comes over the radio: a search party has found Emmett Till at the bottom of the Tallahatchie River; a seventy-pound cotton gin fan was tied to his neck with barbed wire; he was beaten and shot in the head, and was decomposing. Gerry's father lowers his magazine, removes his glasses, rubs his eyes, and says: 'Oh my Lord, it's happening again.'

He goes to the kitchen and Gerry hears him mixing another bourbon and water, then the back screen door opens and shuts. His mother and one sister still at home are talking about Mississippi and rednecks, and the poor boy, and what were they thinking of, what kind of men *are* they? He wants to follow his father, to ask what memory or hearsay he had meant, but he does not believe he is old enough, man enough, to move into his father's silence in the backyard.

He phones his girl, and after supper asks his father for the car, and drives to her house. She is waiting on the front porch, and walks quickly to the car. She is a petite, dark-skinned Cajun girl, with fast and accented speech, deep laughter, and a temper that is fierce when it reaches the end of its long tolerance. Through generations the Fontenots' speech has slowed and softened, so that Gerry sounds more Southern than French;

she teases him about it, and often, when he is with her, he finds that he is talking with her rhythms and inflections. She likes dancing, rhythm and blues, jazz, gin, beer, Pall Malls, peppery food, and passionate kissing, with no fondling. She receives Communion every morning, wears a gold Sacred Heart medal on a gold chain around her neck, and wants to teach history in college. Her name is Camille Theriot.

They go to a bar, where people are dancing to the jukebox. The couples in booths and boys at the bar are local students, some still in high school, for in this town parents and bartenders ignore the law about drinking, and bartenders only use it at clubs that do not want young people. Gerry has been drinking at this bar since he got his driver's license when he was sixteen. He leads Camille to a booth, and they drink gin and tonics, and repeat what they heard at college, in the classroom where they met: that it was economic, and all the hatred started with slavery, the Civil War leaving the poor white no one about whom he could say: *At least I ain't a slave like him*, leaving him only: *At least I ain't a nigger*. And after the war the Negro had to be contained to provide cheap labor in the fields. Camille says it might explain segregation, so long as you don't wonder about rich whites who don't have to create somebody to look down on, since they can do it from birth anyway.

'So it doesn't apply,' she says.

'They never seem to, do they?'

'What?'

'Theories. Do you think those sonsabitches—do you think they tied that fan on before or after they shot him? Why barbed wire if he was already dead? Why not baling wire, or—'

The waitress is there, and he watches her lower the drinks, put their empty glasses on her tray; he pays her, and looks at Camille. Her face is lowered, her eyes closed.

Around midnight, when the crowd thins, they move to the bar. Three couples dance slowly to Sinatra; another kisses in a booth. Gerry knows they are in high school when the boy lights a cigarette and they share it: the girl draws on it, they kiss, and she exhales into his mouth; then the boy does it. Camille says: 'Maybe we should go north to college, and just stay there.'

'I hear the people are cold as the snow.'

'Me too. And they eat boiled food with some kind of white sauce.'

'You want some oysters?'

'Can we get there before they close?'

'Let's try it,' he says. 'Did you French-smoke in high school?'

'Sure.'

A boy stands beside Gerry and loudly orders a beer. He is drunk, and when he sees Gerry looking at him, he says: 'Woo. They *did* it to him, didn't they? 'Course now, a little nigger boy like that, you can't tell'—as Gerry stands so he can reach into his pocket—'could be he'd go swimming with seventy pounds hanging on his neck, and a bullet in his head'— and Gerry opens the knife he keeps sharp for fish and game, looks at the blade, then turns toward the voice: 'Emmett *Till* rhymes with *kill.* Hoo. Hot*damn.* Kill *Till*—'

Gerry's hand bunches the boy's collar, turns him, and pushes his back against the bar. He touches the boy's throat with the point of the knife, and his voice comes yelling out of him; he seems to rise from the floor with it, can feel nothing of his flesh beneath it: 'You like *death? Feel* it!'

He presses his knife until skin dimples around its point. The boy is still, his mouth open, his eyes rolled to his left, where the knife is. Camille is screaming, and Gerry hears *Cut his tongue out! Cut his heart out!* Then she is standing in front of the boy, her arms waving, and Gerry hears *Bastard bastard bastard*, as he watches the boy's eyes and open mouth, then hears the bartender speaking softly: 'Take it easy now. You're Gerry, right?' He glances at the voice; the bartender is leaning over the bar. 'Easy, Gerry. You stick him there, he's gone. Why don't you go on home now, okay?'

Camille is quiet. Watching the point, Gerry pushes the knife, hardly a motion at all, for he is holding back too; the dimple, for an instant, deepens and he feels the boy's chest breathless and rigid beneath his left fist.

'Okay,' he says, and releases the boy's shirt, folds the knife, and takes Camille's arm. Boys at the bar and couples on the dance floor stand watching. There is music he cannot hear clearly enough to name. He and Camille walk between the couples to the door.

Two men, Roy Bryant and John William Milan, are arrested, and through hot September classes Gerry and Camille wait for the trial. Negroes sit together in classes, walk together in the corridors and across the campus, and surround juxtaposed tables in the student union, where they talk quietly, and do not play the jukebox. Gerry and Camille drink coffee and furtively watch them; in the classrooms and corridors, and on the grounds, they smile at Negroes, tell them hello, and get smiles and greetings. The Negro boys wear slacks and sport shirts, some of them with coats, some even with ties; the girls wear skirts or dresses; all of them wear polished shoes. There is no trouble. Gerry and Camille read the newspapers and listen to the radio, and at night after studying together they go to the bar and drink beer; the bartender is polite, even friendly, and does not mention the night of the knife. As they drink, then drive to Camille's house, they talk about Emmett Till, his story they have read and heard.

He was from Chicago, where he lived with his mother; his father died in France, in the Second World War. Emmett was visiting his great-uncle in Money, Mississippi. His mother said she told him to be respectful down there, because he didn't know about the South. One day he went to town and bought two cents' worth of bubble gum in Roy Bryant's store. Bryant's wife Carolyn, who is young and pretty, was working at the cash register. She said that when Emmett left the store and was on the sidewalk, he turned back to her and whistled. It was the wolf whistle, and that night Roy Bryant and his half-brother, John William Milan, went to the great-uncle's house with flashlights and a pistol, said *Where's that Chicago boy*, and took him.

The trial is in early fall. The defense lawyer's case is that the decomposed body was not Emmett Till; that the NAACP had put his father's ring on the finger of that body; and that the fathers of the jurors would turn in their graves if these twelve Anglo-Saxon men returned with a guilty verdict, which, after an hour and seven minutes of deliberation, they do not. That night, with Camille sitting so close that their bodies touch, Gerry drives on highways through farming country and cleared land with oil derricks and gas fires, and on bridges spanning dark bayous, on narrow blacktop roads twisting through lush woods, and gravel and dirt roads through rice fields whose canals shimmer in the moonlight. The windows are open to humid air whose rush cools his face.

When they want beer, he stops at a small country store; woods are behind it, and it is flanked by lighted houses separated by woods and fields. Oyster shells cover the parking area in front of the store. Camille will not leave the car. He crosses the wooden porch where bugs swarm at a yellow light, and enters: the store is lit by one ceiling light that casts shadows between shelves. A man and a woman stand at the counter, talking to a stout woman behind it. Gerry gets three six-packs and goes to the counter. They are only talking about people they know, and a barbecue where there was a whole steer on a spit, and he will tell this to Camille.

But in the dark outside the store, crunching on oyster shells, he forgets: he sees her face in the light from the porch, and wants to kiss her. In the car he does, kisses they hold long while their hands move on each others' backs. Then he is driving again. Twice he is lost, once on a blacktop road in woods that are mostly the conical silhouettes and lovely smell of pine, then on a gravel road through a swamp whose feral odor makes him pull the map too quickly from her hands. He stops once for gas, at an all-night station on a highway. Sweat soaks through his shirt, and it sticks to the seat, and he is warm and damp where his leg and Camille's sweat together. By twilight they are silent. She lights their cigarettes and opens their cans of beer; as the sun rises he is driving on asphalt between woods, the dark of their leaves fading to green, and through the insect-splattered windshield he gazes with burning eyes at the entrance to his town.

STEPHEN DUNN

Stephen Dunn was born in Forest
Hills, New York, in 1939. He has
published seven collections of po-
etry, including *Local Time*, which
won the National Poetry Series
Open Competition for 1986, and
Between Angels. He teaches at
Stockton State College in Pomona,
New Jersey, and in the M.F.A.
program at Columbia.

TUCSON

A man was dancing with the wrong woman
in the wrong bar, the wrong part of town.
He must have chosen the woman, the place,
as keenly as you choose what to wear
when you dress to kill.
And the woman, who could have said no,
must have made her choice years ago,
to look like the kind of trouble
certain men choose as their own.

I was there for no good reason myself,
with a friend looking for a friend,
but I'm not important
except as a register, a rabbit
in the night-forest, atremble and alert.
They were dancing close
when a man from the bar decided
the dancing was wrong. I'd forgotten
how fragile the face is, how fists too
are just so many small bones.
The bouncer waited, then broke in.
Someone wiped up the blood.
The woman began to dance
with another woman, both in tight jeans.
The air pulsed. My hands were dead
giveaways; fidgety, damp.
We were Mexicans, Indians, whites.
The woman was part this, part that.
My friend said nothing's wrong, stay put,
no one in here carries a knife,
it's a good fighting bar,
much better than down the street.

LETTER ABOUT MYSELF TO YOU

To Joe Gillon, age 35,
four weeks to live

Joe,
the other day I tried to get my class
to believe something Keatsian and beautiful
about death. What scholastic rot,
true on cool days far away
from the latest personal taste of it.
Next time photos of Dachau, a little
real blood between the lines.
I used to believe in words, how they could
come together happily, and change.
Now I just pray they don't distort.
Cancer's my sign. See what I mean?
I just wanted to say *cancer*
the way a boy first says shit
in front of his parents. There, it's out.
Listen, I'm four years older than you
with a tennis date at five.
That's not guilt, it's another broken piece
among the puzzle's broken pieces,
it's the silence that comes back
after "Why?" is shouted in an empty room.
I need to know if love's absurd
to you now. Or meaningful, perhaps,
for the first time? Your wife,
do you want to make love to her,
or to everyone else? Do the ethics
of it matter, now, at all?
I need to know if rage helps,
if it feels good to spit
in an invisible eye? If resignation

is as sweet as sitting back
in a Jacuzzi with a telephone
and someone due to call?
Here, two thousand miles away,
I feel a tick in my cells;
you've brought out a selfishness, Joe,
please believe is empathy.
I'm writing this in the afternoon,
that time of day I'm most lost.
A wind is blowing insignificantly.
My cat, Peaches, curls on my lap,
humming like an extra heart.
What good are words?
I'm feeling that impotence which wants
a Lazarus to rise
everytime someone loved is sinking.
Rise. Miracle. Heaven.
There, I've said them, sadly,
to make you laugh.

PAM DURBAN

Pam Durban grew up in South
Carolina. She is the author of *All
Set About with Fever Trees* and
the recipient of a Whiting Award
and the Rinehart Award in Fiction.
A former associate fiction editor
for *Crazyhorse*, she teaches at
Georgia State University.

IN DARKNESS

The summer Jennifer was ten, her grandfather Turner said she must learn
to be silent with the rest of them. It had been a time of abrupt decisions—
loud voices, suitcases packed in the middle of the night, lights snapped
on, cars that scraped the low spot at the end of the driveway, tires that
squealed all the way back into the garage—and she'd discovered that the
way to get along was to make herself small and to follow wherever they
led. In May, her mother and father had decided that this year she would
spend two months in Hamilton with Grandma and Grandpa Turner be-
cause Mommy was going away for a while and summer was Daddy's busy
season at Kodak. "Besides," they'd asked, crouched in front of her grin-

ning and looking excited the way they did when they wanted to make something sound like fun, "wouldn't it be great to be in Hamilton for that long?" She'd studied them, and then she'd said yes, because she understood that *yes* was the only answer they'd hear. And when her grandmother said she must choose one dress to wear to meeting on Sundays, she chose a plain blue dress with a round collar and red smocking at the waist and wrists. And when her grandfather said she must learn to be still with the other Quakers, she left behind the colored pencils and paper that had distracted her through other summer meetings, and she sat with her hands folded like the rest of them, waiting, watching the sunlight slowly take the room, one wall at a time, dissolving the white boards in light.

The meeting house was a gaunt one-room building with gray benches and plain tall windows. The people (like their house, she thought) were also plain and clean. Sitting among them that summer, Jennifer counted colors in the room—her red smocking, green shutters, red stovepipe on the wood stove—and secretly felt proud to find herself among them. The women wore dark dresses, muted patterns; the men smelled of smoke, they wore white shirts, gray pants. After the greetings, the shifting, and coughing had subsided, they were quiet together. At first, there was just the ordinary comfortable quiet of people sitting together in a room. But then the silence stirred and came to life. Every Sunday she listened and watched for the moment of the change, but she always missed it. From the bare polished floor to the sharply pitched roof the silence moved among them and deepened, the way light fills a room through a clear window. It was as if the silence had always been there and the people came into it one by one until no one was left outside. And when the people were listening together inside the silence, their faces changed—they softened and rested as if the silence had stopped in front of each person and quieted each face. No longer fierce, sad, hungry—the way her mother had looked before she left for Pittsburgh—they looked like people who'd found something they'd lost, something they recognized. Her grandfather said they were resting from toil. For Jennifer, there always came a moment when the room was so deep in stillness, the light so clear, they might all have been floating in an ocean of silence and light. Each time, just at this moment, a shiver danced straight up her back and she wished she could stay there. She shut her eyes then and tried to hold onto the feeling but it faded in front of her and was gone by the time someone said "Amen."

At home, in her grandparents' house, she often checked her own face, expecting to find a change. She stared into the dark, bright eyes, and sometimes, just as she turned away from the mirror, she thought she caught a glimpse of another expression similar to the one on the people's faces when the silence was deepest.

Every Sunday as they drove home, she'd ask: "What were the people looking for?" And every Sunday, Grandpa Turner prompted her, his eye with its wild, white eybrow fixed on her in the rearview mirror: "What do we say?"

"Light," she'd say, bored with the answer. The leaves of the young willows that lined the streambed beside the road flashed silver when a breeze stirred them, and she wondered if that was the light they meant, the underside of what you could see.

"That's correct," he'd always say. "We call it light."

"But where does it come from? What's it for?"

Sometimes her grandfather would only say that the light was invisible, and this light was what made us live.

"How can you see it then?"

"With other eyes," he'd say. She giggled at the thought. He looked stern as a mountain when he talked that way. He said the people were looking for the light inside them and the only way to find the light was to be very still, to go into the dark and look.

"The dark?"

"What you see when you close your eyes," he said. "That's what we are, and the light is inside the dark."

Her Grandmother Turner would get impatient then and say, "It's what we have in common, Jennifer. It's what we all have been given and what we want and give to each other." But no one could describe this light or say it starts here, ends there, this is its shape; and if we all had it in common, then why did we have to work so hard to find it, why did we have to be so still?

"Because," her grandfather said, "that's how we're made. This is the light that banishes the inner dark," he said.

"What's *banish?*" It sounded black and cold and far away.

"Sent away," he said. She understood then. Love did it. And love was what you waited for too. "Just you wait," they'd say. "Just wait till your mother comes home, what a good time you'll all have again."

So she waited. She couldn't remember a slower summer. The days in Hamilton passed as heavily as the man who came in June to set the beehives in her grandfather's orchard. Dressed in padded gray clothes and gloves, with a net over his face, the man moved among the apple trees in his clumsy dance. Always before, she had raced him, keeping to the edges of the orchard, taking pleasure in her bare legs and the speed with which she'd outrun him. That summer, she sat and watched him from the top of a small grassy hill nearby, feeling as swaddled and hindered as the man in his quilted garments. Even the bees seemed sluggish that summer. Some years, they worked fast, speeding from blossom to blossom, their legs furred with pollen. Some years, they buried themselves so deeply in the blossoms they might have been parts of flowers. But that year it was cold and damp until late June, and the bees, if they left the hives at all, flew clumsily from tree to tree and dropped heavily into the flowers. It wasn't even fun to run after them, they were so easy to follow. That was the summer she found out about waiting. The Quakers waited too, but they got what they wanted. She waited, but the trouble was she didn't know what she was waiting for, only that it would be different once it came. It seemed she'd have to wait even to know what she was waiting for.

Late in July her father took her back to Webster's Crossroads. Her mother arrived August eleventh on the 2:05 bus from Pittsburgh, and her father took a vacation so he could be with her. They talked from the time they left the bus station in Rochester until they passed the last suburb and dropped into the valley where Webster's Crossroads lay. The closer they got to home, the less her mother talked and the more she stared out the window. Finally, even her father was quiet. At home, he'd taped balloons to all the door frames and they'd lettered a paper banner that read *Welcome Home*. Her mother blushed and smiled and fingered the edge of the banner and then she set her suitcase in the front hall just inside the door. When Jennifer and her father grabbed the handle she said, "Just leave it there, please, I'll get it later."

"Not on your life," he said.

Mommy got very patient then. She pressed her lips together: "Just leave it there, I said." But he picked up the suitcase anyway and he said: "Margaret, it's all right, just relax." Her mother walked heavily upstairs then and took a shower and had a drink and Jennifer understood, with a sinking feeling, that whatever was supposed to have begun when Mommy came home had already begun and ended.

Later, after dark, her mother gathered Jennifer up into her lap and tried to tell her their story about the great tree that grows between heaven and earth and about how the stars over the valley behind the house are really the buds and leaves of this tree. But she forgot one part of the story, mixed up another, and Jennifer grew more and more restless until finally she interrupted: "Mother," she said, "you know Pegasus? Well, he's just stars in the *shape* of a horse." Her mother sat very still, blinking hard, and then she leaned over and kissed Jennifer on the top of her head and said, "Right you are, honey," and she went inside. That was her mother's first day at home.

The second day was no better, nor the third. They visited every boring place they'd ever been. They visited the two wineries nearby, and as usual her parents sipped wine and allowed her one small sip. They visited every musty antique store along the highway. She knew the contents of these stores so well she could have walked through the rooms blindfolded, naming the things no one ever bought: stuffed rooster, butter churn, dented milk pail, photograph made on tin. That was boring enough, but Conescus Lake was the last straw. She and her father had been there to swim almost every day since she'd come home. Now she had to be ordered out of the car and lifted into the rowboat, the *Hughes III*, named after the three of them. She would have been content to wait on shore, to look up and find the boat, shading her eyes against the glare, and then to go on building her own pathways and walls out of the freckled pebbles that felt smooth and cool as the lake itself when she stroked them with her thumb.

But no. Her mother snapped, her father scowled. They hustled her into the rowboat and her father said she was part of this family too, and she might as well get used to it. He rowed them into the center of the lake where the water was deep and, even in August, cold. And he made them bow their heads and hold hands and swear: "Till death do us part, again," he said. And when he said *death* she thought *the lake*, he means the lake, and she felt a chill, as if the sun had set without warning and the night cold had seeped through the bottom of the boat and was swirling around their ankles like fog. He squeezed her hand and she squeezed her mother's hand but neither of them opened their eyes. She looked around and saw that they were alone on the lake, the sun was sinking, and the shore seemed far away and rapidly darkening. A loon flew overhead, trailing its clear mournful call. Daddy switched on the big square flashlight and set it on the seat up near the bow. Mother held out her hands to its beam, then laughed, tucked her hands back between her knees while Daddy, with a look like glory on his face, leaned over from his seat to hers and brushed back a strand of hair that had caught in her mouth. Then there was only the sound of the small waves lapping against the sides of the boat. The quiet, the dark water seemed to Jennifer as trackless as the silence in Quaker meeting had been. "Light," her grandfather said. "The light is hidden inside the dark." She closed her eyes then and looked for the light and she saw the lake, a dark circle drawn around them, and the boat floating there with the light in the bow. They had gathered the light, she thought, drawing it out of the dimming sky, up from under the water, like fishermen drawing up their nets, until the boat was full of light and they rode with their catch home across the water. As her father rowed them back to shore she felt very solemn and grown-up.

The cookout to celebrate her mother's homecoming was Sunday night. They were grilling hamburgers in the back yard. Her father tossed the long-handled spatula with one hand and caught it behind his back with the other. His wedding ring glinted on his hand. Her mother didn't know, but Jennifer knew, that he'd rummaged through the house looking for the ring, which he'd taken off when she'd left. That broad band of white skin left by the ring had been the first thing she'd noticed when she'd come home from her grandparents' house in Hamilton. They'd said their rings were a sign of the love that would always be inside them. Well, what did the missing ring mean? No, it wasn't that love was gone. "Love doesn't do that," he'd explained one night not long after Jennifer came home from Hamilton. She couldn't sleep, had called to him. The night sounds—wind, sleepy birds, a big hoot owl, loud radio music downstairs—had seemed amplified, confused. She'd tried to concentrate on one sound but another intruded, then another until the sounds merged with the shadows tossed around the room by the sycamore outside her window, and mixed with a memory of her mother in her long dress, wearing a lacy white shawl around her shoulders. Then the sounds and the shadows tangled in a gust of wind, swooped and lifted to reveal the glimpse she'd gotten, before they'd hurried her away, of the girl who'd drowned that summer over in Hamilton. They had lifted her from the water still tangled in the branches of the fallen underwater tree that had pulled her down. "DADDY," she'd yelled.

Later, after he'd soothed her with talk of her mother, he'd said, "Just because Mother is gone right now doesn't mean she's stopped loving us or that we don't care about her, Jennifer." He'd smelled of beer and sounded distant. "No, I care too much," he'd said. And he sounded angry then, as though he were arguing with someone, the way her mother had sounded when she'd said she loved herself too, and that's why she had to go away for a while. That night Jennifer had thought he wanted to hit everything, only he couldn't decide where to begin. Then he'd shaken himself. "I'm sorry," he'd said. "Daddy's sorry." He'd smoked his cigarette carefully and knocked the ash off into his palm and sat there rolling it lightly so it didn't break up. "I believe time will prove me right about this, Jennifer, I do. And you must believe too," he said. So believe was what you must do. Believe in what? "Love changes," he said, "but it doesn't go away."

All summer, she'd watched the band of lighter skin on his ring finger darken, but it never blended with the brown of his hand. There was something repulsive about the white skin, something dead or private-looking, a mark that people shouldn't see.

Well, when Mommy said she was coming home, he sang "I'm Getting Married in the Morning," he put back on his wedding ring, cleaned the house, mowed half the lawn, rushed to Sears and bought a porch swing that he hung on the back porch just off the kitchen. "She has always wanted one of these," he said. That had been on Thursday. His ring fit perfectly down over the blank place, but Mommy didn't care for the swing. The night of the cookout, she asked, "Why the swing, Ed? It's almost autumn."

"Got a porch, Margaret, got to have a porch swing." He fanned the charcoal till it glowed. "It's like two plus two," he said.

Jennifer went over and hugged his legs for making it simple again. She looked up at him where he swayed over her, and she felt so safe she shouted: "Two plus two equals FOUR."

"Not so loud," her mother said.

"Right you are," her father said. "There are porch swings, sweetheart, and true love, flags, blue skies, the tall corn of Iowa, fathers and daughters, mothers and fathers, summertime, wheat fields, Webster's Crossroads, New York, and snowdrifts," he said, "and apples, and even Buffalo, New York."

She yelled "Daddy, what's those," gripping his pants legs, standing on his toes.

"*Are* those," her mother corrected her. "It's just a tide of silliness, Jennifer," she said, shooting her daughter her shy, darting, sideways look, "just a tide and a flood of silliness. He's capable of that sometimes too, no matter what he says." She looks happy, Jennifer thought. The tense lines around her mouth and the dark look around her eyes were gone. She winked at Jennifer.

"It's a new day, Maggie," her father said. Daddy's happy, she thought. She remembered about happiness. Happiness was something to believe in. Happiness was part of the story that would start again—only it would be better—now that her mother was home. Happiness made the story go. Her father came from the South. They'd met in college and had fallen desperately in love. They'd been so happy. Now they lived in New York State where Jennifer was born and everybody loved her because she was so pretty and sweet and made everyone happy. Mommy and Daddy loved Jennifer with all their hearts. And happiness was also what Mommy wanted when she went away—"A chance," she'd said, "for some happiness of my own." Still, Jennifer wondered. How could love and happiness send Mommy away in June and bring her back in August? And how did love and happiness make them speak to each other in those voices that made her shoulders pull tight? How could you ever know about love and happiness if they kept changing that way, like the lake with a storm coming—first silver, then gray?

Her mother went into the kitchen. They listened to her knocking around and swearing to herself. "Mommy's pretending she's forgotten where things are," her father whispered loudly to Jennifer.

"Mommy's not pretending anything." Her puzzled voice preceded her to the door, a slender woman in jeans and a green tank top piped in bright rainbow colors. "Where have you hidden everything?" she said.

"Have I?" he said. "I thought I put it all back in the right places." He winked at Jennifer.

"Oh, you," her mother said, and she ducked back inside.

"Mommy went to Pittsburgh," Jennifer said, carefully, quietly, and her father's hand bore down on the top of her head.

"Yes she did," he said. "And now she's back and that's what we need to think about, isn't it?" Jennifer nodded. *Gone*, they said, was simply a catch, a pause. When *gone* ended, things returned to normal, meaning to love and happiness, she guessed. They said *normal* with grateful voices. But now normal hadn't come back. She couldn't explain. It wasn't like going to her room anymore and finding it familiar; it wasn't like crawling into their bed and taking a nap between them. Since her mother had come home, something didn't fit.

"Found it," her mother said, holding out a wooden salad bowl. His eyes changed, a light seemed to pass over them and he grabbed one of Margaret's fingers and wriggled it. "Eureka," he said, and he held onto the tip of her finger. She almost stumbled, frowned at her feet, at the two of them in the swing, and sat down on the porch's bottom step.

Jennifer climbed down from the swing and went to her mother, who was sucking an ice cube, her knees drawn up close to her chest. She put her arms around her mother's neck and kissed the back of her head and rubbed her nose in her mother's hair. It smelled of milk and made her drowsy. She leaned, her mother turned, and Jennifer kissed the air. "Honey," her mother said, "honey, Mommy loves you but she doesn't want you leaning on her right now, all right? It's too warm."

"Come here, baby," her father said brightly, "Daddy'll hold you." He grabbed her up under the arms and she felt herself slung through the air. He pulled her close and she felt his heart beating against her back. "Stuffy," Jennifer said, and she slid off his lap.

"Did you hear that, Mother?" he said. He laughed but it wasn't funny. "Our daughter's growing up. She said my holding her made her feel stuffy."

"Is that so?" her mother said. She sat still, listening. "*You're a part of this too,*" he'd said. Part of what? Jennifer wondered. Of their love for each other and for her? Of this cheerfulness then and of the way Mommy looked at Daddy as though she didn't know if she liked him or not. She didn't want to be part of that, she wanted to be tiny again, to be nothing but eyes, ears, and skin, to be carried on the warm river of their voices, to rest under the moon and sun of their faces. Her heart thumped so loud she was certain they'd heard, that she'd given herself away, and she looked up, waiting to be discovered. But both of them were staring off in the same direction—past the hemlock trees and over the broken fence that marked the boundary of their yard.

"You know, believe it or not, Jennifer, Mom and I have discovered we have a lot in common over the past few months," he said. He spoke to Jennifer but he frowned at the back of her mother's head.

"What's *in common?*" Jennifer asked.

"*You,*" her father said, and he dove at her. She squealed and ran, knees pumping high in panic until she was past the hemlocks, where she crouched and watched them. From there, they looked like two ordinary people—almost without faces, the way it used to be, her parents who loved her with a love that was vague and warm as the days she washed through dimly. But now, since her mother had gone away and come back, every time she looked at them she saw the lines around Mommy's mouth and the way it pulled down at the corners, and the crease that ran straight up between Daddy's eyes. She unfocused her eyes and tried then to make them those strangers whose soft hands and eyes spelled *love*, into whose midst she'd tumbled one day, a small stone from the sky. She would have liked to have been that way again. When she was little, they'd played a game that her mother called "Just Imagine." "Just imagine you aren't my parents, who would I be?"

"A little speck, a little girl speck."

"Would I have a name?"

"Only to yourself, one you made up."

"Would I be lonely?"

"Very lonely."

"Who would my parents be?"

"The wind and the rain."

"But who would I be?"

"Nobody."

And so on, round and round and back again. Without them you were nobody; with them you were who they were. Her mother lifted her heavy brown hair off the back of her neck. Her father swung and puffed his pipe. Under her breath, she commanded them to freeze, right there, to go no farther.

They froze. Her father's pipe smoke hung suspended and she was Jennifer the magical, Jennifer the powerful, and they would wait for her, she would make them wait until she caught up with them or they became themselves again, until they told her what was different now though nothing seemed to be, how this love that had taken her mother away and sent her back was the same (they said so) as what had created Jennifer in this world. Until they told her how this love they talked about pulled you apart and kept you together. Her mother slapped her knees and stood up. She pressed a finger to her lips and frowned and then she went inside. Jennifer ran back. "What are you and Mommy talking about?" she said.

"Nothing," her father whispered. "Have we been talking?"

"Not funny," she said.

"Not supposed to be funny," he said.

She was about to reply when she was struck by a wish, a wanting so potent she thought that if she could just have that one thing, she would be happy. She wished she could be the boy she knew in Hamilton who cut pictures of motors out of magazines and carried them around in a shopping bag, who could dump them out and explain them. All kinds of motors—washing-machine motors and the engines of cars, giant turbines and the tiny motors that drove electric clocks. He understood what they were for, he said only he knew why they worked, and all the children were afraid to make fun of him. She wished she could be that boy.

"You know Mommy," her father said, nodding toward the door where her mother had gone.

"Daddy, don't talk," she said. "Don't talk." She put her hand over his mouth. Startled, he grabbed her wrist. "Jenny," he warned. Then he seemed to remember, loosened his grip. "Mommy will be back," he said. "She's inside, she's coming back." Jennifer studied him, struggling to match another time with this time. Both times, Mommy was coming back and what was about to begin again was something fine, better than before. She remembered. He'd said the same thing at the bus station when Mommy had left.

He'd held her hand tightly that time too, so tightly the bones had crunched, and she'd understood then—Why, he's afraid. And then she'd been afraid too, afraid the way they said two people were afraid when they were drowning and grabbed onto each other until they both drowned. That day at the bus station, she'd tried to pull her hand away and she thought for one crazy second, as the lights began spinning overhead in small brilliant orbits and he'd loomed over her, that he might topple on her. The bus sighed, released its air brakes with a sharp rush. He looked down at her with his terrible forehead, his unseeing eyes, and he said: "Mommy's gone to collect herself, Jennifer, Mommy's coming back." At times like these, that terrifying picture returned: an exploding Mommy, then Mommy stooping, collecting herself, putting the pieces in a brown paper lunch bag, bringing the pieces home. Love did it. And now she was back. That was love, too. Someday they would explain. Later, Jennifer. Just have faith.

"I'm hungry," she said. The screen door slammed and her mother came out, drying her hands on a dish towel. "Me too," her mother said. "Daddy too. Just as soon as your daddy finishes cooking, we're going to eat."

Over the valley behind their house, the sun was setting in a swirl of blue and gold. It was the kind of sky that prompted her mother to sigh and declare their view the prettiest view in the world. Down below, at the beginning of the woods, where it was already dark, a gray mist climbed the wheat field. When the mist reached their house, Jennifer thought, night would begin.

When the hamburgers were done, she refused to sit on the ground. "Fine," her mother said impatiently, "then sit on the bottom step here and pretend we're on a camping trip and we're the only people in the world."

Jennifer shook her head no.

"O.K.," her mother said. "Just sit there and be stubborn then."

"Thank you," she said. She'd noticed that when people didn't want to do something, they became polite and then there was a fence around them that no one could cross.

They gave her a plate with the world's biggest hamburger on it. It was like a cartoon hamburger, the kind she ate with her father every Saturday at the drugstore: no onion, no mustard, a frill of lettuce, and the reddest red tomato. Twice she tried to bite into it, twice the bread slipped, and a pinkish mix of catsup and mayonnaise splattered onto her plate. It was the most beautiful hamburger in the world, but she couldn't eat it. She began to whimper. "Well, what is it?" her father said.

"Can't," she said.

"'Course you can," her mother said. Her father watched her mother but her mother looked at neither of them, just kept chewing her own hamburger in small fierce bites and staring straight ahead.

"Honey, you like hamburgers," her father said. "You've always liked hamburgers. I've never seen a kid cry so much over nothing, have you, Mother?"

"Yes," she said.

"Well for Christ's sake, what's she got to cry about?" he said.

"Why don't you ask her, you're the word man," her mother said. This was a joke between them: "You're the word man," her mother said when she wanted to tease him. "You figure it out." But she wasn't teasing now.

"I'll do just that," he said. "Jenny," he said. "Jennifer Lynn. Stop that now and tell me what's wrong." But Jennifer couldn't stop. She was away and flying down a long in-drawn breath, taking in air to fill an empty place that seemed deeper with each breath, as though air had no power to fill it.

Her mother knelt beside her. "Breathe," she said. "Jennifer, breathe."
She clapped her daughter on the back and Jennifer breathed, wailed, and
jerked her shoulder out from under her mother's hand. "It's too big for
her," her mother said wearily. She rose from her knees like an old woman,
first on one leg, then the other. "She wants you to cut it up for her," her
mother said.

"Well, doesn't she know how to ask?"

"I don't know," her mother said. "Where'd she learn this trick? Who
taught her anyhow? She didn't do this before I left."

"That's right," her father said. "What did you think, that she'd just sit
here and wait for you, that she wouldn't change at all?"

"Right," her mother said.

"Right," he said. And the way they said it, *right* was a big engine that
pulled a long black train out of a tunnel. You saw the engine and you
sensed by the way it labored that it was pulling a weight, but you couldn't
see, you couldn't, and you trembled against that seeing.

"O.K. then, love," the man said. He sounded tired too. Against the sky
where the stars were backing away, his face looked worn and huge. When
he picked up the knife, Jennifer shrank violently and flung herself side-
ways on the grass and cradled her head in her arms. "Well, Christ," he
said. "Now what?"

She felt her mother kneel down beside her again. "There's no reason for
any of this, Jennifer," she said. She opened one eye and stared at the
ground. She felt the earth against her belly where her shirt had hiked up
and it was cool and damp as though in the ground it was already autumn.
Her mother began to rub Jennifer's back in wide, smooth strokes. Jennifer
felt drowsy. For the first time since her mother had come home she felt
safe again, back in the darkness with nothing to do. Her mother's voice
went on and on, gently now: "You've got a mouth," she said. "See." She
pried Jennifer's face away from the ground and held her chin and pointed
to her mouth. "See," she said. "You've got a mouth like my mouth and
like Daddy's mouth. You can use it like we do and ask for things," she said.
Jennifer rolled over. Moist dirt clung to her stomach, and the sky kept
going away away away and below the sky, poised on the edge of the valley
where in winter, when the green was gone, their exposed house looked so
frail a hand could knock it down, there were only herself, her mother, her
father, and the silence where the secrets of things lay hidden. She hated
her mother's words then, hated the whole idea of needing or wanting any-

thing, of having to crack that silence and ask and want, with a cold and definite hatred. And they called this love—what you needed and could neither ask for nor understand, what you closed your eyes and felt for blindly. She vowed to herself then, as solemnly as if she'd written the promise on a sheet of paper and dropped it into her secret place—the knothole of the basswood tree near the creek—never to want anything. Her mother searched her face and Jennifer stared back at her and, with the power of the knowledge of the new way she would be warming her, in pity and anger, she said: "*Your* mouth, Mother." And thought: That's a curse. When they said "*Don't curse*," they meant what she'd just done, not the words but the feeling that caused the words. That was a curse.

Her mother grabbed the knife out of Ed's hand and chopped the hamburger into pieces and slapped the plate back onto Jennifer's lap. "Now *eat*," she said. "Eat, I said, before you dry up and blow away." Jennifer relaxed. What a wonderful thought. What fun that would be, to become small and weightless, to catch every breeze that happened by.

"Well," her father said. "No long faces now. You can eat later," he said, and he scooped her up and carried her back to the swing.

"Ed," her mother said, "I just got her settled down, honey."

"Well, she's upset," he said. "She can eat later."

Margaret flung her arms in the air and gave up. Jennifer sneaked her thumb into her mouth and gave over to the drowsiness and the cool dark. She was too old to suck her thumb, but they wouldn't notice because they were talking to each other and rocking the swing. Softly at first, with wild chilly voices, the peepers chimed in over and around them, first in small groups, distinct chirpings from different corners of the yard, then louder, more unified, and soon the night was riddled with their noise. He said: "Not to change the subject, Maggie, but I saved something just for you because I know how you love those lakes." Her mother always said she loved the Finger Lakes because they were classrooms. She went on nature walks and bird walks and flora walks, saw Canada geese, loons, killdeer, heard the lunatic pheasants chuckling as they ran, followed the reedy marshes west and south and came home with a knapsack full of leaves, feathers, stones, and roots that Jennifer danced and begged to hear about. She said they each had a language. Her father winced at that. "Well, I have to have something that speaks to me that way," she'd say. "Someday," her mother would say, "you can go with me, Jennifer." Now Jennifer thought: The next time she asks, I will say "No thank you." She felt the satisfaction of that refusal as if it had already come true.

"Are you listening?" her father said.

"Don't I look like I'm listening?" she said. He shoved his face close to hers then and studied her. "Now that you mention it," he said. She blushed and bit her lip.

"Anyway," he said. "They took a sounding in the middle of Seneca Lake last month and guess what? There's no bottom to the damn thing, at least not one they could find. I have a newspaper clipping somewhere."

"Imagine," her mother said. "Must be an underground river or something down there, imagine that."

"Monsters," Jennifer said.

"No, no monsters," her mother said. "Creatures, maybe, but no monsters."

"Monsters," Jennifer said. Anything could be monsters, she thought. Sometimes the peepers were monsters. Sometimes it seemed they tried to shriek louder than anything around them. Once her father had been playing the stereo on a summer night much like this one. Her mother kept shouting at him, "Turn it down, turn it down." He pretended to misunderstand her—"You want it what?"—cupping his hand to his ear like an old man. The more she'd shouted, the louder he'd turned the stereo, the wilder the peepers had sung.

"You're quite some philosopher," her mother said gently. He looked pleased. He tucked his chin and beamed at her. They're trying to do something, Jennifer thought. They're doing it right now.

"Where does the lake go?" Jennifer asked. They looked at her blankly. She felt her face redden. Well, maybe once in a while you could want a simple answer, as long as it wasn't about you *personally*.

"Who knows?" her father said. "China, the center of the earth maybe."

"Oh no," her mother said. "The water would turn to steam at the center of the earth."

"Right," he said. "Only I wasn't talking about *really*, Margaret, remember?"

"At least you think," her mother said, as though pursuing some thought of her own. "At least you do that. A lot of people don't, you know. They're the miserable ones finally, don't you agree?"

"Oh I don't know about that," he said. "They may be happier, especially if they've never known much."

"I don't think so," her mother said.

"Well, if they don't know," he said, and a sly soft look came over his face, "how do they know they don't know?"

"I think you always know when something's missing," she said.

"You don't do so badly yourself in the thinking department," he said. He stroked her thigh with a faraway look on his face.

"Thank you," she said. She reached to tuck up her hair.

"You learned a lot while you were away," he said. She folded her hands suddenly. "I learned enough," she said.

"Enough?"

"Enough," she said.

"Enough for what?"

The swing stopped and her mother stared at him. "I'm back aren't I?" she asked. She looked at him as though she were measuring him. Why did they talk this way? What was it for? Jennifer felt the boat, the way it had rocked the instant he'd said "*death do us part.*" It was her mother pushing the swing again.

"O.K.," he said. "Don't get mad. I just want to know, that's all."

"It's too complicated," she said. "You don't want to hear right now. It's late," she said. "I'm tired and I'm not thinking clearly. Besides, don't command me that way, Ed. Really, I don't like it."

"Who's commanding?" he said. "Look, I'm happy. Look, here's to us," he said, raising his glass of water. "All right then, to us," he said again. "To us and to whatever you learned that brought you home."

"Stop it, Ed," her mother said.

"Do you want me to understand?" he said. "I just need to understand, that's all."

"Of course I want you to understand," she said. "Later. Let's just enjoy ourselves for once." Jennifer nodded. That was good. If she were in charge, they would just listen to the peepers and to the wind in the hemlocks. Because the longer you talked, the more you wanted to know, and then you had to go on. You turned into one of those people at Quaker meeting, always looking, always wanting something. Or you turned into Mommy and Daddy.

"Great," her father said. "Fine, great. I'll forget it. Remind me if I step out of line."

"Eat," her mother said, and she shoved Jennifer's plate back into her hand. Carefully, Jennifer began to peel the bits of hamburger free from the soggy pieces of bun and to set them in separate piles that did not touch one another. When she finished that chore, she picked off the tomato and lettuce and started to work on the catsup, squeezing the bun, scraping the goo with her thumbnail and wiping it on the side of the plate. She wanted to get down to the plain bun again.

Her father pushed the swing. Her mother pulled Jennifer close to her. She began to sing: "*Sweet and low*," she sang, "*sweet and low, wind of the western sea.*" Jennifer's lullaby. When her mother sang, the wind blew across the western sea, that dim, milky sea, smooth as a brow soothed by a soft hand. Only tonight, when she closed her eyes and waited to hear the western sea, she saw the shore, and there were people walking up and down on the shore, turning shells with their toes, and the houses that lined the shore were brightly lit. She saw it as clearly as if she was there. She kept her eyes closed, trying to find that calm smooth place the lullaby always made, the cool place, smooth as a northern pebble. But it was no use. As her mother sang, the people walked up and down, in sunlight, on the shore of the western sea. Her mother's voice couldn't stop them.

"So come on, Margaret, could you tell me, please, what you meant back there about what you learned?"

"Whenever you care to listen," she said, "I'd be happy to tell you."

"What should I do, telephone first to make sure you're free?"

"Oh stop it," she said, "won't you?"

"No I don't think I will this time," he said. He stood up. "I don't think I will stop it just now. I think I'll hear what you have to say." He watched her as if he were having trouble seeing her, but he kept looking. Her mother sat still and seemed not to breathe. Then she clapped her hands. "Jenny," she said, "time for bed."

Her mother's hand stopped her protest. She'd been tricked. So this was where love took you, and happiness—it was some big secret that they promised, then took away. "No fair," she said.

"No fair is right," her mother said. "Now kiss us and go get ready for bed and we'll come up and kiss you goodnight in a few minutes." Her mother held her. She held her for a long time, and she let her go and then she held her again. "Don't slam the screen," she said.

Jennifer lingered in the kitchen, listening. "Go on, Jennifer," her mother said. "We'll be there soon." The burnished copper bottoms of the pots on the wall shone back at her and the quart jar of honey shone like congealed sunlight. She lifted the jar off the shelf and held it close to her face and tipped it so the pale gold honeycomb settled heavily to one side. She turned the jar slowly, trying to follow one cell all the way through the comb. She traced it with her finger on the outside of the jar, keeping her eye on that one cell, following until she came to the point where that cell met another and she lost the one she'd followed among all the others, all intricately, delicately, surely connected to one another. "Jennifer," her father called. "Are you dawdling?"

"No," she said.

"We're waiting," he said.

It wasn't like any going to bed she'd done before. It wasn't like being carried piggyback up to bed and it certainly wasn't like being lifted out of the car half asleep and being carried up to her room so that the trip between the car and the room was lost in the warm blot of her father's body and the covers closed over her like warm water. That had happened to another girl. No, she was going on her own this time, toward the small blue night-light in the upstairs hall. And then her room opened in front of her, yellow and white, like summer—yellow toy chest, bookshelf, yellow-and-white checked canopy over the bed. And there was the windowsill, the ant farm, the turtle asleep on his rock under his plastic palm tree, and beyond the windowsill, across the ghostly fences, over in the dark, the ponies at the farm down the road still cropped grass. She was sure of it. And beyond the ponies and the grass and the last lights, to the east, there was Hamilton and her grandparents, dressed in their plaid flannel bathrobes by now, and beyond them, yet connected to them, the meeting house, gaunt and silent and dark now, and waiting. But below her window, underneath the slanted tin roof of the porch, her parents were talking. She couldn't hear them. She pressed an ear to the screen and listened. She thought she could almost make out their voices, low and quiet at first, then angry, sharp. Her mother said, "All right then, Ed, all right." And then he asked her something, he wanted something, and their voices dropped and there was only the keening of the peepers, going wilder and higher, spreading out, until the whole sky disappeared down the broad whirling throat of the sound.

Then the porch light went out. One minute the grass was white, the next it was dark. Jennifer drew back from the window. They were gone. She heard them come inside. They always said, "Jennifer's a brave girl." Well, she guessed she knew a little bit now about being brave, about why you had to be brave. It had something to do with the light's going out that way. It was because of love somehow, and because of what you wanted. You had to be brave, you had to wait and have what her grandfather said was faith, which was a special kind of waiting, a special kind of bravery and love that kept you standing in the dark, in the silence, looking for the light inside you, believing it was there.

She heard them start up the stairs. She jumped into bed and turned out the light. It was important that they should pick their way through her toys and books in the dark to find her. She pulled the covers over her head and imagined how they looked, coming up the stairs. They had their arms around each other. Her father's arms were dark and his shirt was white except where her mother held on to a handful of cloth at his waist. Soon they would stop at her door and see the mound of covers and catch on to the game and they'd say: "Well, where's our Jennifer? Who's that underneath those covers?"

"Let's call her, Daddy," her mother would say. And they'd call—"Jennifer"—they'd call softly, making their voices sound far away. And call again while they tiptoed across the room and she waited, shivering with excitement close to terror, for what was sure to happen. For the moment when they'd each take a corner of the bedspread and draw the covers back slowly and say, "Well, look who's here." For the moment when they'd pull back the covers to reveal—Jennifer the fair. She hid her face with her hands, to keep from them how it shone.

CORNELIUS EADY

Cornelius Eady's *Victims of the
Last Dance Craze* won the Lamont
Prize. His other books are *Kar-
tunes* and *Boom Boom Boom*.
Born in Rochester, New York, in
1954, he teaches at the State Uni-
versity of New York at Stony
Brook.

SHERBET

The problem here is that
This isn't pretty, the
Sort of thing which

Can be easily dealt with
With words. After
All it's

A horror story to sit,
A black man with
A white wife, in

The middle of a hot,
Sunday afternoon at
The Jefferson Hotel in

Richmond, VA, and wait
Like a criminal for service
From a young, white waitress

Who has decided that
This looks like something
She doesn't want

To be a part of. What art
Could describe the
Perfect angle of

This woman's back as
She walks, just so,
Mapping the room off

Like the end of a
Border dispute? Which
Metaphor could turn

The room more perfectly
Into a group of
Islands than that? And when

The manager finally
Arrives, what language
Do I use

To translate the nervous
Eye motions, the yawning
Afternoon silence, the

Prayer beneath
His simple inquiries,
The sherbet which

He brings personally,
Just to be certain
The doubt

Stays on our side
Of the fence? What do
We call the rich,

Sweet taste of
Frozen oranges in
This context? What do

We call a weight that
Doesn't fingerprint,
Won't shift

And can't explode?

RUSSELL EDSON

Russell Edson has published eight
collections of prose poems, includ-
ing *The Intuitive Journey and
Other Works* and *The Wounded
Breakfast;* a book of plays, *The
Falling Sickness;* and a novel,
Gulping's Recital. He reports that
he was born in 1935 "in a bed with
my mother" and that his current
employment is "patience and con-
sciousness, with a bit of courage
thrown in."

ELEPHANTS

A herd of elephants stands in the yard, old pieces of tusk lying in the
grass at their feet.

They endure through winter and summer, slowly evolving their monu-
mentality.

It is said that the eye of a fly can actually see the hour hand moving.

The body collects itself gradually from carrots and chops; works late
into the night translating these things into fingernails and pubic hair.

The night is falling, and nature sucks its teeth at my window. I pretend
to be living my own life . . .

THE MEETING

A man met himself in a street one day.

He said, are you me?

No, you are me, said the other.

We are two, yet we are the one, he said.

No, I am the one, you are the other, like a shadow or an echo, said the other.

Are we not twin brothers? he said.

No, we are the one, but I am more of the one than you, who are as a reflection of the one whom I am more of, said the other.

It doesn't matter which manifestation of us is the more essential to the idea I have of myself; it is not lessened in me for residing mostly in you, he said.

Then both men walked into the other and disappeared . . .

JOHN ENGELS

Born in South Bend, Indiana, in
1931, John Engels teaches at St.
Michael's College in Vermont.
Among his seven books are
*Weather-Fear: New and Selected
Poems, 1958–1982* and *Cardinals
in the Ice Age,* which was a selec-
tion in the National Poetry Series.

IN THE PALAIS ROYALE BALLROOM
IN 1948

for Zimmer, most marvelous ofay

Just at the end of the first set I step out
in my white tux, my white shoes
onto the sequined dais at center,
into a golden spot, another focused overhead

onto the spinning, mirrored ball,
spills and whirls of gold light everywhere,
like stars, like comets hurtling across
the blue cloth ceiling of the Palais Royale Ballroom

in South Bend. And I wait,
Kenton and the boys riffing quietly behind me,
Milt Bernhart disconsolate among the brasses,
June Christie waiting, even June, for this

is mine to do alone, and everyone
knows it; and everyone
is waiting. And then
I see out there beyond the light

the dancers begin to take notice, to turn,
to gather themselves into a circle around me,
arms linked, swaying, others, little
eager knots of them, hurrying to get back,

the word having spread, even
unto the streets. And they gather around me and wait,
knowing what is to come, the air growing dense
with the fragrances of gardenias, camellias, carnations,

the light that is like stars and comets
careening over the ceiling of the Palais Royale Ballroom.
They wait, and suddenly I raise to my lips
the red-gold Olds trombone,

and hit high G so clean, so sweet, so un-
endurably sustained, that the girls
I am remembering myself to have loved beyond desire
go faint with desire,

and the song is "Summertime," and I am alone with it,
and play it out, drive through
to the last sweet resolution of the last phrase.
And then, my solo finished, the great band

riding it out behind me, the song diminishing
forever into the sky beyond the starry sky
which was the ceiling of the Palais Royale Ballroom in 1948,
my lips still numb from the embouchure, I think of it

as if in fact it might have been,
as if those dancers to whom too late and far too late
I have thought to offer this as a memory
might truly have gathered themselves around

and have remembered such a thing: the song
held in its starry, high, unlikely register,
the surging of their bodies to that song:
that fragrance of light again.

I DREAM OF ROY HANNA

With whom one morning at a crossroad
outside Peoria—cold, exhausted,
bound east from Reno to South Bend,
and having waited for eleven hours
without a ride—I fought,

though briefly, then
traveled on with, parted from,
and never saw again, not
for these past thirty years, until I dream
of waiting with him in the cold dawn

and of the sky whitening, of how the trees
ooze fog, the line poles take shape
and the wires come out from the dead
silence of the memory: the bird-
bearing wires suddenly come out,

strung and singing over the black road,
and his face comes out, unfolds, petal
on petal, as mine must unfold
before him. I dream of the long
shrilling of wires overhead,

and the two of us grown irritable
with waiting, somehow grudging
the coming of light,
having all night been each
to the other no more than a clumping

of shadow. I dream
of the waiting for light, and then
of the light itself, of the slow
revelation of place, and of ourselves
fixed there in that slow

emergence and disclosed obligation
toward all which looks at us and at which
we look back and perhaps
see. I dream we lurch
together, accidentally touch,

one or the other of us thrown
off-balance, in an instant both angry, bumping,
swinging at the other, glaring and turning
away, in the end seeing how the light spills
redly everywhere, becomes

dawn. I dream
of how we stand apart from one another
in what seems reprisal,
in the frail tissues of dawn visible again
each to the other. The light

sweeps over us.
There are shadows of wires
on the black road, and the air
sings. We stand together, the light
around us, our shadows bright with ice.

Well, we ought to have waited
far more patiently, with more love; as it is,
in the end, our angers ebbing, we undertake
to warm what extremities of ourselves
might remain warmable; in time arrive,

part, never meet
again, though the shapes of love
or anger with this measure of radiance
persist: in the dream
we glare out each at the other,

our young faces in the thin light
of the instant before dawn
perfectly recognizable, names and all:
small wells of shadow at the corners of our mouths
where our bodies turn in, entering themselves.

JOHN ENGMAN

John Engman is the author of
Keeping Still, Mountain. The re-
cipient of a Bush Foundation
Fellowship, he teaches at the Uni-
versity of Minnesota. He was born
in Minneapolis in 1949.

ONE MINUTE OF NIGHT SKY

I worked for a year in the cellar
of an airtight clinic, trudged through a valley of cabinets
in a gray smock. My job was filing bulging folders of the dead:
I carried a wire basket through the alphabet, dumping envelopes
of aneurysm, cancer and cerebral lesion into yawning racks.
I could travel decades in a few steps,

stop and page through a chart until
I was in the blue hills west of brain damage, dwindling hills
and rivers of red that met in flatlands on a black horizon,

tickertape from the electroencephalograph. Stapled on last
reports of death there was a small snapshot from the morgue,
a face no larger than my thumbprint.

    The work made me sick.
Reading histories of tumors and fatal transplants
until the lines on graphs convulsed and snarled like wiring
come loose in a circuit for the mind of God. Once, I saw
close-ups of the malignancy which killed a man my age,
nothing much on the X-ray,

    a blemish vague as memory,
a burr which swam through nervous systems into his brain.
I could have sworn he was staring back at me from his worn
snapshot but, of course, he wasn't. He couldn't. His eyes
were shut. I put him away with unusual force and heard
his chart jar the rack, as if something

    small had gone off, a mousetrap.
The next day I quit. For the first night in weeks, I slept.
But in my deepest sleep, even now, if the chemicals balance
and tissues are ripe, a synapse forms the memory: iron
spring slips, the trap shuts, my eyes fly open and all
    the darkness around me wakes.

    Supposedly, each human being
has a built-in mechanism for one minute of knowing
he or she will someday die. One minute of night sky: life
going on across the street where someone greets darkness
with tins of food and drink, where someone listens, pauses
by the door and throws the bolt and lets the animal in.

ELIZABETH EVANS

Born in 1951, Elizabeth Evans
currently teaches in the creative
writing program at the University
of Arizona. She is the author of
Locomotion, a collection of short
stories, and the recipient of vari-
ous awards, including a James
Michener Fellowship.

AMERICANS

Left hand holding open the pages of the strong, green journal lying on his
desk, Oyekan wrote:

> apple of my eye

Mrs. Scotty Hillis had given Oyekan the journal not long after his arrival
in the U.S. A sweet lady. Right to this very room she brought the green
journal, and three baked yams in a yellow dish. "I hope you'll be happy
here," she had said.

> apple of my eye

The blonde-haired girl who sat next to Oyekan in Statistical Methods once told him he was "the apple of the teacher's eye." Oyekan did not know the expression, but felt it made easy sense, quite unlike Mr. Scotty Hillis's "If wishes were horses, beggars would ride," or, yesterday, the remark of Oyekan's friend, Joe, at the barbershop: "Oyekan's got the Hillises eating out of his hand." *Eating out of his hand.* When Joe said this, the barber had made a smile, but still it had not sounded nice.

Absently, Oyekan reached across his open journal to the chart hanging on the wall above his desk. "Border Changes in Nigeria." He slid a finger between the chart's colored transparencies. The top transparency—yellow—made his finger appear varnished; the second and third, dark as the back of a turtle.

Truly, Oyekan thought, his friend Joe was not himself lately. Truly, Joe was a good man: One day a month he did not eat so that money saved might be sent to poor peoples of the world; soon he would go to Micronesia with the U.S. Peace Corps; already, he volunteered at the medical center each Wednesday evening! And, too, Joe and his sweetheart, Peggy Dixon, had kindly taken Oyekan to all manner of places: U.S. lectures, films, parties, museums. America! Peggy Dixon herself a black girl, living in the U.S. just as comfy as a white boy like Joe! And no one staring when they held hands.

Peggy is the apple of my eye

wrote Oyekan. Then turned from this terrible, irridescent sentence—from where had it come?—and using his burnt sienna marker added quotation marks and, beneath the sentiment, the words:

says Joe Hart.

Better. Yes. Soon Joe and Peggy would come to take Oyekan to the Internationals' Barbecue. And Joe had hair of the marker's color, the color of the slim pipes running along the ceiling of Oyekan's basement bedroom in the fine, brick home of Mr. and Mrs. Scotty Hillis. Over Oyekan's head went the pipes, then straight into tidy holes in the panelled east wall; and beyond, to the shadowy, sweet bathroom where, since April, small mushrooms occasionally erupted at the toilet's base.

Our son this, our son that, Mr. and Mrs. Scotty Hillis had said the day Oyekan toured the big house and basement bedroom he was to use during his stay in the U.S. They showed him photographs in the adjoining recreation room: golden Lee Hillis throws himself into a swimming pool whose surface appears dangerously white, a bath of mercury; handsome Lee on a motorcycle, still just long enough for the photographer to get the shot. At the time, Oyekan reeled from the long flight from Lagos, the fact of Minnesota. At least a week had passed before he understood the son to be not away, but dead, killed while engaged in an act which Mr. Scotty—face blotched red and white with grief—accorded the ominous, giddy name of "hang-gliding."

A world away all of that seemed now, days when Oyekan did not know Mr. and Mrs. Scotty, or Joe and Peggy!

Oyekan laid down the burnt sienna marker, peered through his open door into the recreation room's dark. Only the blond shafts of the pool cues showed distinctly, but Oyekan knew the location of everything: the mini-tramp; the TV; the low table called, mysteriously, "the coffee table"; the photos. There were no photos of the sport of "hang-gliding," so Oyekan could only imagine its aspect; but, on the north wall, there *did* hang a photo which always struck Oyekan as extraordinary in that it contained not only Lee Hillis but Oyekan's friend, Joe, and Peggy Dixon, also. This made sense, of course. It was the Hillises who first introduced Oyekan to the couple. Many times he was told that Joe Hart had been best friend to Lee. Still. Visible proof. The dead son, Joe, Peggy. Whenever one wanted to examine:

All wore swimming suits, and Lee Hillis appeared to laugh, perhaps at sunburned Joe, who, it seemed, had just kissed Peggy Dixon. Joe and beautiful Peggy smiled at one another with secret, impenetrable happiness. A smear of the white ointment on Joe's nose streaked Peggy's cheek— which made the picture not quite so nice, it gave Peggy the look of a lost tribeswoman, caused a heaviness in Oyekan's heart—

But stop! Soon his friends would arrive. He would tell them his good news:

At first, Oyekan had misunderstood Mrs. Scotty's tears at breakfast. Both he and Scotty Hillis had handed her their napkins, and, in her considerate way, Mrs. Scotty dabbed at her sweet, moon-round face with each in turn. Oyekan supposed that she cried at the memory of the dead Lee. The old wife of Oyekan's father still cried at memory of one baby who died of measles some eighteen years before, when Oyekan was only five years of age; and, unlike Mrs. Scotty, the old wife had six children who lived.

Mrs. Scotty was too old for more children. Her hair was white as rice.

Her hands lay motionless on the shiny table top, as if choked by their own thick, violet veins.

Oyekan looked across the breakfast table to Mr. Scotty. Was he glum, also? Mr. Scotty favored the word "pep." "I think a brisk walk would pep us up," he often said after dinner. Or, "Let's all go to the club for a swim! That'll get the sleep out of our eyes!" But this morning Mr. Scotty sat quiet while Mrs. Scotty wept. He chewed his bite of the English muffin. He wiped the crumbs off the breakfast nook table into one palm with the meaty side of the other.

Oyekan rose from his chair in the big blue and white kitchen. "What is it, please?" he pleaded. "May I help, then?"

"Oh, these are happy tears, sweetie," Mrs. Scotty said, "aren't they, Scotty?"

Mr. Scotty made the noises of a man digging heavy soil. "We'd like you to stay on with us, Oy," he said finally. "Like family. We thought Lee— the plant's growing every year."

The plant meant Hillis Carton, an impressively large and dusty concern which made waste paper into boxes of cardboard.

Mr. Scotty continued: "You're a bright fellow, Oy. We know you've got opportunities back home too but we're awful fond of you and there's a place in management for you right now, and more, you can bet on that."

Oyekan could not believe it! A dream!

Mrs. Scotty removed from her hair the single metal clip she inserted each night before bed. Absently, she worked its hinge: opened, closed, a hungry, long-beaked bird. "I can't imagine what it would be like around here without you now, Oy," she said.

"No, now—" Scotty Hillis lifted his hands. "No pressure, Edie. You don't have to answer right off, Oyekan. You sleep on it, see?"

As if he should need to "sleep on it"! Tears started to Oyekan's eyes. Did Mr. Scotty see this? Had he, too, felt as if he would begin to weep, or had shame at Oyekan's tears caused Mr. Scotty to carry his breakfast dishes over to the sink just then? His back to Oyekan and Mrs. Scotty, Mr. Scotty had said, "I know Peg and Joe would be happy if you stayed, Oy. I'd be willing to bet on that."

Yes! In a fit of high spirits, Oyekan now performed a series of pull-ups off the top of his bedroom door frame, dropped to the floor for sit-ups. Twenty-five, fifty, seventy-five.

"Hey, Oy, do twenty-five for me." So his friend Joe would tease if he were here. And then return to the reading of books of social injustices. And Peggy Dixon? Smiling, she would sit on the handsome red and gold bedspread, once Lee Hillis's, now Oyekan's.

One hundred! Happy in his brief exhaustion, Oyekan lay back on the carpet, fingered the gay loops of orange and brown and red. Everything about Minneapolis—its astonishing latitude and longitude, Mr. and Mrs. Scotty's generosity, the garage doors which went up and down at the touch of a button, clear lakes where handsome citizens canoed past homes gray and solid as fairybook castles—everything here affected him like the whiffs of Parson's Ammonia received when cleaning his bathroom: fascinating, purifying, liable to bring tears to his eyes. Bundles of energy thrilled the air! He stretched out a hand, laughing. He could grab a fistful of that energy, compress it—like the Minnesota snow, weightless flakes which, shaped into balls, became hard, might crack the windshield of an automobile.

A knot of poem forming in his belly pushed him upright:

> Your hair is dark and kinked as my own
> but, dressed with sweet oils,
> becomes a cloud of rainbows.

He would give this poem to Joe. To give to Peggy. But that made no sense! The excitement of the day had made him foolish; Joe's hair was neither dark nor kinked—

Gingerly, Oyekan lifted his fingertips to his new haircut. A terrible mistake! Yesterday he had accompanied Joe to the barbershop, where Joe—who always wore his hair in a battered left-hand parting—told the barber he wanted something "different." And when the man finished? Rusty curls rose out of the top of slender Joe's narrow, shaved head like froth on a glass of beer, so painfully awful that, as a comrade, Oyekan had felt the only thing he could do was to climb up in the chair and say, "Me, also."

He rose from the bedroom's bright carpet. Shyly, as if going to meet a stranger, he examined his reflection in the mirror which hung over the little bathroom sink.

How did he appear? Yesterday, when the barber had stopped his clipping, whisked away the silky apron, Oyekan had made a little joke: "And now I believe I am Frankenstein's Monster!"

But the barber said, "Hey, Joseph, look at your handsome buddy, here, he looks like that Carl Lewis guy, doesn't he?"

Elizabeth Evans 149

Oyekan did not know any Carl Lewis.

"He's a celebrity," Joe said. "Come on, I'll buy you a beer and you can sign my napkin."

Oyekan squinted at his reflection. They did not have a mirror at his home, but a neighbor let them look in hers before town meetings and such. Americans were forever telling one another they resembled celebrities! Since arrival in the U.S. Oyekan had been told, also, he resembled Mr. Harry Belafonte, a boxing star, and the singer Michael Jackson. At home, he resembled only his mother.

Ay, suppose Peggy Dixon thought him a fool, an imitator of Joe's drastic gesture! Suppose, also, that on the way to the International Barbecue, in the confines of Joe's Datsun F10, he smelled of Mrs. Scotty's sauerkraut dish of last night.

Twice he brushed his teeth. The guide prepared by the Rotary Club stated that U.S. Americans found foreign students "unfamiliar with accepted practices of hygiene." Oyekan and the other Internationals laughed about this at Orientation, but it was not so funny the time a lady at the Union cafeteria backed away from Khabir with a show of disgust. "My friend does not want to be in your nose!" Oyekan told her. Scandalous! But she had not understood. Khabir had not understood. Oyekan had forgotten to use his English.

"Oy?"

Mrs. Scotty stood in the doorway, so cheering in her bright golf skirt with black dogs following one another about the hem.

"I believe you are already to the barbecue, Mrs. Scotty."

"On our way, sweetie. I just wanted to tell you"—she shifted a bright green lunch bucket decorated with flowers and birds and such from one hand to the other—"if you *do* decide to stay, Oy, I could write your mother for you. If you like—"

Oyekan's face grew hot. People gathered in the sunshine outside his mother's little house, chewing on cane, trying to hear the conversation inside, between his mother and brother. Biki, too, and at her side the old gray and yellow dog which followed her always, to the fields and the pump and the market. Biki might understand; before he left she teased that he would be like Daniel Ojay who went to U.S.C. to study chemical engineering and never returned, broke his betrothal. Oyekan's mother, however, would not understand. His mother would pull on the clothes and hands of Oyekan's brother. She would plead: "How can this be? Is he in trouble there? Is he in jail? Is he sick?"

"I thank you, Mrs. Scotty," said Oyekan. "But should I stay, I would have to write—"

"Of course. Of course, you would, dear." She lowered her head after that, as if afraid; the exact gesture of his mother when she learned of the scholarship to the U.S.!

"Mrs. Scotty," Oyekan began, but, outside, Mr. Scotty began to honk the horn of his auto impatiently, and Mrs. Scotty hurried towards the door.

"I know you'll make the right decision," she said. "I just know it."

The thick tires of Mr. and Mrs. Scotty's auto rolled past his bedroom window, for one moment his room became dark, then the light returned.

Suppose Peggy Dixon called and said that Joe did not wish to go to the barbecue today, but that she and Oyekan might go anyway?

Oyekan *did* want to see Joe, of course, but he had such news today, and lately, Joe appeared most often deep in thought, and, then, to draw him forth, Peggy Dixon told noisy tales; after Oyekan's Honors presentation, it had been the story of a drunken cousin drowned in an attempt to retrieve a bottle of whiskey from a flooded building called a "fallout shelter." Ho, ho, ho, this made Joe and Peggy laugh and laugh.

Oyekan was sorry, but he did not see the humor.

That same night, at Peggy's apartment, he and Peggy and Joe had watched an old television program in which a man received a wound and discovered himself to be a robot. As if they saw themselves in the robot-man who did not know himself to be a robot, Peggy and Joe cried; they cried, they laughed! Sometimes Oyekan did not understand Peggy and Joe at all. Oyekan was no robot! His blood ran hot in him, thank you very much! Joe was a good friend, a good man, but if Oyekan were Joe, he would not act so silly before Peggy Dixon. He would not rush off to Micronesia, leaving her to be sought after by other males, no way!

Maybe Joe did not like Peggy Dixon so well after all, for in his place, Oyekan would write her poems and drive her about, perhaps on a motorcycle like Lee Hillis's, certainly not in a rusty Datsun F10 with gravel and squashed fast food containers in the back. He would show good posture and never fall down on the floor laughing during the "Saturday Night Live" television show, an act Oyekan witnessed after Joe and Peggy believed him gone, after the robot television show.

He had been wrong to watch. His dear friends! They had not even wanted him to leave. All the way to the door, Peggy teased, "Won't you stay on just a bit, Oyekan, now we're having such fun?" Peggy Dixon's eyes were flecked with green. She spoke with the accent of the American South, her voice soft and deep as pillows. Down the dark little hall she called to Joe, "Joseph, come on out here and instill a little guilt in this friend of yours so he won't go breaking up our party." Smiling, they both watched for Joe to appear at the end of the hall, Peggy holding in her fingers the cloth of Oyekan's jacket that his hand might not fit through the sleeve, but Joe did not come.

After a while Peggy Dixon let go of the sleeve. She looked beyond him, out the apartment door, her gay voice suddenly sad, "You didn't like me telling that story about Roy drowning in the fallout shelter, did you?"

"You are a good storyteller, Peggy," Oyekan said, "but I think your stories have the problem that they lie. They pretend to ask only for laughter. This is not right. A story may lie and lie, but all its lies must tell the truth in the end."

"Woah!" Joe stood at the end of the hall, his feet clad only in athletic stockings. "It was so quiet out here I figured you'd gone, Oy!"

"I'm trying to get him to stay, Joe," said Peggy. She turned back to Oyekan, smiling. "Come on, now, we'll make you a fine big bowl of popcorn. Popcorn with butter on it!"

But Oyekan left. That he might stand in the open, second-story stairwell of the apartment building across the way and, leaning over the balustrade in a manner which caused passersby to stare, observe whether or not Peggy and Joe behaved differently in his absence:

They watched television, made popcorn. Then a neighbor had threatened to call police officers if Oyekan did not move along, and so he had missed whatever came next.

Where were they now, Peggy and Joe? Oyekan looked at his digital watch: 1:23 PM. The clock radio beside his bed read one thirty-one. They might be late, or not yet due.

Last fall, when the couple came to Mr. and Mrs. Scotty's for dinner, the night Oyekan met them—why, no sooner had he and Mrs. Scotty stepped into the dining room to insert the clever extra piece in Mrs. Scotty's shiny table than Joe and Peggy had begun to kiss! And not in a polite way, but with hands moving, mouths open!

To still himself, Oyekan reopened his journal, noted yesterday's high and low temperatures. The coldest day of the year since Oyekan's arrival: January twenty-third. He used to imagine reading from the journal to his family. Everyone laughed at such cold, his stories of foolish American University girls, the loss of his new penny loafer shoe in the first snow. Back then, the journal drew him on, it extracted the gifts he wanted to share. Now, he felt the others would understand nothing of his recent entries; and the early entries no longer amused him, showed only what a bumpkin he had been.

The ringing of telephones still made Oyekan jump. Even when one knew one was to receive a call, even if one waited with the hand holding the phone, the ringing happened behind one's back, nasty as Oyekan's auntie's monkey throwing its messes. Oyekan put his fingers in his ears as he walked into the recreation room. He had lived twenty-two years without a telephone and never felt the lack. This would be a rule in his U.S. home: No Telephone!

"Are you ready?"

"Peggy," said Oyekan. The high school graduation photo of Lee Hillis sat on the stereo. It seemed that daring, golden boy offered advice: Oyekan could say, "I have a surprise for you and Joe!" But, in fact, he could say only: "I am thinking perhaps I will study this afternoon, Peggy."

"Oy! Mr. and Mrs. Hillis helped plan this! Besides, I personally know the picnic features ham, po-ta-to salad *slathered* with mayonnaise, and watermelon from Texas! Chocolate brownies with chocolate icing! Food our kidnapped ancestors ate to ease their aching hearts!"

Kidnapped ancestors. As if both descended from slaves.

Joe Hart took the phone from Peggy. "As you can see, Oy, she's on," he said.

On. Which meant, Oyekan knew, excited.

"My, my!" Peggy called as he walked briskly around the car and slid into the back seat. Embarrassed, tantalized by the possibility that she truly did believe his haircut handsome, he said, sternly, "You do not have on your seat belt. Either of you."

"Oh, Oy!" Peggy pulled at her belt with a great sigh. Her lips bore the hot red color of the flowers planted by Mrs. Scott that very morning. *Geraniums.* Her hair was sleek, bound into a tiny, most elegant knot at the base of the neck; and, to his surprise, she wore a long skirt similar to that worn by women of his own region. "I do believe I'm getting fat as a hippo!" she cried.

"No, no," Oyekan began; but there were Joe's eyes in the rearview mirror, watching, they flickered away as if he did not mean for Oyekan to see!

Too late! Oh, terrible, terrible, Joe knew what lay so deep in Oyekan's heart, and so now did Oyekan also!

Heart jumping, mouth suddenly dry, Oyekan hurried on: "Now, me, I first became a stick in the U.S., you may see this in photos from the Thanksgiving Day. My skin became gray like ash, my clothes no longer fitted!" He forced himself to look, once again, into the mirror, to grin. "Now, however, I am a slick dog, man! I eat Mr. Scotty's chocolate chocolate chip ice cream each dinner. My belt size is thirty-four inches. This morning, Mrs. Scotty tells me I cannot wear my old shirts anymore, I am not decent!"

Peggy Dixon smiled at Oyekan over her shoulder. "This one boyfriend to Mama, now he loved ice cream. That was Floyd Barstow. Y'all remember Floyd, the one she was carousing with the time she met up with Daddy and *his* honey on that painfully narrow bridge—"

Joe interrupted with a laugh, "And Floyd's car and your dad's car got wedged together—"

Peggy Dixon clapped her hand over her mouth.

"Go on," said Joe.

She shook her head. "No. I don't want to tell that. Oy, you tell us something sane and good. Tell us—what you hear from home. Tell us news of your Biki!"

Oyekan smiled, but pretended to take the words of Peggy Dixon as outcry, in no way a genuine request. He was sick at heart, and this—American politeness! They thought betrothal crazy, but that their politeness required they act as if Biki were his heart's desire, that he had chosen her for the foolish reasons they chose one another! In this way, they were bad as children—worse! Like monkeys trained to drink tea from a cup!

Joe slowed the car. "We want ten-nineteen. Ten twenty-seven. And—this must be it."

Oyekan peered up a long driveway to a large and angular home. Tending the barbecue grills on the wooden porches which wrapped the house were Mrs. Scotty, and Professor Reitz, too, her lower half encased in a pair of vast and surprising pink pants.

The car came to a crackling stop on the gravel drive. Miserable, ashamed—what right did he have to be angry with Joe!—Oyekan tried to make a little laughter for his friends: "I am the apple of Professor Reitz's eye."

Peggy Dixon smiled, bent for the big covered bowl at her feet. "Is

Oyekan practicing his ironing?" she asked. An old joke. All three laughed as they climbed from the car. "Irony is commonplace in modern literature," the teacher of American novels had told Oyekan's class; Oyekan had misheard.

Peggy Dixon set her bowl on the roof of the car. Sunshine shot through its translucent contents. That would be her gelatin dessert embellished with pears and the delicious fluffy bits called marshmallows. "I'm tired of irony," drawled Peggy Dixon. "I do believe modern literature could use more ironing."

"Hey." Joe laid his hand on Oyekan's arm. Forgiveness? Oyekan glanced towards Peggy Dixon, busy rolling up her window.

"Joe," Oyekan began in a quiet rush, "if you believe I have overstepped—"

"This is Lee's shirt, isn't it?"

Oyekan looked down in confusion at the shirt front. "Yes. You see, Joe, Mrs. Scotty—"

Joe shrugged. "Forget it, man. I just wondered." He winked. "It looks good on you."

"So be it, Joe," said Oyekan, though he did not believe the wink of his friend sincere, "so be it. Do you wish me to carry your dish, Peggy?"

Joe laughed, his head turned towards Peggy Dixon, now busy with the hiding of her purse beneath the front seat. "Peggy's a big girl, Oy," he said. "Hell, she *used* to pick me up and carry me into the bedroom whenever the urge hit her."

"Joe!" Peggy rose from the car with a movement too quick, bumped her head on the roof, but Joe did not stop to offer apologies, he crossed the lawn, through girls in blue jeans, and men in turbans, dashiki, Muslim women in their headdresses of gray and black wool. Under high pine trees, a group of Indian students played volleyball. "Hey!" called a plump girl in a purple sari as Joe passed through their game, but play continued uninterrupted, a score was made.

"Oh," Peggy moaned. Oyekan did not wish to look at her. The image of Joe in her arms—his heart shook his chest; it was swollen, inflamed. He did not know whether he wished to weep on the shoulder of his friend, or smash his fists into his face.

"Look at this girl," he said, angrily, and indicated with one jerk of his head a Vietnamese he remembered meeting on another such occasion. Mathematics, her area. A vain and giggling girl. Today she wore a leopard-print bikini of impossible size. She stood beside the diving board, shivering, jiggling her knees and shoulders. "Such a fool, to come to such a party in such clothes."

Peggy Dixon shook her head, whispered, "No, I reckon she's got her sights on some fellow at this picnic, Oy, and she's putting all her merchandise on the counter. Who's she got to love here, poor thing, folks all in Viet Nam or dead?" She sighed. "Now where do you suppose a body's to put her dish? I do hate the first minutes at big parties. Someday, somebody—I *know* it—is going to mistake me for help and send me out to wash up glasses!"

Oyekan softened at this admission. She was so pretty, so kind, and here was her forehead all wrinkled with worry! "Not at this party, Peggy," he said. "Though here we are maybe all potential dishwasher material!" He laughed. "Do you know, such a thing did happen at Mr. and Mrs. Scotty's golfing club? In the coatroom, a member asks if I might bring round his car!"

"No!"

He held up a finger, tapped the air. "I only report this to show it happened, and still I live to tell the tale." He smiled. "Undiminished, yes?"

"Undiminished," said Peggy. "You"—she pulled her long fingernails along the back of her hand. Faint trails of roughed skin remained when she finished, and she looked up from them, as if quite surprised, and embarrassed, too. "You—do you think she's pretty, Oy, the Vietnamese?" she asked, and then, before he could answer, "Do I ever remind you of anybody from home?"

The question lodged in his chest, hot as the heart shown by Jesus Christ in the room Gloria Dei Church loaned for practice of English conversation. As if for answer, he looked at the tiny Vietnamese—so strangely sexual and sexless in her silly clothing, one leg extended before her now, as if she imagined herself to pose in a magazine of American fashion.

Peggy Dixon brought her face close. She stood, perhaps, thirty centimeters taller than his betrothed, her eyes of green flecks almost on a level with his own. She resembled no one, anywhere.

But one learned to parlay such terrible questions in America, and, with the sleeves of Lee Hillis's old shirt rolled above his biceps, his feet springy on their cushion of sock and running shoe, Oyekan felt—almost American. He found an American grin. He asked Peggy Dixon: "When?"

Peggy Dixon covered her mouth with her fingertips. "Don't you mean 'who'?"

Still grinning, Oyekan shook his head, no. But this made Peggy Dixon look away, her eyes suddenly sad, he did not understand—

"There's Mr. Scotty," she murmured. She waved at Scotty Hillis, down on the lawn, a set of brightly colored wooden mallets and balls in his hand. "You're getting burned, y'all!" called Peggy Dixon. "Better get that head covered!"

Scotty Hillis nodded and smiled. To Oyekan's relief, Peggy Dixon looked back at him, laughing.

"Mr. Scotty enjoys a small consequence," he said.

"He's a sweetheart," said Peggy.

"He's a bear!" Mrs. Scotty, coming up from behind, put an arm around each. "And don't you two make a handsome couple!" She flushed, widened her eyes, as if she, too, were startled by her words. "With Oyekan's haircut, I mean! I can't quite get used to it! How'd Joe's turn out, Peggy? I haven't seen him yet."

Peggy Dixon smiled at Oyekan, happy as a bird, as if she had not heard the most embarrassing words of Mrs. Scotty! "Well, Joe wanted something different," she said with a laugh, "and different he got. I don't doubt but the boy'll be a big hit in Truk, or wherever they all send him off to!"

Mrs. Scotty laughed at this also, her face tilted up to the sunshine. "So!" She rubbed her hand briskly up and down Oyekan's arm. "Scotty says I'm not to pester you, Oy, but I'll bet Peggy and Joe agree you should stay!"

"Oyekan?" Peggy Dixon leaned forward, squeezed his hand, hard. Perhaps she did indeed remind him of someone from home, he had not recognized this until she put on the traditional skirt, but no, it was the smile, so sleepy, secret. And not from home at all: the smile offered Joe in the photograph in the recreation room! The smile after the kiss. For him, Oyekan.

"Mr. and Mrs. Scotty are most kind," Oyekan said, so stupid, so stupid.

Down on the lawn, Joe held a handful of the wire hoops which Mr. Scotty bent to press into the grass. Mrs. Scotty was saying to Peggy Dixon, "I guess I don't have to tell you Oy's like family," and Mr. Scotty was talking, too, he lifted up his red face to point in the direction of Oyekan, he waved and smiled, and Joe looked up also, his face white as tooth, bone.

Perhaps Joe meant to smile, but could not. Oyekan himself could not smile. Teeth pressed together, he looked at Peggy, at Mrs. Scotty—both of them waiting to be so happy, already they were weary with waiting, their smiles dimmed by something on his face.

"Oy?" said Peggy Dixon.

Oyekan backed into the picnic line, now traveling behind him past the many bowls of food, gathering baked beans and brownies and salads.

"Excuse me," he said. "Excuse me, everybody, please."

The door to the big house stood closed. On the small pane of glass which allowed those inside to look out at callers was a note which read: "Picnickers: Please use bathhouse loo!"

Oyekan pushed open the door, however. He stepped inside. Dark and the chemical cold of conditioned air filled the house, a shock after the bright afternoon. Quickly, he passed through many rooms of beige carpet, brick, wood. He meant to convey acquaintance with the house should anyone see him, but to his surprise all rooms stood empty, quiet, curtained against the sun.

He sat, finally, in the single chair of a small room he took to be a kind of office, walls lined with books and, too, dolls from foreign countries: a little fellow with a load of straw on his back; a Spanish dancer with wide skirts of orange and red and pink; a Scotsman playing the bagpipes. He fitted his back to the chair. He took deep breaths to calm himself. In, out. Out. The sound of the picnickers reached him as a kind of rustle, a small and uniform wave of gaiety which washed against the outer walls of the big house.

Oyekan sat in the chair for a very long time, long after he grew used to the dark, and knew that the slim shadow caught in the room's pale curtains was not a fold of the curtain's cloth, no, but the Vietnamese from the deck, in hiding, too.

CAROLYN FORCHÉ

Carolyn Forché was born in De-
troit in 1950. Her books include
Gathering the Tribes, which
won the Yale Younger Poets Prize,
The Country between Us, which
won the Lamont Prize, and
Flowers from the Volcano, trans-
lations of the poetry of Claribel
Alegria. She currently lives in
Washington, D.C.

THIS NEED NOT HAVE BEEN SO

We were there, our tracks leaving
bowls of water, a quarter moon
ladling light over the sand.
Where it ended, we stood some distance
apart, the beach sucked from beneath
us, the wind torn open, in your whisper
the words *the rest of my life,* in mine
this has happened before.

The same wedges of water moving
toward us, gulls biting scraps
of light from the sea, the same.
I have seen your face in the faces

of others: a young boy peeling eggs
for me, a morning sun red through
a bandage of mist and the man after
months of hunger, whose teeth came away
in his hands, who stood where you stand
saying over and over *Korea*.

In Salvador beside Antonio, whose
hands were lost, who touched me
only with his wrist: *can you find them?*
Years ago, the one who thought I was
his wife, in the bed where I was
that woman, held like candles, those
flickering touches along me, wet
faces flattened by wind, left
at a window burning and as if
we are dying we tell ourselves
only the truth.
We resemble each other.

You have met me where women lean
from doorways, their wet linens
hung in the wind, their mattresses soaking.
In the refugee camp, rocking a child
as if it were alive, to that one, singing.
When in so many countries I asked
for nothing and you pressed currency
into my hands, so that now as this water
rises around our legs, as it wraps us,
with my skirt in my fingers saying
take me with you, you brought me back
to my country.

And now what do you see in my eyes,
the age, the cache of ammunition?
It is only the horns of boats
calling and lost, it is Antonio's
missing hands washing up, it is
how I would hold them to my face.

H. E. FRANCIS

H. E. Francis divides his time be-
tween Madrid, Spain, and Hunts-
ville, Alabama, where he taught at
the University of Alabama until his
retirement in 1988. His first book,
The Itinerary of Beggars, won the
Iowa School of Letters Award for
Short Fiction. His most recent
books are *Naming Things* and *A
Disturbance of Gulls.*

THE CLEANING WOMAN

She would say nothing about the man, her husband, Ripley Samples—
Rip. If it were any workday, she would go down the street with absolute
regularity, moving in any weather with something of the relentlessness of
his ship, dressed always in the same unsullied green most people like to
discriminate the cleaning woman by and, in cold weather, the dark green
overcoat and deep brown knit cap and matching gloves, carrying what
looked like a laundry basket in which she carted the boy.

　She would not take a job where she could not bring the boy and set
him, while she worked, in a quiet place apart from the eyes of whatever
woman was paying her for the day. She had been carrying the basket so

long, if anyone thought about it, that a time when she had not carried it seemed beyond memory. Anyone would think that, with time, the child would have outgrown the basket, would be walking beside her, separating from her to go off to school or play as she went off to work. But the flesh lay in undeveloping and soundless anonymity in the basket, like one of her limbs severed irreparably and carried around as part of her identity.

She had rented after her husband's death—when there was no insurance money from him or the ship from which he had dredged oysters—the rear room, the ex-kitchen, of a small ramshackle cottage back of town by the crick, a single large room whose door was sealed off from the rest of the house, with a toilet stuck as an afterthought in a cubbyhole at one end. She paid fifteen dollars a week every Monday at six P.M. without fail, the only time she ever had any dealings with the owner, until the man and his wife moved out, leaving her sole inhabitant, still at fifteen dollars, a kind of house sitter who was free to use the other rooms now if she wanted to, but who would use only what fifteen dollars paid for.

She had only what possessions she needed, mostly for the boy, and it was the oil burner she valued most—for heat and cooking and the constant bucket of hot water ready to keep the boy clean.

Her only large possession was the dory, the only vestige of Rip's ship, which he had had to fight to get her into that night and shove off, crying, "Row, goddamn it, Wanda, row," until she did row, knowing it was useless not to—because he had made up his mind. After, it was the only thing she let anyone do for her, haul the dory from the crick, where she had rowed and moored it that night, to her back lawn, that long patch of ground where each spring she broke ground to plant the vegetables she would can, the corn and string beans and tomatoes. The dory lay there now, overturned, long since peeled and penetrated by salt, sun, wind and water, looking like the shell of some extinct species bleached bone gray. People passing still said, "That's Rip's dory," though nobody could understand how it had come to be moored hundreds of yards away from the harbor and Hulse's Oyster Factory and the old Socony pump.

The summer following Rip's accident she would pass every Tuesday morning at 7:55—I could time her exactly—pass alongside the house I'd rented, round the corner and go down the street. So near eight, I thought, she must work nearby. She was a rhythm that summer, carrying the basket under one arm, adeptly braced against her hip, shifting hips without the least flagging in her motion.

From casual talk at the Wyandank or Meier's or Helen's, where I ran into people whom I had all my life known casually, all I had was that it was a baby the widow was carrying, the last evidence of a man whose bones might be lying in the black silt of the harbor. But I was roused to no more curiosity until the following summer, when I realized that it was the same basket and that its contents were no larger, so I could ask directly and I suspected from the way they spoke of her—men especially, who are usually the more meticulous and reliable gossips—that her presence in their lives was as natural and relentless and as close as blood or the sea around them. Local events outlive international holocausts, and mention of Rip's bones or the baby brought silence or anger or shame, sometimes indirectly, and I was startled, drinking or playing cards on the long porch of the antiquated Wyandank—once a thriving hotel which embodied a good bit of national history—very startled at the way the word "Rip!" seemed to burn old Hulse's lips; and it was Frank, the bartender, who later explained that Rip had cost Hulse a fortune by setting his oyster business back at least a year.

"It happened at night, midnight or maybe one in the morning, though nobody knows exactly the details, how Rip maybe did it, but the results yes—Hulse's factory and dock and the pump burned, and Rip's ship too, maybe even Rip, because they never did know—they didn't find him—if he got killed or got away, skipped town."

"Without his wife and baby."

"Wife. There was no baby yet."

It was Frank's stare, too deliberate and still, which demonstrated a vague discomfort, a fear of lowering his eyes, as he did his voice, to reveal that other feeling which her mention seemed to evoke—shame.

I followed Frank into the bar, the soft dark, where bottles and glasses and leather and old mahogany gave off muted underwater gleams.

"Which Samples was he?" I had lived most of my summers on the island, and my mother's people had their roots here.

"They're all one. Made their living off the sea since the time when. Big in whaling times. Nobody'd believe that now. Their house went to pieces, torn down now to make the new rest home. All of them've lived on Carpenter since—you know those fishermen's houses."

I knew the row of shoe boxes hidden just behind Main.

Over that afternoon and many others, into dusk and the few drinks, I felt the figure begin to emerge: Rip had grown tired of working for others, of the drinking and carousing and whoring when the ships came in with a big haul and the men collected their share; he had grown tired and persuaded his brother to mortgage the house they owned and shared for a down payment on Briggs' *Defender*—half a wreck, in dry dock, and headed for the graveyard—which he and the brother could restore. He would pay the mortgage and pay the brother for his share of the work on the boat, which he did resolutely. Working on that relic, they—or at least Rip—became a sight, a legend, even a laughingstock to some in town, where a man's image is pretty fixed, though a Samples could always claim old blood.

They cleaned up the ship, painted and decked it out, set it in operation; and with some pride Rip got himself a crew, three men, the mortgage outstanding and the ship, certainly, precarious. From the Wyandank porch you face the harbor—restaurants and galleries, docks, the New York train still as a blacksnake on the railroad dock but shimmering alive in the water below, Shelter Island, the far tip of Hulse's buildings, and no end of nothing beyond. And Rip's ship, the small oyster boat, came to assume a presence. It might have been docked at Hulse's, vaguely undulant, gathering darkness and anonymity now before the waterfront lights made a retreat against the infinite dark. I, who had seen it, could know it quite clearly now, somber gray, its pilothouse narrow and upright, the suspended dory, the side ramps rusting somewhat, all the deck streaked and scraped and rutted to raw wood from chains and oysters.

Then it was Ripley Samples I began to see in dark and day with his three men dredging for oysters, filling the ship so heavy its stern rode almost level with the waves, in all kinds of weather struggling, and returning to old Hulse's dock to deposit the catch, collect the cash, divide it among the men, and then appear with scrupulous haste at the bank and at home to make his payments, keeping whatever pittance remained to live on after buying supplies for the ship and crew. He had not let up working from the time he had decided the ship would be his, free and clear; but nobody could abide him—he was absolute, strict to the letter about times shipside and being in fit shape to work, about the men's share of the haul, cash deducted for food, rations doled out aboard ship.

So over the years he went through any number of crews—I would meet some of his ex-crewmen, locals, on this or that dock—and he became almost legendary as a test, which teased men into taking jobs with him, some oldsters but mostly the young who'd quit school or got into trouble, dope or sex or stealing, and wanted or had to straighten up.

When I left the island in the fall, it remained dormant, the story, his history, the part of it which cankered, until I went back to buy the old family house sold years before when my grandfather had died, now up for sale again; and it was at Lawyer Weems' office, signing the papers with the seller, and afterward, getting a little acquainted with Weems alone—who did some writing himself, he said—that he talked of the renovation being done all over town and how there soon would be no more eyesores like the place behind me.

"Who lives in it?"

"The last of the Samples—you know the family."

I nodded. "Last?"

"His brother was blown up in a ship accident a couple or three years ago. Grim."

"You knew him?"

"I know everybody. I do most of their business—did most of Rip's until he died, or at least what little he had until he stopped coming to me and took things into his own hands."

Rip seemed to have left his traces everywhere.

"He made a go of the ship," Weems said, "had a reputation for being the most driving man around, but his crews were always satisfied with their share, though he worked them at breakneck speed and they'd gripe about his hard exactitude. He wouldn't give in one red cent, kept tabs on the New York market, insisting the locals pay him the day's closing rate, making himself obnoxious, until two or three buyers refused to deal with him. Mostly he sold—he had to—to Hulse, a client of mine too. I'm divulging no confidences; it's all common knowledge.

"But Rip claimed Hulse was cheating him, claimed Hulse took advantage, after Rip had docked and delivered, to lower the going rate per bushel for oysters or miscalculated the count, so Rip came to me to sue for what Hulse owed him. I couldn't set two clients at odds and told him so. Naturally I had to take Hulse's case when he threatened to go elsewhere with his business, and Rip accused me of siding with Hulse because of the business he brought in, so went to another lawyer. The judge—you've met Tasker?—ruled against Rip. After that he turned renegade."

Perhaps at that instant the picture I had of Rip, however shadowy, set him against sun and storm, tall, lean and implacably hard in mind as well as body, a strider who could halt abruptly and demand with a fixed challenge, with a smoldering calm.

"But Hulse did in fact go on offering to buy his haul and Rip did sell to him. It came to a head when Rip—who, it seems, was calculating the difference in bushels between what he delivered at market price and what Hulse claimed he delivered and paid him for—one night after collecting, rigged a chute and dumped oysters to the tune of his loss onto Hulse's beach so they'd rot there.

"But in no time Hulse managed to trump up a claim against him for threatening the public health. Rip was called into court again and Judge Tasker ruled against him, fined him the worth of the haul plus court costs and the cost of the work of cleaning the oysters off Hulse's sand—or jail.

"Rip paid, but the next time he sold to Hulse—that was the mystery, why they both kept at it—he made an exact calculation and reduced what he delivered by the amount Judge Tasker had fined him.

"So it seemed Ripley Samples had beaten Hulse to the draw, though, some said, selling to Hulse under any circumstances was desperation to support a wife; for by then he had married the Polack girl, Wanda, from Easy Street back of town, where once he'd drunk and played poker Saturday nights in the Polack barns until he had been stabbed near the heart, almost fatally, in an effort to prove he'd been cheated. 'Keep your money! It's the last game I'll ever play with your kind,' he'd said. And it pleased them all, when he was forced out of the harbor, to bandy those now popular words about, with plenty of laughs and smirks to Rip's detriment.

"The wife, Wanda, he kept in a small rented cottage back of town too, near the crick. The brother had long since taken advantage of the chance to take the house over in his name, assuming Rip's mortgage payments and freeing Rip's money to pay double on the ship."

"Maybe," it came to me, "Hulse was buying from Rip only to delude him until he could work something against him?"

"It's possible he was afraid of Rip and was biding his time until he could do something that wouldn't fail."

It was the *afraid* which made Rip grow in my head. I had created by then a fair image of Rip, but for a while, too busy moving into my house, his story hung suspended except whenever I caught a glimpse, rare now since moving out of her accustomed path, of Wanda. Then Rip, vague and precise, would seem to be standing there on the sidewalk where she had appeared but an instant before.

But my mind could push it no further. It was one of those cases where I am led to the edge, but not yet close enough to want to leap free into some strange sea and struggle toward a revelation which I can accept and believe as if it were an inkling of undeniable truth.

And it began to come not long after the move, when I looked out the back window one day—had he not been shorter than I envisioned him and neither so tanned nor energetic in his movements, I'd have sworn my imagination had forged reality:

It was the brother, Halsey Samples, and he was standing outside the fisherman's cottage which he and Rip—and the family before him—had lived in together, a one-and-a-half-story, brown-shingle house behind mine with full windows downstairs and half windows up, ceilings surely barely high enough for a man to stand under, upstairs rooms for children to sleep in or for storage. In fine weather I worked in the yard, and the brother, sullen coming and going, would after a time nod; and when I joined the club at the crick for cards and company and plenty of town talk, with some regularity he would be there, sullen too, alone at a table by the great window, staring across seagrass and crick, marina, the two cemeteries and sandy beach to nothing beyond. "Always was morose," the bartender said. "Worse since his brother, who ruined him."

"His own brother?"

"There was a big fight before the accident. Halsey came off pretty bad, beaten blue. The talk goes, somebody threatened he'd better not help his brother oystering."

"But who?"

"Halsey must know. And worse—the next day, the day of Rip's crash, Halsey's boss—at the shipyard—let him go."

"Why?"

"You can ask Halsey, but you won't get a word out of him."

But I did get a word. One early afternoon the mail truck stopped at his door with a registered letter. From the truck Dennie said, "You can just bet Halsey won't budge even for mail."

I offered to sign.

Late that afternoon I caught Halsey to hand him the letter. It was our first confrontation. He opened the envelope then and there. And instantly, at the dark pain that came over his face, a visible sinking into far time, I wanted to turn away, but I said, "You could stand a drink?"

For a fraction his eyes faltered. Then he nodded, forlorn, but his dark eyes kept to that paper.

"It's his license. They gave him back his license." The paper quivered, and the voice, heavy and harsh.

"Him?" I dared not look up.

"Rip. My brother."

"But—" I could go too far.

"You knew him?"

"As a kid, maybe—his name, your father's, uncles'."

He began then to tell it—in the yard, under the maple, with some bourbon—not because of the drink, though that helped, but perhaps because some impetus, released then, could not stop releasing whatever of truth he held in him that a stranger or the license or the moment or simply time had made way for.

"Old Hulse, he pulled every string to get Rip cut off all down the coast. Rip *had* to sell at below the going rate or let the oysters rot on the ship or dump them and waste the men's labor. And with Rip's luck, who could keep a crew? Bad enough what the crews turned out to be. His reputation got around—made it tough—he took crews too far out, too long, and maybe sometimes just to keep them on he was forced to sell to old Hulse cheap. Rip had his moment—dumped a load to rot at Hulse's—I suppose Weems told you all that?"

I said nothing.

Halsey retold it with such tautness of speech and stare that I was tempted to follow his eyes to see who it was he was talking to. I felt *him*, the other, Rip, talking through Halsey, *at* somebody or something. And I could begin, through Halsey's eyes, to see Rip, hear, feel the breath of him, when Halsey said, "I talk too much," and rose and crossed the yard to his cottage, his head down, with that quick walk that was sometimes like skulking. And I felt bereft, left high and dry, abandoned, but I did not underestimate an ear, which most men long for, and the moments came— early afternoons of burning sun or late afternoons of silver and shadows, or nights by the living room lamp as salt air flurried the curtains—when he let me into his darkness.

So I could see Rip better and especially clearly on a night much later, sitting in Halsey's front room, Halsey telling how the times Rip came it was always night. To Halsey the dark had come to be filled with Rip's presence even when he was out to sea oystering. And Rip brought night, carried darkness in his shadowed eyes, in the face sunk too close to bone, the lamp sending glints, stars that flickered and fell diamond-white and hard in his eyes:

Rip shoved into Halsey's front room.

"Bastards!"

"Now what?" Halsey said—no greeting, too appalled, despite the rush of pleasure in his blood, at the bone of his brother, the hang of clothes on a body gone thin, degenerated. Halsey said he jerked under Rip's hand, not in disaffection but at the unbroken stride of Rip's fury.

"Bastards! They won't renew my dock lease."

"Why, dammit?"

Rip threw himself into the armchair, too still then, hands gripped still, hard brown as his face, legs bones under his trousers.

"I can't dock after tonight, that means. They've cut me out of the harbor."

"How'll you make a living?"

"Oh, I'll make it. Bastards! Next it'll be the license."

"How'll they manage that?"

"You know them!"

"Then go to—"

"I've been to my lawyer! You know what the bastard said? Try farther south, the Carolinas maybe! As if they hadn't already cut me off all the way down past the Jersey coast. I offered to pay him whatever was legally fair, even mortgage the ship "

"Mortgage your ship!"

"But it'd take months, he said; they'd have the ship in no time, he said. Meaning—he won't fight Weems. Weems—and Hulse, sure—have the whole North Fork sewn up."

"You could live here—as long as it takes."

"That wouldn't be long, the way they work."

"What'll you do?"

"Live on the ship—I've just about been doing that."

"And Wanda?"

"Wanda and me'll settle that."

"And how long can you keep that up?"

"You can just bet old Hulse won't turn me down with a load. It's what he wanted—me to sell to him, then to nobody, then go crawling back to the greedy son of a bitch. Trying to prove he was generous and fair! We'll see!"

"You can't manage the ship alone."

"That's right."

After would come evidence from this or that bum, scum, some stranger who had been with the ship, slumped now against a piling or sitting on a curb or sponging at the train depot snack bar, who would bear witness to Rip's tough demands, his niggardliness to the red cent, his energy and sleeplessness, and the tongue-lashings of old Hulse and his crowd, who he claimed had cohorts up and down the coast, who sometimes "bribed" or "made offers" to the scum to bring back news of what Rip was up to. There would come too the fury of owners whose docks Rip would tie up at deep in the night and set out from before the motions of morning business began. There would be some nights when his ship lay in the bay as if abandoned while he stole home to that cottage back of town to Wanda, but the ship would be gone before morning. And there would be fines too, which he appeared regularly to dispute and ultimately pay. There would be the wonder where he came by his supplies, fuel, for he had exhausted the town, the area, and could no longer hire even the untrustworthy men who had turned out to be bloodsuckers, thieves, free riders to New London or Bridgeport, Brooklyn, Jersey.

All the time that he had still been selling to Hulse, clinging to town (was it because of the woman and bones in the cemetery and the places that fill a man's head?), he must have been tallying his increasing losses—what Hulse, if he would admit it, owed him—which he swore to his brother he would collect come hell or high water.

"And he did decide to make old Hulse pay—I know it," Halsey said. "He had some plan—that was written all over him," though Rip shared only silence, restrained fury, an energy which he surely was storing up for the right motion, which must have come to him the night of his final visit to his brother—in the dark again, as Halsey had learned to expect, though it was not the dark which upset, but Rip.

"Not an ounce of flesh to spare then," his brother said, "and eyes too deep, dark. You sure wouldn't want to run into them in an alley. But no matter what he's feeling, Rip could sit still, all control, hours—fixed, waiting. And I knew this night he'd do whatever it was, and I had to stop him—I *would* too. I told him I'd do anything to help—and it *was* help I wanted to give, though *he* couldn't know what kind, or me either—yet. And I was half in my jacket. I followed him out, when he turned on me. 'No,' he said, 'I shoulder my own.' Maybe he knew about the threat—to the house, and me too, if I didn't get him to leave off oystering around here—for good. All the oystermen were down on him for selling cheap to Hulse. They hadn't gone to Wanda yet, maybe because she was pregnant. So when I tried to go with him—I wouldn't take no—he turned on me and clobbered me, left me cold on the front stoop, bleeding—because he maybe thought I was lying or wanted to protect me—I don't know; but everybody in town still thinks I got beat up covering for him or protecting him from somebody, thinks I had a hand in what he did—well, let them!—everybody except, I guess, Wanda."

"Wanda?"

"She says—said, 'I know you'd've helped if you had the chance.'"

So it was Halsey who had got me at last to that night: the fall. Dark, and no moon, and no rain. A quiet season for town. Few activities. Silence. Perhaps two thousand TVs flickering. Then sleep.

I had got that far, though from the very beginning at the Wyandank it had been old Hulse, bitter: "Months without the factory buildings!" Or, Frank, the bartender: "The biggest fire in hell knows when—three days smoldering." And later the men at the club: "Nothing left to the ship but what was metal." Yet I always sensed in their talk the defiance they could not overcome, or maybe shame.

But I did not have *him* yet: I would like just once to have arrested their memory, vision, at the right moment and seen for myself who the man was they thought they looked into. Yet finally, if I could take it as far as I might, if it were to come to the end, I would know it was that—that I had *not* seen him, would never see him—which was the wonder, the blessing: I could thank not knowing him for releasing whatever it was I was seeking:

Because he had become a demand in me.

By winter I had come to know the cottage where he and Wanda had lived together, came to know too that house empty but for the rear room she still rents. I had gone there one night because she was the best cleaner around. The single bulb on a cord glared across the dark. The dory made a black mound in the shadows. She said, "I've got my steadies. There's only seven days to a week."

So I was not prepared when one breakfast time down Main Street came the unchanged image in the green coat and brown knit cap and gloves, and with that basket, came up my walk and rang the bell.

"You wanted a cleaning woman." She stood, all health and sturdy, her round face bit red and alive from the cold, clear her skin and brown eyes. "Old lady Welsh died."

"I'd like somebody steady," I smiled.

"I can start right now. Eight hours every Thursday, pay at the end of the day, and I bring my boy—that's understood."

"Of course. I'll show you—"

"I know this house. Pantry and sink's what I need first."

On Thursdays the house took on vigor, her hard breath, the biting clean odor of her skin. There would be only the briefest hiatus now and again, when I knew she would be tending to the basket, talk quiet and factual— she might be speaking to me or anybody.

Her presence brought Rip in. Her silence made him grow so that there were days when my questions almost insidiously broke into words, when, after she had gone home, I was certain I would come upon him behind a door, at the foot of the stairs, sitting in the shadows, waiting, hard glints in the darks of his eyes. Sometimes I felt the press, as if he could not, nor I, wait much longer. So I counted on her Thursdays to make him grow in me.

And it was a day between Thanksgiving and Christmas when she was in some way agitated, her rhythm askew, that she stood in the study doorway and said, "I could give this room a good hurry-up cleaning, and I wouldn't touch a single paper, honest." She must have seen how off guard I was because she backed off so I said quickly, "It can stand a cleaning, can't it!" And a smile almost—yes—burst from her, the first spontaneity, white teeth in a splendor of gratitude.

And it occurred to me afterward, in the stillness of night, that she had obliterated or celebrated something. And in the morning, during my usual meandering downstreet, I stopped in to talk to Eaves at the *Times* and ended by finding the day, December 7, a Monday, and with the front-page story, how sometime in the early morning hours fire destroyed the Hulse Oyster Factory buildings, the dock, pump, and Ripley Samples' ship, *Defender II*. At press time the fire was still blazing, spread by gasoline from Hulse's private pump, the old Socony landmark, and there was no possible way to discover who, how many, had been on the ship. Articles on the following days added little. A day in December. So it was neither celebration nor obliteration, but a translation into utterance of a kind, or the eloquence of work—and to a man, to me, as if to that other one, Rip. Somehow I was getting nearer.

That same morning I found too—at the town clerk's office—the other date, which would have been, yes, some four or five months after the fire, when what they had made together was born: that son.

And when his day in April was nearing, I left for the boy some new clothes and a stuffed whale, ostensibly from the Easter bunny, not knowing whether she would accept them, for people said she had refused all public benefits, had turned from charity after the fire. "And me so able-bodied?" she'd said.

At the end of the day she was standing again at my door. The study, on the second floor, views the backyard and over low houses the bay and near island, and pours sky and sea forever in.

"Why, I thought you'd gone, Wanda."

She said, "Rip thanks you."

"Rip?"

"He's Rip too. In the hospital I said, 'It's a boy, ain't it?' It was Dr. Sperling. He nodded. 'Rip said it would be,' I told him."

For a flicker, as her eyes sought the window and faltered on the sea— clear and serene, shimmering with late sun—I believed we understood each other.

And I made then my appeal to her. I said, "My own children are words," and as I said it, I was ashamed.

"Children?"

I knew it was insidious, but I could not stop then, I had to go on while she was standing there, while it was Rip out there, and the sea, perhaps even *then*, that last night, all of it—in her thoughts.

"Because," I said, "it's the only way I know to make things live."

"How's that?"

"In words, stories—"It was mean, paltry, low, but I watched her. She waited.

I said, "We use the way we have, our only chance sometimes."

She was staring at the water again—I wanted to know what she was seeing—and she was even impelled a few steps toward the windows. She said again then, roused, "Rip thanks you," and left.

I sat there gazing at where she'd stood. Then I went over and stood in her place, in her footsteps, and looked out: from there the fisherman's house, his, rose to sight. Was that why she had come to me, taken this job to be near that; or maybe near the brother, who looked like him, reminded?

But inadvertently Wanda herself would tell me no, not because of Halsey: "I got no truck with Halsey. No need to abuse people's judgments. *You* know." And it might have been because she knew Halsey and I talked now and again, or because she thought Halsey might tell it differently, or even because of the Easter gifts: whatever, she gave utterance and, once released, there was the inevitable motion to talk and to afterthoughts.

"His brother don't know about the dory neither, and it's better you get it straight and true, no lies, cause I know now it's for Rip, it won't go reckless from this house, at least in cheap talk."

July was a swelter. She sought whatever breeze to set the basket in for air. She kept wiping her face with an old rag. "Whew!" Her husky legs she kept set wide apart for air. She would not talk on my time, she was all business, and in the study she would not sit. Did she need the goad of the view—cottage, sea, the ship out there, Rip—each time she stood in that doorway?

"That night he come after dark. I almost never seen him in day no more. He couldn't dock and they pulled his license too, so I guess you'd say he was running illegal—see? They's a lot of them at sea are crooks with no license. Nobody'd stay with a ship had to steal in even for supplies. Rip knew that. But it was how long he could keep going—I *know*, even if he'd not admit it to himself. He said he'd get the license back—he wrote for it—and be back at the docks with crews too when he made them all see they were wrong, he knew they were, he'd prove it. He come that night like his old self: You come with me, he said, quick. Where to? I said. The ship. No, Rip, I said, not this time. And he grabbed me—I'll never forget—and whispered so mean, and him never mean before: You're my wife, you'll do's I say. You get dressed—now. He needed me for a crew sometimes in a pinch when not even his brother was around. It wasn't far—you know, by Gull Pond, the dory hid in tall seagrass. When we got to the ship, I didn't know how he done it alone, the nets so full and the boat deep, and he knew he couldn't pilot and handle the winch and even out the load too. I was almost afraid to go aboard. How much you got on this damned boat? I said, and he said, Just do what you're told. Seemed like we run two hours, him making me lower the nets while he shoved the load in place, the shoveling to keep the oysters level and me every minute thinking Holygod, water's going to come pouring in. You never done it so full before, I said. Shut up, he said. And it sure stinks of gas, I said. I told you shut up, he said. I never seen him so fast, hard, like I wasn't there but to be his right arm, a thing he could make do. Why'd you think I got a Polack wife, he'd say sometimes at home, if not to work her ass off? But me asking now, What're you up to? and What, Rip? and him no word at all then, both of us sweating like fools, even bundled against the cold and me pregnant and about to say I can't no more when he said, It's done. He lowered the dory and loosed it, said, You go home now—harder than he'd ever been—and that's what done it. I said, Whatever it is, you can't! Don't Rip. You can go too far. He said, It's some others've gone too far. Now you get in that boat, Wanda. No, I said, you can't. And he hauled off and let me have one I couldn't believe—Rip, what never one time smacked me before. I fell. My head pounded. I knew then it was bad. Rip: I'm staying. You grab those oars, he said. Rip! He shoved the dory off. He said, Go to the crick. You never saw me—get it? I didn't answer. I sat there. I couldn't move. I didn't till he said Row, goddamn it, Wanda, row! like mine and his life depended on it, so I knew nothing could change his mind and I rowed to Stirling Creek and moored the dory and went home. But I sat up. I waited—it would come, I knew it, but not when or what. And then the fire whistle blew, I went out—the sky was burning. I thought I'd die that night—I would have too, but for him, not even born yet: he saved me."

A great breath quivered her body.

"And nobody saw?"

"Not a thing. Not him nor me. Nothing."

"And Rip?"

She was seeing sea again: empty, it filled her eyes.

"Nothing."

And was it that—not a bone or a grave? Out the window, far to the left, almost on the edge of things, are the stretches of stone and shrub, trees, walls—the Protestant and Catholic cemeteries. A widow is not complete until her man is laid in the ground in a final place she can know.

She went downstairs then, and home.

What it must have cost her to break silence! Though she could not know, she had brought me to the brink, and she could not know the tumult; she had left me seething with it. I stood in the window, watching the motion of the water, watched till the air itself became a sea moving, and dark came down, slow, long, and stillness and shadows moved, moved, and I heard the sea, saw it come through the window, felt it under the ship, moving. I looked out at the harbor where the lights came one by one piercing dark, and the harbor made the one small coil of light in the growing dark. My legs twitched, my hands; I felt a fierce energy, nervous, I couldn't contain it. I was seething with what was to be done, had to be done, waiting for Wanda to row off, listening, until I had to cry out *Row, goddamn it, Wanda, row!* I said it aloud, I said, "Row, goddamn it, Wanda, row," and listened in the interval of quiet; then I heard the oars scrape in the locks, the splash, then the suck of water, listened, so still my head and skin would burst, bones shatter, watched till there wasn't a streak or ripple—she was gone in the dark. It would be only a few minutes I had to wait before she hit Stirling Creek, a few minutes more to the bank by Pell's Fish Market to moor the boat and then a few more to walk to the house. Wanda! My breath cracked—too loud. *Wanda.* The boat was making heaves. On the left I could see the Orient Point lighthouse, far, and all the night beyond, black—pitch—and on the right the harbor, all the lights long pins in the water. I could feel the laugh, it broke in my throat: I knew every foot of this harbor since a kid on the boats, I knew exactly the factory at the far end, knew blindfolded I could shoot the boat direct, right past Preston's shipyard and Claudio's restaurant, the railroad dock, straight to the end—that pump. *Cheat a man of his living, you son of a bitch!* I switched the ignition on and *Jesus!* for a second it was thunder. I throttled slow. I couldn't stop the *put-put,* but *Jesus* too loud, too. But the ship made the line, it headed direct, I held: it moved toward the harbor, smack into the middle of the mouth of the harbor. But so slow! I could hardly breathe. I could feel my breath hard. And it was coming— the long dock, the main building, long and gray and the spots spraying light down, and the old Socony pump straight up and hard, waiting—I could see it clear now, green and white and red. I eased the throttle all the way. The ship glided, scarcely a heave, cutting straight, straight. It would not veer now. I went out on deck. Even at full speed the ship reeked gasoline from the open drums planted in the hold. And I sloshed gas over the deck, ropes, old clothes, pilothouse. The boat was whining, taut and stretched to groaning, heavy in the water but cutting fast—and the dock growing bigger, the buildings, and that pump: fifty yards, less, less. I lit the torch—*You and your kind, Hulse!*—it leaped flames; I grazed the deck with it, hurled it into the hatch, and shut myself in the pilothouse. The air whipped a fast blanket of fire over the deck, flames swept around the pilothouse. *Here's your haul, Hulse!* I clutched the wheel, headed straight for the pump. *For my son,* I shouted, *so someday he'll never forget!*

"Never forget!" I shouted. My hands leaped for the pane, but my own voice halted them.

The silence was so sudden my breath thundered in the study.

But I was exultant. I had done it, I had been there, seen—for a moment I had brought Rip back, and it had come such a burst over me—for *him,* that son, who would someday bear witness without shame or fear and justify his name.

Somewhere in my mind I saw the ship strike the dock, hurl the pump down, ride up half out of the water, penetrate the building, jar, tremble and settle suspended there—and then explode, again, and again. The sky throbbed red. The rest was fire and ashes and bones.

Outside, darkness returned, not a star. Only the lights of the harbor were burning, still and white. And there was nothing. No one. The voice faded to the shadow of a sound. Rip receded. I could no longer see him clearly . . .

But I could envision Wanda standing alone in the dark, watching the sky burn that night and feeling the stirring of the son she carried inside her. Who could know how far she would carry him? Here in my study, I had made my appeal to her in his name. Looking out over that empty sea, what had she seen? Whatever it was, she had broken silence. She had spoken. What more could she have done?

Then she had gone to that cottage back of town.

In the morning she would set out on the endless round. Who in town after so many years of going down these streets in day and dark, knew the way any better? Children would stare with wonder or curiosity or sometimes taunt in deviltry. The men at the Wyandank or Meier's or standing on any corner or any dock, and the women glancing out frosted windows or sitting in good weather on this stoop or that porch, would speak or nod, lower their heads or drop their eyes until she passed and then raise them to follow what she carried in the basket, which must move them to ponder many things.

And sitting at breakfast, I would know it was Thursday because there would be her firm step on the porch before she rang the bell and opened the door and called out, "We're here!"

JAMES GALVIN

James Galvin is the author of three
collections of poems: *Imaginary
Timber, God's Mistress*, and *Ele-
ments*. He was born in Chicago in
1951 and received an M.F.A. from
the University of Iowa, where he
now teaches. He served as poetry
editor of *Crazyhorse* from 1978
to 1979.

ALMOST NOON

The water, you remember,
Was so cold it took our breath
Until we laughed. The sun didn't shine down there at all
Except at noon. You remember. No one
Ever took your picture there, but this one:
Granite walls, deep water, cedar, your favorite spot,
Where I threw your ashes into the falls.

I like the hat you're wearing, Father's straw one,
Though it casts your eyes in shadow.

I can tell what time it is
By how much of you is missing.
The children can go swimming now.

Sometimes things happen this way,
And I can't talk about it.
There are smaller, darker shadows gathered in your ears.
They are planning an invasion. Listen,
You can't even hear them.
You are turning to the camera, saying yes.

LITTLE ANTHEM

Cool in brindled shade below the springbox,
Willows muster and fold over
In green vaults
To assemble and reassemble the place
My mother planted watercress
A long time, now, ago.

That deep in green was hers,
Safe from deer and safe from horses.

Shallow water doctors the light,
And the vague silt settles down
Vegetable and feathery
Like the inside of a living eye.
The watercress is a secret floating country,
Its own green flag,

With history.
It's quiet here,

Despite the water's
Small gasps of surprise,
But the noise Ernie raised
Repairing the springbox lid
Was an old man's pissing and moaning
And a glorious hurling about of tools in rage.

Father gave orders to stay clear of Ernie,
Whose meanness came from dying slowly,

But my mother sent me down for watercress.
Above my head, a cat's paw hit the tree.
I knelt and touched the atmosphere
Those numb leaves lived in.
Keeping myself small, I tore up handfuls.
Howling, Ernie sent his hammer arcing.

One of his eyes was made of glass
And it wavered toward me.

What desire
Held me there against which fears?
When my bowl greenly overflowed, I stayed.
When his fury lost its way in sadness, I stayed.
When he set to work again,
I stayed.

And what I stole from him
Was mine.

GARY GILDNER

A professor at Drake University,
Gary Gildner was born in West
Branch, Michigan, in 1938. He has
published eight books of poems,
including *Blue Like the Heavens:
New and Selected Poems*, and
three collections of stories. His
memoir *The Warsaw Sparks* re-
counts his experiences coaching a
baseball team while serving as a
Senior Fulbright Lecturer at the
University of Warsaw during
1987–88.

THE WAKE ON GOOSE RIVER,
NORTH DAKOTA

At my uncle Jimmy Lynch's wake
we were everyone except tight Grandma
working loose to drink
the good dead man to earth,

when Grandma spilled the beans
to God, i.e. aloud she squeezed
her beads to save us from dam-
nation on this dark, queer night.

What brought the trouble up
was Jimmy's plane & Heaven;
or, our joke to buzz the saints did
rage with Grandma's recipe for Bliss.

Alas, she went to bed & we without
a leg to pull took up the Piper Cub.
Three facts amazed us:
1. the ground below was Climax, Minnesota

2. we scooped the loop & heaved our guts &
3. we landed.
At which point we drank our health
& hoped we scared the Devil shitless.

ALBERT GOLDBARTH

Albert Goldbarth was born in Chicago in 1948. His many books include *January 31*, which was nominated for the National Book Award, *Original Light: New & Selected Poems, Popular Culture*, and *A Sympathy of Souls*. He is currently Distinguished Professor of Humanities at Wichita State University.

CAMERA LUCIDA

. . . reflecting light by means of a mirror,
so that the image is projected . . .

Night: the birds
in the branches not so
much birds as vague-shaped
ancillaries of night.

I wonder how Niels Bohr felt,
there in Manchester, every atom
in the ashy autumn air of 1913 suddenly
showing him its quantum spectrum!

Probably, nobody knows. Though
in the photos, Margrethe
leans her black shape into his black shape and
something continuous, yes
maybe down to the atoms, happens against
the stiffness of his collar
and dry, November-gray twig tracery.

Once, you talked to God by slitting
a mouth in the throat of an altar-bound beast.
It was a different way
of saying these birds
may really be a link to the living
cosmic matrix, a croupier
in Vegas has his, a cosmetician redoing
a rougey camouflage under an eye has hers,
why not? Birds' notes are sprockets
tonight, their song is the lubing
smooth of the large machinery.

When Madame Curie looked up
for the first time
after the hundredth time, the night said
radium. And then she looked up,
through something weary, and saw her husband
Pierre in a place
beyond being weary, and many buttons
later—this was an age of
many buttons, and she'd worn her high blue frock—
they slept with the window open to ivy.

It was dark. They couldn't see the ivy,
the leaves were ratchets
engaged. And so they turned in their sleep.

There are times for disliking machines,
but not tonight.
The moon is the sun,
as a mirror is light
in a camera lucida, and tonight we're all
that little much
of the sun, together, our skins accepting
projection of that
other-hemisphere blaze.

That's us. The gears
of sun's diffusion, all through the night.

If I dialed, you'd answer.
I don't know exactly what Bell carried
in his head of his father, a woman's
glove on the hardwood mantle, a child's sour kiss . . .
But there are times for machines.
The birds are cranking it up. It's
night, it's a time of interlockings.

PATRICIA HAMPL

Patricia Hampl was born in St.
Paul, Minnesota, in 1946. Among
her books are two volumes of
poems, *Woman before an Aquar-
ium* and *Resort and Other Poems*,
and a memoir, *A Romantic Educa-
tion*. She teaches at the University
of Minnesota.

MOZART DURING A SNOW STORM

Hands are clapping in Vienna,
the child Mozart takes his bow.
Ladies reach for the triangular
iced cakes of intermission;
the small chapped Viennese hand
touches my forehead.

Snow is falling, snow
is falling in the twentieth century.

All the brief white threads sift
through the air like silence breathing
its own thin life between
the quick notes of the sonata.

The dense, heavy stars of afternoon
stud the brain with slowness.
We slam in iceboats across
our bleak landscape. We are going
backward, we are going forward,
history is this slick surface.

So much whiteness in one lifetime.
The children are shrill in the snow,
they are making a man.
A shovel scrapes like a thought.
In the bedroom a sheet is taut
across the double bed. We are like
everyone who has ever lived.

LAST LETTER

for Jim White

Everything is more beautiful today.
I'm sorry, it's not right when you're dead
for the first time this morning,
but the splats of rain hit the black
asphalt like hoofers, exhausted and heavy
under the transparent strokes of dance.
The pink geraniums (do you like pink?
                    I want to know if you like pink)
are hanging in a basket from the cafe awning
as dry as tissue paper on a package.
They're wonderful, like an escape.

The lights of things have turned on
more intensely just now as yours
has clicked immaculately off.
The women at the next table are saying
something is cute, real cute.
One of them is wearing earrings
the shape of hearts. *No way
would I follow that oaf around
like she did*—they're talking about love,
the only subject, darling,
except for this new one of yours.

Listen pal, here's what I meant to do:
call you this weekend, go for
chicken salad sans at the Sky Room
and you'd whisper again the truth:
the really great waitresses
always chew gum. You approved
of their dismissal of us, charmed always
by any artist who couldn't be charmed.
You posed glamour
as the first honor of friendship

and we said darling
to each other like movie stars.
Your white, naughty smile:
Tell me again, Trish darling,
how we're going to claw
our way to the top.

The woman with the hearts at her ears
is saying that after 30 years of marriage
you can't expect . . .
and that the girl *wasn't* a gold-digger . . .
She says when you order prime rib
you just better not think
you're going to get it medium rare.
But the only words today
are endearments: darling, sweet angel one,
caro, caro (we liked to be affected
and spoke all languages for their flair).

Just this instant a cat streaked by outside,
wet and matted as carpeting in a vestibule.
His brown and black stripes were green in the rain.
A green cat, Jim, bet you never saw that.
And the hearts are gold, pressed tight against
each lobe, not hanging—in case you thought
I meant the hanging kind. No, pressed
like two kisses. And she's looking at the cat too.
She may be thinking something, about the cat
or about something else. I couldn't say for sure.

I'll keep describing things, getting the colors
right, taking down the dialogue, packing
the report with metaphor so it's art,
letting the world be unlikely and eccentric.
I call it honesty, as you do. But today
I call it keeping you alive just a little longer,
using the present tense though that's dishonest now,
and it is unholy, darling, to hold you
a second longer than you held on to us.

JAMES HANNAH

James Hannah was born in Lufkin,
Texas, in 1951. He is the author of
Desperate Measures, a collection
of short stories, and the recipient
of a National Endowment for the
Arts Fellowship. He teaches at
Texas A&M University.

BREAKING AND ENTERING

The glossy photographs were tucked neatly in the briefcase at Paul's side.
That morning, when they were first passed to him, he had quickly turned
them toward the light so the glare would obliterate most of their madness.
Now, as he drove toward his home, he tried not to think about them. In-
stead he thought about the beach house in Crystal City he and Nancy had
talked about buying. How badly he needed the soothing calm of the coast.
If only he could go there now, escape from the photographs and the expla-
nations to the newspapers and all the rest of it . . .

As he turned recklessly into his driveway, his mind on Crystal City, the
heavy bumper of the New Yorker shuddered against the gatepost. Paul
winced as the wood splintered and the huge car, forced by the broken

root of the post, slipped off the concrete driveway and sank a neat trench through the late-blooming mums.

Angrily he yanked the wheel, and the whining power steering pulled the car crossways, the grill coming to rest in the hedge under the children's bedroom window.

"Goddamn it to hell." Paul pounded on the padded steering wheel with his damp palms. But he refused to look at the damage. It'll wait, he told himself. And with a loping step he skirted the sideways car and ran up the steps.

Paul wanted to avoid Nancy, but the front door opened onto a long hallway and she stood at the far end in the kitchen, her profile toward him, her small, tightly packed body in a bikini with his chef's apron over it. She tore at a head of lettuce. On the tile counter near her wooden salad bowl were scattered tomatoes. At this distance and in the muted light of early afternoon, they shone like splotches of blood.

Carefully he closed the door but so intently had he been watching her in his anxiety to escape unnoticed that she seemed to sense his gaze and looked around with a shudder.

"Oh, Paul!" She dropped the lettuce into the bowl. Her hand brushed against the tomatoes and several skittered to the floor.

"Hello." Paul waved with a flick of his wrist, and as Nancy bent to pick up the scattered vegetables, he trotted down the hall to the bathroom. With the door closed he crossed to the lavatory and spun the taps to full force. Their angry sputter reminded him of his promised repair—this, like other chores, methodically outlined on the refrigerator door, stuck there with small magnets in the shapes of crayons and miniature potholders and bunches of grapes. Next to his list was hers and under theirs, the children's. It was an orderly arrangement, a system that worked, that they were all happy with.

He took off his trousers, laid them neatly over a towel rack, and sat on the toilet to let the pain in his bowels, the ache that had been there for hours—through the long series of meetings instigated by the photos and the news they brought—twist and cramp his intestines. The sweat collected on his forehead. Through the partially raised window he could hear the distant splash of his children in their backyard pool.

"Paul?" Nancy pecked at the door. "What's wrong? You're home an hour early."

His hand brushed the briefcase that leaned against the tub.

"Paul?" She rapped again.

"Nancy." His voice was rough and instantly he was sorry. "Nancy, it's nothing. A touch of diarrhea."

"Oh."

He could picture her with a forefinger on her cheek, her lips pursed and twisted to the left as she thought.

"I'll get the Kaopectate out of Judith's room. It'll do the trick."

"In a minute." The twisting rumble under his navel made him grimace. "I'll be fine in just a minute."

"Nonsense," she said, her tone the one she used on recalcitrant children.

After a few minutes, when the pain had dimmed, Paul moved his hand across to the rough leather of the case. The sharp click of the latches echoed off the tile.

The light entering the small window was filtered through the leaves of the huge live oak outside near the garage. So, as he arranged the pictures cautiously on the rim of the tub across from the toilet, they took on a green tint. Where the glare of the harsh fluorescent lights had aided him in his office, here the dull underwater light took some of the edge off. But not enough.

Mr. Shaw lay near the front door, his pajama bottoms wet with blood to the knees. The flap was open, the flaccid penis dark pink against the white cotton. His head lay over one end of the metal grating of a floor furnace. What sort of impact did it take, the FBI agents had wondered, to force the skull so far down into the metal?

Mrs. Shaw was in the kitchen. The three children were scattered in between. The oldest daughter had been stuffed in the narrow space between the washer and dryer. It was early last night, Thursday night, when her date had found them all.

Paul reached out, brought his hand up from his sore gut and touched the photograph of the youngest, the only boy. Some Legos protruded from under the body. Frozen in the policeman's flash were two posters: the ominous helmeted head of Darth Vader and the anorexic beauty of Charlie's Angels.

"Hey, you still in there? Here's the medicine." Nancy turned the handle. "Paul, you've locked the door." She rattled it in frustration. "Paul, answer me."

"I'm better. Just fine now, as a matter of fact." He cocked his head to the side at the sound of his weak voice. "Be out in a few minutes. Think I'll shower." He sat anxiously on the edge of the sweaty seat until she left.

Slowly he gathered the pictures and placed them in their manila folders.

Then he stood and began stripping off his shirt and tie. It's not your fault, they'd told him. Anderson, the agent in charge, had patted him on the shoulder and smiled.

No, it's really not, Paul told himself and turned to look in the mirror. He turned off the roaring taps and listened to the few final drips fall in the basin.

He knew he was a good lawyer. A fine tax lawyer and hell with contracts and leases. And quite a politician—they all said that. For a moment he smiled and then he reached down for the case and stood naked in the green light.

No one could have known it would happen, Anderson had said. You try to sense everything but you're not always going to bat a thousand. Not forever.

As United States Attorney for three years, he'd never personally tried a case. Oversaw them all, sure, but left the details to his assistants. He was excellent at delegating authority.

It's one of those things, Anderson had said, lighting a cigarette. Paul could almost smell the harsh odor now. He had been amazed at the steadiness of the agent's hand.

But Paul had helped get Cox, the murderer, into the Federal Witness Protection Program over a year ago after he had agreed to testify against some of his cronies who ran an interstate extortion ring based in Austin. In turn, they'd gotten some aggravated assault charges against him dropped. Sure he was violent, Paul thought. His record showed that clearly enough. But not crazy. And Paul's assistants, the agents, everyone had assured him of the necessity of Cox's testimony. Cox had probably only seen the Shaws once or twice since he'd moved a block down the street from them. Paul shook his head slowly. Still, it was his name, Paul Winslow, scrawled leisurely across the bottom of the government forms.

Paul stood in front of the mirror, his head light, his naked feet sticking to the damp tile floor. Political appointment, the newspapers had called it. Well, weren't they all? He nodded at himself in the mirror.

The children splashed and screamed outside and Nancy whistled along with the radio as Paul showered furiously.

Later, after he had dressed, Paul locked his briefcase, shoved it as far up under his desk as he could, and came out to sit next to Nancy on the screened-in porch that overlooked their pool and backyard. The children, their numbers increased by six or eight friends and neighbors, seethed like a hive.

"Need this?" Nancy asked and picked the plastic bottle of medicine off a low table.

Paul slumped in the vinyl webbing and rubbed his tired eyes. "No, I'm okay now."

"I saw the car and the fence." Nancy reached across to stroke his thigh. "What's the matter?"

Paul looked straight ahead at the pool and stopped her hand by covering it with his own. "Some problems downtown. Some reorganizing going on. Justice wants me to step up some white-collar crime investigations. It'll make county officials mad as hell." He wasn't lying or inventing any of this. It was really happening, although smoothly, without a hitch. "I'm sorry about the flowers. And they were doing so well despite this heat."

Nancy shrugged and smiled. "I'll call the insurance company about the fence and fender. The flowers you and I can replant. You with such a knack for landscaping." She stood and stretched, still wearing her bikini. Paul noticed the three-inch scar over her spine, midway down her back. It was from surgery for a slipped disc. He marveled at how long ago that had all been. Like another life really, he thought.

She waved at the children and turned to go. "Want a drink?" she asked over her shoulder.

"Listen. Sit for a minute."

Nancy pursed her lips and twisted them to one side as she leaned against the door.

"I'd like to get away from all that bullshit downtown for a while. You know, let the rest of them sort it out themselves. Anderson said"—and for a split second his thoughts crowded together all the agent had really said during the last few hours—"he said nothing was going to break soon anyway." Paul shifted uncomfortably in the chair. "So, what if I drive down to Crystal City and look at that beach house Lynne told us about?"

Nancy straightened and reached over to give Paul a strong hug. Laughing, he shrugged it off. "What do you think?"

"You know damned well what I've thought for months. Wonderful!" She raised her hands over her head and pirouetted awkwardly on the concrete. "Marvelous! I'll go call Lynne and get the realtor's name." She danced out of the room and left Paul with only the noisy children clustered around the diving board at the far end of the pool, their shouts mixed with the nervous bark of a distant dog.

"Wasn't it a strange name?" he spoke over his shoulder. "Like Bo or Ho or Mo?" But Nancy had already passed into the sprawling house.

In his youth Crystal City had seemed like paradise. Then there had been a ferry run by the highway department instead of the huge dramatic hump of the causeway. And his father, the smoke from his pipe brushed flat by the steady breeze, would hold him up from the observation deck and turn him to all the sights—the burned brittle hull of a World War I troopship; the gas flares from the dozens of oil wells; the gulls at the stern begging crackers; porpoises roiling in the oily wake of the ferry.

Paul slowed the car and switched off the air conditioner. On the other side of the bridge, the island flattened into the precise symmetrical lines he loved so. Hurricane Carla had destroyed much of the old beauty, and he almost stopped once or twice on the outskirts of the small central town of two or three thousand. The grand houses were utterly gone. The gentle southern concave curve of the bay that had sheltered the single row of gulf-facing mansions was a riot of broken pilings and kudzu that topped every tree and bush with a tangled conformity. Often all that remained were broad steps littered with the coruscating grit of broken glass.

He had seen the news pictures years ago, of course. But he had no idea the damage had been so tremendous. The ferry had been a portion of his childhood, a memory he loved in part because it had vanished.

The sea breeze blurred the windshield with salt as he swung the car sharply toward the white glare of the town.

And here too he shook his head in disbelief. This side of town he remembered well because here, docked immediately behind the stolid pastel faces of the fishermen's houses, were hundreds of shrimpers and beached dinghies, all the paraphernalia of the sea. Here the gulls flew in and out of the gables and landed on the low stone walls topped with shells and bits of broken colored glass. But now these houses were left to the bitter sea air and the pastels were gone, the wood bare and soft and pitted. The streets were littered with trash—a pile of soiled disposable diapers against a step; sidewalks paved with flattened tin cans. Behind the houses only an occasional fishing boat in terrible disrepair swayed lethargically in its moorings.

And in every doorway he detected the flat lustrous eyes of Oriental children. Their black hair glistened against the duller darkness behind them as gulls dipped and rose near the eaves.

He stepped on the accelerator, stirring up the flotsam in the street, then loosened his tie and mopped his forehead with a wad of tissue from the glovebox. Some of the houses he sped past looked burned out with precision.

He rolled up the window and turned the air conditioner on full blast. Quickly the coolness dried the irritating patches of sweat on his stomach. He remembered that there had been trouble with some boat people relocated here. They had been too industrious for some of the others; had encroached on the natives' domain. But he hadn't really paid much attention to all that.

For a moment he considered making a U-turn where the palm-lined street widened. He could recross the causeway and be home in a few hours. After one seafood meal further inland—he'd promised himself that treat—he could go back. But instead Paul drove on into the small resort.

Carefully Paul parked the large car in front of the tiny Chamber of Commerce building. It was a gaudy storefront concocted of a maze of seashells embedded in cement, their millions of indentations filled with cigarette butts and crumpled foil gum wrappers. Its one cloudy window was filled with colorful brochures.

Paul straightened his tie and brushed his hair in place before he pushed open the door. The light inside was dim, a tint of aquamarine. Nets fuzzy with dust dry-rotted overhead. A wire rack built for a thousand brochures, folders, and maps held a dozen or two dog-eared remnants.

He cleared his throat cautiously and walked to the low counter. On the other side, in a space no larger than a comfortable closet, three people were busy. A thin woman dressed in an out of fashion heavy black suit sat talking on the phone, its obsidian receiver matching perfectly her black, looping earrings. Her thin legs were crossed and he noticed the heavy mesh of 1940's stockings, their wide seams almost vulgar. Her shoes, black with stiletto heels, tapped idly against a corner of her desk.

Immediately across the counter a black man with the dry, thin look of a pharoah's mummy swayed on his broom handle to an internal song.

"Excuse me." Paul heard the unused croak of his voice. He spoke to the third person, directly across from him. She was a gigantic woman; her huge breasts rested on a belly the size of a truck tire.

"Excuse me, miss." Paul felt tired from all of yesterday's madness and

James Hannah 199

this morning's long and dispiriting drive. He wished he were home mowing the lawn or watching Nancy toss a salad. A cool dip in the pool would have done wonders.

The woman rose slowly, her chair moaning. As she crossed the two yards, Paul looked away quickly to the destitute wire rack at his side. As always, he politely avoided witnessing another's misery or pain or misfortune. He was the first to glance elsewhere.

She finally arrived after a struggle with her unwieldy body. Her head barely cleared the counter and she whistled and wheezed. It took another few seconds for her flesh to settle. She spoke between gasps for air.

"Yes, sir, can I help you?" Her eyes were miniaturized by her glasses. Paul was caught by them. He'd never seen lenses perform such tricks.

"I'm trying to find a realtor here in town. I'm new . . . just got in . . . we used to come here when I was a child though . . . years ago." Paul laughed uncomfortably. "Anyway, I'm looking for a beach house to buy. We got his name from a friend but no phone number."

Her tiny eyes tightened as she smiled. "Sure, we can help. Who is it?"

"Louis Bo."

For a second Paul felt everything stop. Only a single tick of the clock. A microsecond gap. The woman on the phone dropped a heel click and the black sweeper broke his sway. The eyes of the huge woman flickered like a cat's.

"Louis Bo's hard to find, you know. Very hard to find. Works out of his father-in-law's store in South Crystal." She threw her thick neck in the direction he'd come. "But we've got a dozen other realtors who'd be glad to help." With a sudden flick of her wrist she grabbed a brochure from under the counter and slid it across to Paul. He scanned the list politely.

"Could you give me directions to Louis Bo's store, then?"

"*Louis* Bo." She pronounced the first name as it would be spoken in French. There was obvious disgust in her tone.

Paul glanced at her.

"Listen," she added, leaning across the formica counter as much as her weight would allow her, "we've had years of trouble from all of them, you know. You're from . . . ?"

"San Antonio."

"Yeah, well, you've heard about all the shrimping trouble them people brought in." Her eyes rolled microscopically behind her distorting lenses. "Vietnamese." If she were outside, he felt she would have spat at her feet in contempt.

Paul's stomach tightened. He didn't want any of these problems. Not any of them. "Listen, I'm sorry about all that, really I am. But I don't think it has anything to do with me and buying a house on the beach. Mr. Bo or not." He wiped his forehead with his wilted handkerchief.

The fat on the woman's shoulders heaved and quivered to a stop and Paul realized she must have been shrugging. Deftly she wrote an address on the back of the realtors' list and flipped it across to him. "Vietnamese," she muttered as she turned away.

Outside at the car Paul opened the door but paused. He'd forgotten to ask where the Ramada Inn was. Idly he searched the long strip of downtown for a service staion.

"You know what I'd say?"

Paul jerked around to see the black sweeper deep in a narrow alley, his head and broom barely discernible.

"What's that?" Paul squinted to see him through the glare of the seacoast sun.

The sweeper glanced over his shoulder and mumbled something.

"What's that?" Paul asked. "I can't hear you."

"I'd say Louis Bo's a fine man. Finer than most here. And something else, too."

"Yes?" Paul shaded his eyes.

"Some houses here just . . . whoosh," and he tossed his free hand skyward.

Paul nodded and sat for a long time in his car with all the air conditioner vents turned toward him.

After checking into the Ramada Inn and eating a mediocre club sandwich in the Inn's restaurant, Paul retraced his drive into South Crystal City. With the help of reticent children's pointing fingers, he found the narrow storefront off the main street facing onto an alleyway that sloped precipitously to the littered oily sand of the bay.

Inside the door he waited for his eyes to adjust, but a minute later he realized they wouldn't. The store was dark except for a weak orange glow from a single lamp near the cash register at the rear.

Paul had to feel his way between the rows of foreign labels—sauces and jars of crystalized spices. He stumbled into a rack packed with pungent seaweed, and thrusting out his hand to right himself, he jammed his forefinger into a solid wall of cans. Quickly he tried to juggle the falling tins but one escaped and rolled across the gritty floor and up under an old box cooler. Paul reshelved the scattered cans and picked his way more slowly.

The concentrated odor of everything on the dark, dusty shelves was almost nauseating.

Finally he reached the counter. It was sandbagged with canvas sacks of rice—thousands of pounds of the stuff buffering the shopkeeper's refuge. "Hello," he said, relieved to have made the journey from the door safely.

"Yes?" A tall old man, dressed in the folds of a blue suit two sizes too large, set a bowl of soup on the counter and stood. The skin of his face hung in loose folds like his suit.

"I've come to see Louis Bo."

The old man's hand abruptly described an arc in the air before him. "Go away. Get out." And, his high voice breaking off, he turned to straighten an immaculate display of rock candy.

Paul started to leave, but he wasn't ready for the troublesome trip back through the groceries. He tried to steel his voice, but it sounded unnaturally high, as reedy and fragile as the old man's.

"I've come to see Louis Bo. I want to see him in person."

"Louis Bo doesn't want to see you, you hear me?" He picked at the display, destroying its symmetry. He didn't look up. His downcast eyes were hidden in the pearly folds of skin. "He's tired of all of this." Again he waved his hand but this time the movement was more subdued, more gentle. "Get out of here. You don't belong here." The old man's voice hissed in the pungent air. He turned his head up, his black eyes glaring. "Go on."

"But listen," Paul wiped his shining face with a sour handkerchief, "I'm not part of 'all of that'. I don't know anything about it. I'm from out of town, you see."

The old man's face trembled and his voice was dry with emotion. "Oh God, then you're the one Louis talked about. You're the newspaper man he said would come and tell the truth about everything. Thank God." The old man started around from behind the counter.

Paul caught the old man's sleeve. "No, no, you don't understand. I'm here to look at a house, that's all. That's all. Nothing else."

The shopkeeper's shoulders sagged and he pulled his arm from Paul's grasp.

"All I'm interested in is a summer place for my family. I came here as a child and I've always loved it."

The old man sat heavily on his unpadded stool and poked at his soup with a spoon. For a minute they were quiet. From the street came a rush of language as a crowd of children ran past. Finally, the old man stood again and drew an ancient pen from his suit. He sighed and looked into Paul's eyes. "You don't know how awful it's been." He shook his head and then he shrugged. "Give me your name and phone number. Louis'll phone you later."

After writing his brief message and fumbling his way to the door, Paul looked back toward the dim light. He could barely discern the tall shop-keeper who sat reorganizing the demolished display.

Out in the alley he hardly noticed the bright yellow wrecker whose engine started as he passed it and turned the corner toward his car.

"Hey, you."

Paul didn't hear the man's voice coming from the partially rolled-down tinted window. He noticed the yellow wrecker coasting, keeping abreast of him, but he was thinking of seeing the beach house and returning home as soon as he could—maybe checking out tonight. Then he saw the paradoxical nature of his thoughts. How could he live—even a month out of each year—in a town he was so anxious to leave? He stopped a few feet from his car in amazement. How could he bring his children and Nancy *here?* But he quickly told himself that North Sound would be different—controlled access probably; certainly tight security; walls around each house. But still, there was all of this to avoid. And then he looked up at the yellow wrecker that had stopped, its engine mumbling, almost at his feet.

"Hey, you!"

Quickly Paul stepped back against the low wall that surrounded a dingy house. The palms of his hands brushed the peeling paint.

The low voice, scarcely audible over the noisy motor, came from behind darkly tinted glass. The glare on the windshield was blinding. Paul started to reach for his U.S. Attorney ID to ward off this man, but somehow knew it would just provoke him.

"What do you want?" The rough wood prickled his palms.

"You know Bo, huh? You find him back there?"

"No, he's not there." Paul's words rattled in his dry mouth.

"Why you so interested in Louis Bo?"

"I'm interested in a house he has for sale . . . on North Sound." For some reason he expected the address to help.

From the cracked window he heard voices, and the static from a CB.

Paul wanted to break and run for his car but he was too old to run away in such heat. Trying to calm himself he noticed details of the wrecker—its elaborate paint work: the rear, hoist and all, a flat black; the rest at least a half-dozen shades of yellow and orange. "Matthew's Wrecker Service" was painted on the door in fancy script.

"It's okay with you if I buy from him?" The firmness of Paul's tone surprised him, but he really was tired and right now all he wanted was the quiet of his motel room. He turned, his palms white from the chalky paint, and walked toward his car.

Slowly the wrecker moved with him.

"You'd be better off with someone else. You know, someone not Oriental."

"A gook," another voice mumbled and the wrecker cab filled with harsh, ugly laughter.

"That's my business, isn't it?" Paul spoke softly as he unlocked his car door.

"Maybe so. But you know," the voice came across flat like the monotone of a public-address voice, "you might be better off staying away from Bo and all them goddamned slopes. You hear me?" And with the last word, the window slid up and the wrecker burned rubber, slipped sideways for a second, and sped down the quiet street.

Paul laid his head on his arm stretched along the roof of the car. "Jesus Christ," he muttered to the hot, ticking metal.

Once inside his motel room he fastened all the locks and took a long shower, alternating bursts of scalding hot and icy cold water. Then, for a while, he lay on the queen-sized bed with only a towel wrapped around him. He was furious and terrified. And after an hour, he dressed quickly and threw his bag on the barely rumpled bed.

The hell with it, he thought. He'd call Nancy and explain the misery of Crystal City and everything else. She'd get a laugh out of his strange dance with the townspeople.

Now that he'd made his decision, he let the motel room soothe him. As he repacked, he relished its peace and order; the spotless tiled bathroom; the neatly tucked drapes. Everything was carefully placed. Even unwrapping a cellophane-sheathed drinking glass brought some comfort.

Crossing over to the phone he stopped and drew the heavy curtains. Beyond the opposite side of the square of rooms, a few dark thunderheads had blossomed inland. Lightning flickered across and through their purple flat bottoms.

As Paul sat on the bed and looked out, the phone purred twice.

"Hello?" he said.

On the other end there was the strange hollow silence one sometimes gets on the phone—the reverberating emptiness of silence in a deep well.

"Mr. Paul Winslow?" The voice was thick and flowed viscous with all the syllables clinging together.

Paul immediately recalled the yellow wrecker and stood to look out the plate glass window and down to the clear blue water of the motel's swimming pool.

"Mr. Winslow, are you there?"

"Yes, yes I am. Who's this?" Paul focused beyond his own reflection in the glass.

"Louis Bo, sir. I hear that you want to look at the North Sound property. It's a good piece of real estate. Very nice. The people who just moved always said . . ."

"I don't believe I'm interested any longer," Paul spoke quickly. "I don't think it's right for us, for me and my family, after all."

"But Mr. Winslow, you've not even seen it yet. How can you know that already? Really, you must give yourself a chance."

Louis Bo talked on, extolling all the house's features, but Paul didn't listen. Instead he watched the pool below. Around it the other guests sat and smoked and drank beer from plastic cups. The middle-aged men's chests sagged, cellulite dimpled the backs of the women's thighs and legs. Children pushed and pulled on the diving board; teetered, screaming, and fell thrashing into the blue of the chlorinated water. It could have been a pool party at his house.

On the highest board a young boy bounced restlessly but never dove. Paul put a hand to the warm glass, the heat of his palm spreading a thin fog outward across the window. For a moment he rested in the scene; in the immaculate, clipped grass and the precisely trimmed hedge.

"So, you see, you owe it to yourself and your family. Don't you think?"

Paul shook his head into the receiver. "I was just about to leave when you called."

"But what can it hurt? And you've come a long ways."

Paul sat on the edge of the bed. He could hear the noises from the pool but they came through the thick glass jumbled and distant.

"Okay . . . I guess so."

For the first time the ingratiating and thick voice laughed—a long, horsey laugh. Then he gave Paul the complicated directions.

After hanging up, Paul set his packed bags near the door and went down to the lobby to check out. But instead he walked past the desk and out into the stifling heat of late afternoon. He sat at an uncomfortable wrought iron table near the pool and drank strong instant tea and sweated through his fresh shirt.

Twice Paul got lost in the intricate maze of sumptuous beach houses. He only relaxed after he found his way and began noticing the sturdy high cedar fences and the carefully kept lawns. Most of the houses were vacant this late in the season, but several showed lights in the dusk.

Cautiously he slowed and stopped before a grand, two-story white house that sat far from the road and right on the beach. As he emerged from the car he delighted in the smack of the waves and the heavy mist blown in on the freshening wind. Overhead he noticed the occasional streak of lightning from the same front of clouds he'd seen earlier from the room.

Paul cupped his hands and bellowed Bo's name over the surf. But there wasn't an answer. And since there weren't any cars close by, Paul tried the massive double gate. The wind tore past him as it swung open. Already he was damp from the heavy mist, his hair plastered flat on his head. The salt trickled onto his lips and into the corners of his mouth.

At the top of the steep stairs Paul rattled the handle of the French doors and tried to peer inside but couldn't make out a thing.

He made a quick circuit of the wraparound balcony, trying windows and doors, but everything was tightly locked and shuttered. On the sea side he sat on the edge of a broken chaise lounge, careful not to tip it. Here the mist was thick. And blown in constantly by the breeze it dripped from the railing in fat drops.

Far off he heard the bass mumble of an engine and the swish of tires on the wet pavement. It sounded like a truck approaching.

"Oh, Jesus," he muttered, and walked to the corner near the steps.

He looked down the dark street and through the thickening mist he thought he could discern the silhouette of a truck, the faint glow of its yellow paint and the webbed tackle of its hoist.

"Sonofabitch," he spoke, loud enough to be heard over the waves below. He tried to wipe away the water and sweat that ran down his face. Under his wet shirt he felt the prickle of his skin.

Edging forward, he reached for the knob again. The loose panes rattled.

Paul's breath stopped for a second. Over the rumble of the surf he believed he heard the slam of a truck door.

Facing the door squarely and pulling his fist back to his chest, he rammed it through the glass as hard as he could. The pain was sharp and immediate but he ignored it and fumbled with the lock inside until the door opened.

Inside he slammed the door and leaned against the glass. The enormous room before him was beautiful. Even in his fear he saw its luxury and comfort—cream carpets, sunken wet bar in a far corner.

But then he felt the sticky flow of blood down his right arm. Paul brought his hand up close to his face and watched in amazement as it pumped rhythmically from an ugly gash down his wrist and across his palm.

Frantically he searched the house. He ran from room to room hoping to find something to stanch the flow. He trailed the blood everywhere, spoiling the thick carpet and ivory wallpaper.

In the huge, echoing bathroom he twirled the stuck faucets that belched a burst of air and rust.

Then he heard the distinct sound of a door opening. And then the crunch of glass under a shoe.

He stopped with his hands on the taps.

Is this how they felt? he forced himself to ask. This bursting pressure in the ears? This ache in the throat from choking back screams?

Paul glanced up into the dim mirror and could barely recognize his own face distorted and drawn tight across his cheekbones. A swatch of blood colored his forehead and the tip of his nose.

In the mirror was the same fear etched on Shaw's face the instant the grill bit into the back of his head. And standing there he felt that he had broken into some new life and had entered a terrifying and inescapable world.

And there, beyond simple fear, he found rage. He turned from the mirror, ran through the house and lunged headlong into the man standing just inside the door. The force of his lunge carried him and the diminutive man back through the doorway. Screaming, the man sprawled against the rail, and Paul bounded down the stairs. But halfway down he tripped and rolled heavily to the bottom.

For a long time the only sounds were the sea and, above it, their la-
bored breathing.

"Mr. Winslow?" The voice above him was thin with fright. "What are
you doing?"

Paul opened his mouth, trying to suck some coolness from the mist. But
his breath came ragged and rasping. And his torn palm began to burn.

"You've ruined my door. Why, you've bashed it in. That's against the
law." Mr. Bo stood stiffly and searched his arm for bruises.

Paul turned his head and glanced up and down the street. It was empty
except for their two cars.

"What's come over you, Mr. Winslow?" the tiny, meticulously dressed
man asked, brushing his rumpled raincoat. "What's wrong?"

Dazed, Paul shook his head. He started to laugh but couldn't.

"What about my door? What about that?" Louis Bo stood at the head of
the stairs and jabbed his finger at the damage.

Paul thought about all the rest of the violence inside, the spotted cream
carpet and bloody walls, and nodded his head. Gently, with the tips of his
thumb and forefinger, he closed the lips of his wound, but the pain made
him wince and he was forced to release the pressure. The blood dripped
onto his knee.

Paul wanted to lie back along the hard steps and close his eyes, but he
knew that if he did the face in the mirror would return. He turned slowly
to look up at the realtor. "Forget about the damage," he said.

"But my beautiful door."

"We'll take it. We'll take the house," Paul mumbled.

"What, Mr. Winslow?" The Vietnamese stepped down the stairs and
bent over Paul's upturned face. "I couldn't hear you, sir."

"We want the house."

Bo smiled weakly. "You do?"

Paul nodded and pulled himself up gingerly. After all, he wondered,
what else could he possibly say?

WILLIAM HATHAWAY

Born in Madison, Wisconsin, in
1944 and raised in Ithaca, New
York, William Hathaway teaches at
Union College in Schenectady,
New York. He is the author of five
books of poetry, including *Fish,
Flesh & Fowl* and *Looking into the
Heart of Light*.

WHY THAT'S BOB HOPE

The comedian, holding a chunk of flaming shale.
If only *Der Bingle* could see him now! He looked
so puffed and sleepy in that Texaco hardhat,
I could've popped a fuse. Well, like the oil,

here today and gone today. In *my* good old days
Hope was on Sullivan's "shew" so often us kids
dropped TV for longhair sex and smoking weeds.
What a mistake! But now we're past our wild phase

and Bob's back with this burning rock, funny
for a change. No, no old quips now about Dean's double
vision, Phyllis Diller's breasts or Sinatra's aging treble.
He says if we all squeeze the rock together real money

will drip out. We'll live real good and still afford a war
where he'll bust our boys' guts on tour in El Salvador.

EDWARD HIRSCH

A professor at the University of
Houston, Edward Hirsch has pub-
lished three books of poetry: *For
the Sleepwalkers*, *Wild Gratitude*,
which received the National Book
Critics Circle Award, and *The
Night Parade*. He was born in
Chicago in 1950.

PAUL CELAN: A GRAVE AND
MYSTERIOUS SENTENCE

Paris, 1948

It's daybreak and I wish I could believe
In a rain that will wash away the morning
That is just about to rise behind the smokestacks
On the other side of the river, other side
Of nightfall. I wish I could forget the slab
Of darkness that always fails, the memories
That flood through the window in a murky light.

211

But now it is too late. Already the day
Is a bowl of thick smoke filling up the sky
And swallowing the river, covering the buildings
With a sickly, yellow film of sperm and milk.
Soon the streets will be awash with little bright
Patches of oblivion on their way to school,
Dark briefcases of oblivion on their way to work.

Soon my small apartment will be white and solemn
Like a blank page held up to a blank wall,
A message whispered into a vacant closet. But
This is a message which no one else remembers
Because it is stark and German, like the silence,
Like the white fire of daybreak that is burning
Inside my throat. If only I could stamp it out!

But think of smoke and ashes. An ominous string
Of railway cars scrawled with a dull pencil
Across the horizon at dawn. A girl in pigtails
Saying, "Soon you are going to be erased."
Imagine thrusting your head into a well
And crying for help in the wrong language,
Or a deaf mute shouting into an empty field.

So don't talk to me about flowers, those blind
Faces of the dead thrust up out of the ground
In bright purples and blues, oranges and reds.
And don't talk to me about the gold leaves
Which the trees are shedding like an extra skin:
They are handkerchiefs pressed over the mouths
Of the dead to keep them quiet. It's true:

Once I believed in a house asleep, a childhood
Asleep. Once I believed in a mother dreaming
About a pair of giant iron wings growing
Painfully out of the shoulders of the roof
And lifting us into away-from-here-and-beyond.

Once I even believed in a father calling out
In the dark, restless and untransfigured.

But what did we know then about the smoke
That was already beginning to pulse from trains,
To char our foreheads, to transform their bodies
Into two ghosts billowing from a huge oven?
What did we know about a single gray strand
Of barbed wire knotted slowly and tightly
Around their necks? We didn't know anything then.

And now here is a grave and mysterious sentence
Finally written down, carried out long ago:
At last I have discovered that the darkness
Is a solitary night train carrying my parents
Across a field of dead stumps and wildflowers
Before disappearing on the far horizon,
Leaving nothing much in its earthly wake

But a stranger standing at the window
Suddenly trying to forget his childhood,
To forget a black trail of smoke
Slowly unraveling in the distance
Like the victory-flag of death, to forget
The slate clarity of another day
Forever breaking behind the smokestacks.

TONY HOAGLAND

Born in Louisiana in 1953, Tony
Hoagland has published three
chapbooks, most recently *History
of Desire*. He teaches composition
at the University of Arizona and
works in the Arizona Artists in
Education program.

ONE SEASON

That was the summer my best friend
called me a faggot on the telephone,
hung up, and vanished from the earth,

a normal occurrence in this country
where we change our lives
with the swiftness and hysterical finality

of dividing cells. That month
the rain refused to fall,
and fire engines streaked back and forth crosstown

towards smoke-filled residential zones
where people stood around outside, drank beer
and watched their neighbors' houses burn.

It was a bad time to be affected
by nearly anything,
especially anything as dangerous

as loving a man, if you happened to be
a man yourself, ashamed and unable to explain
how your feelings could be torn apart

by something stoical and unacknowledged
as friendship between males.
Probably I talked too loud that year

and thought an extra minute
before I crossed my legs; probably
I chose a girl I didn't care about

and took her everywhere,
knowing I would dump her in the fall
as part of evening the score,

part of practicing the scorn
it was clear I was going to need
to get across this planet

of violent emotional addition
and subtraction. Looking back, I can see
that I came through

in the spastic, fugitive, half-alive manner
of accident survivors. Fuck anyone
who says I could have done it

differently. Though now I find myself
returning to the scene
as if the pain I fled

were the only place that I had left to go;
as if my love, whatever kind it was, or is,
were still trapped beneath the wreckage

of that year,
and I was one of those angry firemen
having to go back into the burning house;
climbing a ladder

through the heavy smoke and acrid smell
of my own feelings,
as if they were the only
goddamn thing worth living for.

GARRETT KAORU HONGO

Garrett Kaoru Hongo was born in
Volcano, Hawaii, in 1951. He has
published two books of poems,
Yellow Light and *The River of
Heaven*, which won the Lamont
Prize and was nominated for the
Pulitzer Prize. He directs the
creative writing program at the
University of Oregon.

MENDOCINO ROSE

In California, north of the Golden Gate,
the vine grows almost everywhere,
    erupting out of pastureland,
from under the shade of eucalyptus
    by the side of the road,
overtaking all the ghost shacks and broken fences
    crumbling with rot
and drenched in the fresh rains.

It mimes, in its steady, cloud-like replicas,
    the shape of whatever it smothers,

a gentle greenery
        trellised up the side
of a barn or pump station
        far up the bluffs above Highway 1,
florets and blossoms,
        from the road anyway,
looking like knots and red dreadlocks,
        ephemeral and glorious,
hanging from overgrown eaves.

I'd been listening to a tape on the car stereo,
a song I'd play and rewind
        and play again,
a ballad or a love song
        sung by my favorite tenor,
a Hawaiian man known for his poverty
        and richness of heart,
and I felt, wheeling through the vinelike curves
        of that coastal road,
sliding on the slick asphalt
        through the dips and in the S-turns
and braking just in time,
        that it would have served as the dirge
I didn't know to sing
        when I needed to,
a song to cadence my heart
        and its tuneless stammering.

Ipō lei manu, he sang, without confusion,
        I send these garlands,
and the roses seemed everywhere around me then,
        profuse and luxurious
as the rain in its grey robes,
        undulant processionals over the land,
echoes, in snarls of extravagant color,
        of the music
and the collapsing shapes
        they seemed to triumph over.

ANDREW HUDGINS

Andrew Hudgins' two collections
of poetry are *Saints and Strangers*
and *After the Lost War.* A gradu-
ate of the Iowa Writers' Workshop,
he has been a Wallace Stegner
Fellow at Stanford and an Alfred
Hodder Fellow at Princeton.
He was born in Killeen, Texas,
in 1951.

REBUILDING A BIRD

The ape stared at the bird, then pulled
the case into his lap. His loose
hands dipped between the bars and cupped
the wings against the bird's green body.
I wondered where the trainer was.
The parrot shrieked *hellow* and fought
his hands. The monkey grappled with
the agitated wings and tried
to shuck her like a ear of corn.
I was too awed to move. The wings

came free and in that coming free
I saw how living flesh could be
disassembled. The red machinery
of meat—joint, muscles, bone—is there
below—as real as what's on top.
I've learned how deep you have to go
to get the surface right. I stood,
and yelled. The monkey looked at me.
The parrot nipped the ape's left thumb
and screamed *hellow, hellow.* Then he
reached in and twisted off her head.
I've spent most of my life since then
rebuilding birds. The skin gives way.
You slide the scapel down between
the joints, you separate sinews
from bone, you probe the recesses
of viscera, and spread the parts
across your desk. Sometimes it takes
three tanagers to rebuild one.
Once I have flayed a body down
to rags, pieces that look most like
confetti, pillowstuffing, trash,
I build it up again with wire
and glue. I try to make it fly.
Not fly out through the actual
like that one individual bird
I've mutilated just as lovingly
as if it were my own damn flesh,
but look as if they flew through death,
like death itself. Such nonsense! I've
left science and moved on to art,
where sins persisted in enough
might lead to grace. But if I took
that bird that I have made, its wings
extended in the attitude of flight,
and sailed it from my roof, the thing
would skitter though pine needles, smack
the ground, and break. It wouldn't be

much to look at and looks are all
it has to offer once the flight
has been dissected from its wings.
But mutilation has its moments too.
It's never far from awe, which is
a sort of holy ignorance
that thrives on surfaces, grows rich
on facts, as it moves down, like knives,
through deeper, stranger surfaces
in search of fire, perhaps. Once
you have dismantled cardinals
the one you see break from a larch
and skim, undulant, across the pond
is never quite the same—it's almost flame,
but even more mysterious
than fire. I watch the distant blaze,
awed and regretful as the gun
rests on my arm. The screeching monkey voice
of a pileated woodpecker will,
sometimes, freeze my cheek on the gun
as if I heard my own soul speak
inside the wild leaves of an oak.
I'm glad to let its mocking voice
escape, though it's the one I want,
to hold, some day, beneath the knife.

RICHARD HUGO

Richard Hugo was born in 1923 in
Seattle. His many books of poetry
include *Making Certain It Goes
On: The Collected Poems of
Richard Hugo.* He also published
The Triggering Town, a collection
of lectures and essays, and served
as editor of the Yale Series of
Younger Poets from 1977 until
his death in 1982.

CONFEDERATE GRAVES IN LITTLE ROCK

Far from these stones, in my country wind shouts
but shouts no name. It hustles north
locked on one heading forever, and salmon enter
rivers on the dead run starting that remorseless
drive home to funereal pools. Children
seem forever preserved in youth by a fresh rain
out of the south, and birds ride thermals
with the easy wisdom of wings.

If I can, I'll die in that weather of home.
This air's not mine. The hum of various insects
compounds the heat. Not one cloud, not
one faint touch of wind. I arbitrarily pick
one name, a 16-year-old boy, John Brock
who fell holding the banner of battle in hands
calloused on his father's farm. He was home
in this heat. He could say: I'm dying home.

I row among the dead stumps in a lake.
My bass plug settles and I reel at the speed
I believe fish swim. Nothing. I'd carve names
on stumps to resurrect the souls of dead trees
and make sure someone remembers the forest
that cracked off one terrible tornado ago.
That air howled "rebel" and the name of a family
destroyed by a blue rain of artillery.

In North Little Rock, poverty's shacks
fill with song. They're singing the last rites of one
more victim of murder—the mean word uttered—
the kind gun fired—the usual forms
filled out and filed—the usual suspect jailed.
They're singing from graves created by wrongs
that go back before wars were recorded
or graves marked by stones.

Maybe the best graves stay unmarked, the right words
never find themselves cut into stone.
Whatever the weather it could be home for one
blood or another. For certain the best wars
wear down for personal reasons. It's hard
to do battle in breezy country where sun
lights the highway and one cloud shades
your car, whatever speed you drive.

LYNDA HULL

Lynda Hull is the author of *Ghost
Money*, which won the Juniper
Prize. Born in Newark, New
Jersey, in 1954, she teaches in
the M.F.A. program at Vermont
College and edits poetry for
Crazyhorse.

1933

Whole countries hover, oblivious on the edge
of history and in Cleveland the lake
already is dying. None of this matters
to my mother at seven, awakened from sleep

to follow her father through darkened rooms
downstairs to the restaurant emptied
of customers, chairs stacked and steam glazing
the window, through the kitchen bright with pans,

ropes of kielbasa, the tubs of creamy lard
that resemble, she thinks, ice cream.
At the tavern table her father's friends
talk rapidly to a man in a long grey coat,

in staccato French, Polish, harsh German.
Her mother stops her, holds her shoulders and whispers
This is a famous man. Remember his face.
Trotsky—a name like one of her mother's

fond, strange nouns. He looks like the man
who makes her laugh at Saturday matinées,
only tired. So tired. Her father pours the man
another drink of clear bootleg gin, then turns

smiling to her. She has her own glass.
Peppermint schnapps that burns and makes her light,
cloudy so grown-ups forget her when she curls
on a bench and drifts then wakes and drifts again.

At the bar, her mother frowns, braids shining
round her head bent to the books, the columns
of figures in her bold hand and the smoke, voices
of men, a wash of syllables she sleeps upon

until her father wakes her to the empty room.
The men are gone. A draft of chill air lingers
in her father's hair, his rough shirt,
and together they walk the block to morning Mass.

Still dark and stars falter, then wink sharp
as shattered mirrors. Foghorns moan
and the church is cold. A few women in babushkas
kneel in the pews. Still dizzy, she follows

the priest's litanies for those who wait within
life's pale, for those departed, the shades humming
in the air, clustered thick as lake fog in the nave.
The priest elevates the wafer, a pale day moon

the spirit of God leafs through, then it's
a human face—her father's, the tired man's
and she is lost and turning through fragrant air.
Her fingers entwined make a steeple, but

all she sees is falling: the church collapsing
in shards, the great bell tolling, tolling.
1933 outside and some unwound mainspring has set
the world careening. The Jazz Age

ended years ago. Lean olive-skinned men
sport carnations and revolvers and in the country
of her father, bankers in threadbare morning coats
wheel cartloads of currency to the bakeries

for a single loaf. The men who wait each night
outside the kitchen door have a look she's seen
in her father's eyes, although it's two years
until he turns his gentle hand against himself.

But now, he touches her face. Her father stands
so straight, as if wearing a uniform he's proud of.
She watches him shape the sign of the cross.
She crosses forehead, lips and breast, and believes,

for a moment, her father could cradle the world
in his palm. When they leave the church and its flickering
votive candles for market, it is dawn. The milkman's
wagon horse waits, patient at the curb, his breath

rosettes of steam rising to the sky that spills
like a pail of blue milk across morning. She prays
that God take care of the man in the grey coat,
that her father will live forever.

ARIAS, 1971

It was her hair I always noticed, rippling
as she walked the hallway to our flat
below the opera singer who'd rehearse
until evening, her arias. China Doll battled
sometimes with her AWOL junkie lover—curses

and plates shattering the wall. Her son
sputtered airplane sounds and beat the radiator
with a spoon, wise already to what smoulders
out of helplessness. I closed my door.
When autumn turned bitter, we taped newspaper

over the panes and those winter nights
we rode the subway from Symphony to Chinatown
where I poured drinks at the Phoenix
and she hustled bars, the gambling houses.
The train rocked and windows gave our faces back

ghost twins, sisters from some other life.
China brushed her hair, coal black, until
it sparked, and if I closed my eyes the rails sang
raven wing, forbidden heart, bright cinder.
One long dusk I sat as her child

practiced his numbers, 5's and the 8's
he'd scrawl like those botched infinities
I'd drawn in high school notebooks
below the signs for man and woman, the sign
for death. China leaned over her spoon,

the match's wavering blue tongue,
over the shadow and soft skin of her arm.
Nothing to lose, she laughed,
nothing. Her strap slid from her shoulder
to show the crescent scar above her breast.

She slow-danced with herself across the room,
vagrant hair swaying. Swaying, her face tilted
heavenward and the low pulse in her throat.
Upstairs the opera singer began again
Desdemona's final prayers for mercy

from a silent God. The aria soared and fell
and carried us out to December streets
milling with late shoppers, their breath chilled,
perishable, the season a paradise of dolls
and trains, the steaming subway vents.

That last time I saw her, we walked the blocks
to Washington, paused at a shopwindow: a pyramid
of televisions all tuned to Walter Cronkite.
His mouth shaped silent phrases. And then it began—
the roll call of war dead. Their names sailing

upward, ash, and we had everything
to lose. Snowing, and the wind lashed
China's hair, a hand
across her face, mine
I tell you, it was snowing.

RICHARD JACKSON

Richard Jackson, who was born in
Lawrence, Massachusetts, in 1946,
has published three collections
of poems, most recently *Worlds
Apart*, and a critical book, *Dis-
mantling Time in Contemporary
Poetry*. The editor of *The Poetry
Miscellany*, he teaches at the
University of Tennessee at
Chattanooga and in the M.F.A.
program at Vermont College.

SHADOWS

Why is there something rather than nothing?
—PARMENIDES

What a consoling poem this will be if the roadside
crows that scatter into the pines as each car passes,
that rise like the souls of the dead in Van Gogh's wide
and confused heaven, are not the signs of your loss.
What a consoling poem this might be if I could remember
the first secret place where the pitiful world did not,
as Flaubert says it does, surface in terrible error
like the bloated bodies of dogs in a stream near his retreat

at Rouen, those poor shadows of the dead, despite
the stones tied to their necks, and surface in the sentences
Flaubert wrote trying to find a secret place for each right
word, a place that did not mean the old disgust for happiness.
I thought I had seen death. I see instead those rising crows
again, remember your leaving, and, scattered here, in shadows
that fall across this page, figures I'd forgotten, shadows
that seem to rise from the faded newsprint, that seem to show
how each private loss is part of a larger loss we might
remember;—yesterday's news is the young boy in Providence
R.I., who followed the consoling words of some killer one night
into woods where animals later tore off his face, or two Palestinians,
two boys, faces covered, who followed one street or another
with a crowd of protesters and were shot, or how, unable to let
death take him, a Bantu tribesman clutched the dirt of his father,
lifting himself again so the Pretoria soldiers could not forget.
Listen, it is nearly dawn here. I wish all these losses
could hide in the shifting forms for these words, that you could hide
in their dream that tries to tell you not to abandon your past
in a few clothes on the shore, no place left to hide.

I didn't know, when you left, about poor Flaubert never finding
the words to dominate the absurd sounds of parrots he kept
hearing, the plaintive sounds of cicadas that always haunted
him, how he would mutilate phrases, how he'd shift sentences,
how each word was, he wrote, an "endless farewell to life,"
crossing out repetitions that meant he only had one voice,
that meant, really, hearing the endless terror of his own voice.
I didn't know, then, about Van Gogh, who was finding
in an asylum, while Flaubert tried to write an asylum for his life,
a style to hold off death, a style that he feared, that he kept
even from his brother. I hadn't read, then, those poor sentences
to Theo, haunted by the power of color and shape, haunted
by shadows of enemies he invented, the way the birds haunt
his last painting, *Crows over a Wheatfield*, where the lost voice
of Christ seems to dissolve into darkness that moment his sentence
was finished, those crows that could be flying towards us, finding
only our losses, or up towards heaven, or maybe they keep
wavering, flying both ways at once, the way Van Gogh's life

would, as he himself knew, painting, he wrote, his own life
in theirs. I can't help but wonder how those crows haunt
all his last paintings. I believe he must have found a way to keep
a secret place somewhere on each canvas, the way Christ's voice
seems to hide beneath the thick paint. I believe he must have found
how the birds carry the painting away from itself, as Flaubert's sentences
were meant to lead him away from what he called the sentence
of his life. And because he saw a halo shimmering around each life
or object the way he had as a young preacher, what did Van Gogh find,
what consolation against all that pain? I am still haunted
by that faceless boy in Providence, the African without a voice,
the Palestinian boys kept from their home, these deaths that keep
announcing their obscene selves. Like Flaubert, I'm going to keep
trying to find some style, some shape for these sentences.
I believe I can hear, in Van Gogh's painting, the poor voice
of Christ which is the voice, too, of Flaubert, and these lost lives
that haunt me now. I believe that the last demon that haunted
Van Gogh was his fear that, outside his frames, nothing was found
to keep the "troubled skies" from his life, nothing even
in his sentences to Theo—"What's the use?" he asked hauntingly,
finally, like the voice of Christ, crying to be found.

Listen, I am writing to you now, on this table crossed
by shadows, that the answer is anyone hearing your voice,
anyone hoping the next news of you is not your loss,
trying by these repetitions to call you back, though the place
keeps shifting because I can't hide the world Flaubert, at Rouen,
fought inside each phrase, and you wouldn't believe a story
with no form for suicide or death. Here I am again
thinking of Van Gogh, listening to Lightnin' Hopkins say
the blues are everywhere, the blues are us, these stories
he sings on the scratched tape, the stories we read
about Van Gogh, the headlines, the poems, the way
the blues rhythms never change, 4/4, as if we needed
something that constant against our fears, as if we knew
how much these sad stories showed us what it means
to go on. Here I am again, listening to the blues,
starting to understand it is my own despair I mean
to fight. Last night, I stood on the bridge where a friend

dove into the shadows of the Tennessee and was afraid
I understood. I was thinking of the faceless boy again,
remembering how the man who found him by the pond where he lay
face down, turned him over, saw what the animals had done
and knelt in prayer, knelt for the pity of it, for the faces
of everyone dead or missing, knowing how he must go on.
I was thinking, too, how the mothers of the Palestinian boys
must also have knelt, must have touched the life
leaking from them, must also have prayed, unwrapped
the cloth around their heads hoping some other life,
not a son's, was missing. I have been thinking how the map
of this table, ever since you left, scatters the shadows
of fears this poem tries to shape, and how Van Gogh's
pictures, the dark secret places in Flaubert's phrases, show
all our words as a care for life, a color we have to hold.

I can't forget that faceless boy. I can't stop wondering
what last thing he touched or saw. I get up, punch
another tape into the player, Charlie Parker, "the Bird,"
taking off into rhythms and harmonies more unpredictable
than Van Gogh's crows—taking notes from what he touched or saw—
dogs barking, the hiss of a radiator, the sudden squeal
of a train's brakes, the rhythm and harmonies of the unpredictable
drunk shifting in a doorway, changing every sad thing
so that the dog's barking, the hiss of the radiator, the squeal
of brakes becomes not a sign of loneliness or loss, but joy,
the notes shifting like Flaubert's words, like the drunk in the doorway,
discovering in each phrase and note some secret place
among the flattened fifths meaning either loss or joy,
among the odd intervals of chords his alto sax remembers,
until he fell asleep for good in an armchair in New York,
nearly 35, "I'm just a husk," he said, in the end, just a phrase
or interval you remember, and I do, in this poem for you
taking these hints from the flights of the bird, Charlie Parker,
who lived beyond death in each note, each husk, each phrase,
above the deaths of the boy, the Palestinians, the tribesmen.

I remember last summer,—finding an old sax player
just waking among the remnants of fieldstone cellars

some quarry workers left half a century ago outside
Gloucester, Mass., a place called *Dogtown*, where he tried
among the sounds of stray dogs Parker would have loved,
to remember the clear notes of the alto sax rising above
the trees, above his memory of the war, unable to sleep
without checking the perimeter, each hour, to keep
all the shadows named and held, unable to sleep at all
if it rained because he couldn't hear the enemy's footfall.
It could have been you there, he said, and I know,
I know all our shadows, *it could have been you.*
And I am remembering the Bantu tribesman, how he could
tell immediately that the difference between dirt and blood
no longer mattered, that the lost children he fought for,
the child detained for questioning and found weeks later
among the smoldering garbage, his tongue cut out
for talking to newsmen, were what his death might be about,
a death that gathered above the tin roofs as the past gathered
—maybe the way it gathered in the eyes of the sax player
who could not forget, as he told it, the way his base
camp was overrun, the way, after a while, the haze
he was seeing was not dawn, not even the smoke of rifles,
but the unbelievable smoke of bodies burning, and the terrible
vapor that rose from open wounds, the sickening stink
that took the place of words, screams, whatever he tried to think.
When things were bad, he said, he could remember the service
for William Williams in New Orleans, how the entire brass
had gathered for the long march to Corolloton cemetery—
the Eureka Brass Band—with its slow dirges, its heavy
hymn notes to "In the Sweet Bye and Bye," the trombones
leading the way, he and his father among the baritone
horns of the second rank—and how they danced on the way
home to "St. Louis Blues," music, he said, you could raise
the dead with, as now, he just wanted once more to hear
the consoling notes of Parker, some sound to drive away his fear.

Listen, I have tried to find for us a shape for all this grief,
a form to make, as Parker and Van Gogh did, our fear
into a strength. It may be that any form is a kind of belief
that the losses, the shadows on this table, the enemy we fear

when the world goes dark, can be contained beyond our moment.
In Berea, Ohio, once, I came across an old graveyard
next to a quarry, centered by a concubine pine, a tree
that grew around its own cones and branches that were bent
around the trunk, as if the tree took as its form the discarded
parts of its own past and future. Now I want to believe
the long embrace of that tree, to touch my hands to your face,
I am touching my own face now, unable to forget that faceless
boy, the frightened sax player, hoping to find here some place
where we can kneel before these shadows, where we can bless
and embrace our pasts. I am blessing the past of a friend, torn coat,
hovering in a doorstep in Belgrade before he escaped the Russians,
who would twist gunpowder out of shells to sell to gangs for bread,
who watched a kneeling soldier smile to slit a prisoner's throat,
who chose not the Danube, but life. Not long algo I knelt in
the park where he played, one secret place where finally the dead
were only distant shadows. I was feeding the few ragged crows
that could have been Van Gogh's birds, leaving them a little bread
and cheese, thinking again of you, of your sadness, of how
form may be only, as Whitman said, another name for the body,
for all the secret places we contain, the only consolation we have
    known,—
and I was gathering you around me, building my own secret place
inside you, feeling you move again unpredictably, like Parker's
rhythms, the shifts in Flaubert's sentences, knowing, having known,
that this poem begins in your body and ends in the same place,
feeling the world move, trying to stay this way forever.

MARK JARMAN

Born in Mount Sterling, Kentucky, in 1952 and raised in Southern California, Mark Jarman teaches at Vanderbilt University. The most recent of his four collections of poetry are *Far and Away* and *The Black Riviera*. With Robert McDowell, he edits the literary journal *The Reaper*

MISS URQUHART'S TIARA

for Chase Twichell

I know this can't mean anything at all,
Except I found the fringed phacelia
Today, walking with my daughters beyond
The baseball diamond, and remembered reading
A story called "Miss Urquhart's Tiara"
So long ago, remembering it surprised me,
Like the Smoky Mountain flower shading white
To the pale blue of skies this time of year,
All the way from the mountains four hours east.

From one flower clouds amassed.
The story built its paragraphs.
And the grass, thick as the stumbling talk
That goes on in my head, tripped me here and there
As when I'm alone I fall into speech
(The habit worries me, when I can see myself
An old man snarled in monologues).
The fringed phacelia. Miss Urquhart.
Strange, their names meant nothing to each other.

Or to my daughters. The toddler doubled
Over a tuft of grass she hugged for balance.
Her older sister drifted at the edge
Of calling range, the fringe of cottonwoods
Along the stream that cuts our neighborhood
And draws the network nobody thinks of
Except in flood, except the city planner
Who, I imagine, knows the map by heart
Like his palm's creasework. All it is is drainage,
Though clear weather clears the water,
And clams, crayfish, snails with turbinate shells
Come to life. There's a faint tinge of odor,
And up the bank, a humped concrete manhole
Reads "Sanitary Sewer." We don't care.
I showed the little one the blue-white flower.
She took it, put it in her mouth, and ate it.
Her sister called. The poplar she stood under
Was the spine of a green book I reached for.

The story of "Miss Urquhart's Tiara,"
Which I hold open in my lap somewhere
On a peninsula, in a hotel,
In a fall noted there for peaks of color
Washed out by rain, was written by someone
You often find in such anthologies,
Reserved for rain in hotels on peninsulas,
Stevenson or Saki, Maugham or Kipling.

In it, two children, brother and sister,
Take a walk one spring day with their teacher
(It may be Scotland, it may be Stevenson).
It's a long walk, but the children keep up
For the first mile. The road's border of nettles
Prickles the boy's bare legs. His sister pales.
A heavy dew crowns weeds and spiderwebs,
And there's a taste of steam in the air.
The sky looks like a pane of whitewashed glass.

Wide shouldered and wide eyed, their smiling friend,
Miss Urquhart, urges them, reaching a hand
To each. Soon they will leave their native land
for—India? (Kipling?)—for a distant country,
And she wants them to have a memory
Of such a day as this that will filter back
Through another climate's heat waves and dust.
But when the children learn it's two miles yet,
They add a whine to the field's insect drone.
Thirsty—they're thirsty. She finds them stalks
Of timothy to chew. They're both too big
To be carried and yet still young enough
To want to be, saying their daddy would.
On they plod, and Miss Urquhart slowly sees
This outing as a bad job, proposed for
The parents' sake, grateful, interesting people
Wound up in packing twine, and for the children,
Wilting and peevish now, but who adore her.

The girl plops down, defeated, in her jumper.
The boy scratches his legs. Miss Urquhart pulls him
Dockweed leaves to rub them, then tells why
They have to keep walking and not turn back.
Ahead there is a church—Oh, they don't care!
Once, I was to be married there, she says.
Now, this is a secret, you can't tell.
But if you'll walk with me, you'll hear it.

Are you married, Miss Urquhart? they both ask.
No, and that doesn't matter one bit now.
I want to see this church again. But if
I tell you why, you have to listen and keep up.
No more bubbling babies. Now, take my hands.
There's a town, too, where we can have our tea.
And she tows the children through it all,
The landscape, the fatigue, the tale she tells.
Hedges back away to give them room,
The dew dries, nettles reach but do not touch.

She was engaged, a long, long time ago,
To the headmaster of the little school
There, where they are going. She was his first.
Whereas, she'd had boyfriends. How many boyfriends?
Boys at church, at school, at dances, boys
To walk with on this very road to town,
Which there, you see, is cropping up just now,
And there's the church, that tuft of sooty stone.
And that's the church where you were to be married?
Yes, and I even know the pastor still.
He'll give us tea. And why were you not married?
You know, she says, not everybody must be.
You can be very happy all alone.
And are you very happy, Miss Urquhart?
I am, very. And why were you not married?
He went away, to Australia. I stayed.
They step into the small, cool church, and meet
The pastor, who gives them tea and takes them home.

He went away because he was not loved.
He gave her a tiara, to wear on their honeymoon
In the capital—Edinburgh or London.
The little crown had been a great aunt's bequest
To him for his bride. He gave it to her
Too soon it seems, because he asked for it back.
Then gave it again, set it on her head.

Then asked for it back, left for Australia.
You can be very happy all alone.
But this part, winding through her on the ride back,
Never reaches the children's ears. She catches
Her breath, repeating, "Gave. Then, took. Gave."
Had she said it aloud? No one had noticed.
She leaves the children touchingly, says farewell
To the grateful, interesting parents,
And turns back into the hidden channels
Of her story. Not is she happy, but how
Did he, who loved her, make himself happier?

The last time they sat up late in her room,
The window held the summer's hour of darkness,
And they were silent, watching through this night
That would end soon, an easy vigil, when,
Speaking to someone else (a dream companion?),
He said, Yes, he had dreamed of Australia
All of his life, the Outback painted
With runes that someday he would read.
Someday. She knew she didn't love him
Enough to tease him for this, but instead
Thought of the tiara in its hinged box,
The almost satiny pearls, the almost cold
Diamonds, the almost tarnished web of silver
They studded, and the ritual of giving,
Then taking it back to have a stone reset,
A broken silver filament resoldered.
Whatever it was worth, it was enough,
She knew it now, to get to Australia.

She turns away, having told the children
Only enough to keep them satisfied
And us only enough to keep us reading.
The front door closes as she turns away,
The street lamps are lit up, Australia
Is a lost continent. But do you know,

Miss Urquhart, that I remember the cool leaf
Of dockweed rubbing up and down my calf,
And how you trailed us, my sister and me,
Behind you like a wake, how we kept up,
Questioning you just as you'd intended,
And getting for all our curiosity
A cup of tea? Today, among clouds
Of fringed phacelia in the deep grass,
When my daughters heard me speak to someone
They couldn't see, they waited for an answer.
So did I, even though I held their hands.
It took them pressing close to close the book.

GOOD FRIDAY

Heat is what I imagine, dust and tension,
And by mid-afternoon the cloudburst,
The sudden coolness, a balm for some, none
For those who had seen a loved one die,
Horribly, nails through his wrists, suffocating,
If not bleeding to death, in the heat, the tension.
The rain covered the gap of his life,
A rattling screen of iridescent beads
Pummelling the dust, cutting off our view.

It does no good to forecast the weather
Backwards. If it was tempest weather,
The nails bit the wood thirsting for sap,
The grain split with a hoarse cough.
Then rain fell. The woods filled with freshness,
Sandal thongs gleamed, faces basked.
Verisimilitude is magic. Jesus struggled
For breath, hanging forward, and said little.
Then someone prodded him, but he was dead.

He lived. He died. He knew what was happening.
The night my father came home from Claremont
And sat at the foot of my bed, forcing up
The news of D.'s death, was a Good Friday.
D.'s bowels had locked and starved his brain
Of blood. He died screaming, and in silence.
There were no last coherent words,
And his young wife (both of them so young)
Had curled between his deathbed and the wall.

All this my father told me.
And the story of D.'s life was told,

Friend by friend, a dozen lives.
A year later there was a gathering
To view home movies of him, and a film
He'd made, mostly a lyric reel
Of widening water circles—
Loved because his eye had seen them,
Turned the lens to ingest the light.

D. died when I was 16. I remember
His twenty-fourth birthday, his last,
The strobe lights' percussion, Zorba music,
And him dancing because that was the soul:
Rhythmless, bare-chested, leaping in air,
Really, I think, in all the sweat and shouting,
To prove a man could dance that way,
In a church basement, a man could
With another man, their wives clapping.

They say that Jesus died at 33.
They say so, and now I think I believe it.
Never have my age and other's ages
Seemed so real, so physically what they are.
I see the skin's grain, the back's curve,
The pools of stamina drawn carefully
To contain the world no longer vast
In possibilities, except that it
Can kill, even in your prime.

And yet, 30, a craftsman in wood,
One finally thought he knew what humankind
Wanted—to be loved, to be forgiven.
Which meant to be loved always.
And yes, perhaps, he was a little naive.
He believed that this was possible,
Loved as he had been by his mother,
His father who trained him to work wood.
He knew the feel of love's grain, its texture.

Knew a way, too, to speak of love.
It had a substance, a heft, like wood
Or nets or sacks of seed or jars of ointment.
Things came to mind, they came to hand,
Unscrolling even from the written word.
The world was made of love, to love.
And he was on the road, finding listeners.
And he was of an age when he knew doom
Waited for him, that people heard what they wanted.

That is, they heard what they lacked.
The glory of it turned the desert green.
The cedars' vertical aspiration said it.
Roads offered their dust, their thieves.
Cities congregated suspiciously, busy
And explosive with potential. Teacher,
They called him (as they called others):
Everyone must be included, loved,
The excluded most of all, who would doom him.

They say he taught three years. They say
Much about him, that his life
Was seamless, like his robe.
And, yet, he was that age when,
Seamed, you put away childish things
And take children into your arms.
They would doom him. He entered rooms
Forbidden to be entered, when the dead
Lay, rising at his call, to doom him.

None of it worked him well. But look,
He lived into his prime,
With all those years to go before
The oil of mother's cooking, the shavings
Of occupational hazard, would paralyze him.
Therefore, the risk of loving this way
Dripped, a water clock; flared, a lamp
Sucking up fuel. It became his disease,
Willed and unwilled, breath held and released.

Mark Jarman   247

Heat is what I imagine, dust and tension.
The scourging I imagine he understood,
The soldiers' reviling, surely he had seen that,
And the way crucifixion worked, the need to
Break legs to bring the strangulation on
(No need in his case; he'd already gone).
In the cloudburst, the downpour of signs,
The saints out walking, puzzled to be raised,
Things were torn, shattered, terrifying.

Today, the lawns are clouded with at least
Six kinds of wild flower. Ground ivy,
Corn speedwell, henbit, chickweed,
Spring beauties, and the dandelion.
My daughters know their names. My wife
And I look at them, the girls and flowers,
And none of us thinks of him, who does not
Haunt us, any more than anyone gone,
When there is such a theodicy of blossoms.

Our four-year-old's lips nearly touch
A dandelion globe, spluttering,
As she learns to blow the seeds away.
One night, the sepals close on golden petals,
Then open, changed. Gone to seed.
Gone to worlds of possibility.
What's love, even eternal love,
But evolution to endure? And doesn't it
Begin here, learning to blow a kiss?

Yes, it is complex, I know.
Look at the articulation of the seed itself,
The filament erect to its parachute
Of downy hairs. How easily
It could be taken as almost cruciform,
How willingly the wind could explicate it:
His breath, his sign. But it is ours,
As we show her how to force the air
Out in a rush, our love she takes as her own.

LOUIS JENKINS

Louis Jenkins was born in Okla-
homa City in 1942 and now lives
in Duluth, Minnesota. His prose
poems have been collected in *An
Almost Human Gesture*. He has
received two Bush Foundation
Fellowships and a Loft-McKnight
Award for his work.

THE PLAGIARIST

A fat teaching assistant has caught a freshman cheating on his exam and
she stands now in the hallway displaying the evidence, telling the story to
her colleagues: "I could tell by the way he looked. I could tell by his hands."
With each detail the story expands, rooms are added, hallways, chande-
liers, flights of stairs, and she sinks exhausted against a railing. More lis-
teners arrive and she begins again. She seems thinner now, lighter. She
rises, turns. She seems almost to be dancing. She clutches the paper of
the wretched student. He holds her firmly, gently as they turn and turn
across the marble floor. The lords and ladies fall back to watch as they
move toward the balcony and the summer night. Below in the courtyard
soldiers assemble, their brass and steel shining in the moonlight.

DAVID MICHAEL KAPLAN

Born in New York City in 1946,
David Michael Kaplan is the
author of *Comfort,* a collection of
stories, and fiction in *The Atlantic,*
Playboy, Best American Short
Stories 1986, and other publica-
tions. He teaches at Loyola Uni-
versity of Chicago.

IN THE REALM OF THE HERONS

When they arrived at the lake, a man called Nye showed Peter and
Megan their cabin and then led them down the stone steps to the water's
edge—"to see something special, little girl," he said, winking at Megan.
He pointed across the lake to the western shore, already burning with late
afternoon sunlight. Giant birds circled the treetops, their wings white
against the sky, their necks folded back into graceful S-curves.

"Sea gulls," Megan said.

"Nope," replied Nye. "Those are herons. They roost in the trees all
along that shore. They nest here summers, then they go south in the fall."
He held up a finger. "Listen, now. You can hear them talking."

They listened. Peter heard a high, plaintive crying.

"They're handsome birds," Nye said, "but they sure make one ugly sound." He wet his lips as if by tasting the air he could hear them better. "In the old days folks used to hunt them for their feathers. For ladies'" — he drew out the word—"*chapeaux*. Now they're protected. Folks still pester them sometimes, though. Kids mostly."

Peter pointed to a white rowboat bobbing against the dock piling. "Does that belong to the cabin?" he asked.

"Yep." Nye said. "Oars are in the cellar."

"I might row a bit while we're here. Would you like to do that, honey?"

His daughter shrugged. When they turned back to the cabin Megan stayed behind. "I want to watch awhile," she said.

"Man named Burnham owns your cabin," Nye said as they walked. "Him and his wife used to come down from Ukiah every summer. Then she died too"—he glanced at Peter, who nodded slightly to show it was all right—"and he came one day, took his tools from the cellar, the clothes from the closets, and just left the rest. Furniture, TV, toaster, the boat, the works. 'You rent it for me, Nye,' he told me. 'You won't be seeing me again.' And I haven't, not for sixteen years." Nye spat on the ground. "People've been making off with things, I know. I tell him I should make an inventory, but he always says don't bother." He studies Peter. "When did your wife die? You don't mind me asking?"

"Four months ago," Peter said.

Nye shook his head. "Don't know what it's like, not to be married. I've been married my whole life. One day I was shooting squirrels and riding bikes and then I was married. I think I'd miss it."

Yes, Peter thought.

"Hope she didn't suffer."

"She didn't suffer at all," Megan said. Without their hearing, she had come up behind them. "She never knew she died."

"Megan," Peter said.

But she was gone, running up the steps to the cabin.

"She didn't want to come here," Peter explained. "I—I thought a vacation would be good for her . . . for both of us . . . she's just eleven . . ." His thoughts began eluding him, like smoke in the chilling air.

It was true: Kate hadn't known she was going to die. There had been no reckonings, no good-byes. "Routine and minor," the surgeon termed the operation to remove a nasal polyp which had been troubling her breathing.

Peter left her the evening before the surgery, and early the following morning—after he'd packed Megan's school lunch and before he'd even remembered Kate was in the operating room—the hospital called, saying he should come. He was met by a tall, jowled man with large-veined hands who introduced himself as Dr. Debcoe, the deputy administrator of the hospital. His words rushed at Peter: *a terrible thing . . . almost never happened . . . one chance in a thousand, in ten thousand . . . a vascular malformation . . . the vicinity of the surgery . . . significant blood loss . . . difficult to stanch . . . transfusions, of course* (here he opened his long ivory hands to show he was hiding nothing) *. . . her vital signs fell so precipitously . . . shock . . .*

Peter was dazed. "You haven't hurt her, have you?" he asked. Debcoe looked at him quizzically, and it was then he realized that Kate was dead.

At the funeral, while Peter cried, Megan sat dry-eyed, nervously crossing and uncrossing her thin legs. When he took her hand, it was so cold it startled him, and they both flinched. During the reception at their house afterward, she disappeared. Peter found her sitting on the floor in the guest bedroom, lights out, curtains drawn against the pale March sunlight.

"I don't want people pawing and crying on me anymore," she said.

"They're only trying to be kind, honey."

"I don't want to be looked at anymore."

"Okay, then," Peter said, "stay up here."

She stood up. "I want to go see Marcie." Marcie was her friend, a small girl with owlish glasses who earlier that day had brought a sympathy card to the house.

"Well, you can't," Peter said. "Not right now."

Megan sighed and sat back down.

Peter cleared his throat. "I want you to know," he told her, "that if there's any—feelings—you've got about Mom's dying"—Megan glanced up—"it's okay to talk about them. You know—get them out."

Megan squirmed, then rested her chin in her hands.

"It's better to get them out," Peter repeated.

She was silent.

"So will you do that?"

"Okay, okay," she exclaimed. "You don't need to say it a hundred times."

But when the door closed for the last time and the final guest had gone, Peter fully expected Kate to come in from the kitchen, slightly breathless from her errands, and tell him she was grateful, it had been a chore, she knew, he had done well in her absence, but now she had come back.

David Michael Kaplan 253

He heard a light thumping and scraping on the floor of the upstairs bed-room, a sound at once familiar, but now strange in the silent house: Megan was playing jacks.

In the weeks that followed, while Peter kept stumbling unexpectedly upon his grief, Megan drew a circle around herself, like the safe zone in a children's game where no pursuers may enter and no prisoners may leave.

"You know, I've never seen you cry," Peter said as they were eating dinner one evening. "Not once since your mother died."

Megan twisted a button on her shirt.

"You've got something in the corner of your mouth," he said. She wiped it off.

"Don't you miss her?" he asked.

"Sure," she said, not looking at him. "Do you think I'm a creep?"

"She's become like a stranger," he said to his sister on the phone.

"What do you mean?"

"Everything's different. She's gotten hard."

"She's grieving, that's all."

"I can't talk to her, I—" His voice caught, and for a moment he couldn't speak.

"Peter?"

"I—I keep expecting Kate to come and explain her to me. Kate did that. I mean, she and Kate—"

"Everybody grieves differently."

"—they were together, somehow, in my mind."

"I know," his sister said. "Give her time."

Silence grew between them. Peter could feel it coming, yet couldn't contain it. It was like trying to keep air in a leaking balloon, or breath in a dying body. In the evening he often found himself outside her closed door, hesitating, hardly breathing, not knowing what he wanted to do or say. Sometimes he would knock and ask her a question whose answer he forgot a moment later; more often, he would just walk away.

He began watching her. Once she was doing gymnastics stretches on the sun deck while he stood behind the kitchen curtains. He held his breath, marveling that she could bend so far without snapping. In mid-stretch, she stopped, her hair half-fallen across her face. Peter drew back.

"What do you want, Daddy?" she called out.

Peter didn't know.

He dreamed one night he was shaking her, yelling words in a language he didn't understand; even though he was hurting her, she kept grinning at him idiotically. Enraged, he shook harder, and she began to come apart in his hands, leaving him holding torn-off limbs from which ran not blood, but something cold and gray, like porridge.

That's why, he thought. *She wasn't a real child after all.*

Horrified, he dropped her arms, and woke. He walked down the hall to Megan's room. The door was ajar. By the glow of the nite-lite, he saw her, eyes open, staring at him warily. She didn't move or take her eyes from him, and neither of them spoke. Peter closed the door. In the morning, he wasn't sure whether or not he'd dreamed it all, but that didn't matter.

We've got to get out of here, he thought.

And so they'd come to the lake. Imagining they would explore the lake trails, Peter rented bicycles, but the only day they did bike, Megan furiously pedaled ahead, complaining that he was too slow. When he grimly set a faster pace, she said she was tired and wanted to go back. They drank slushes at a roadside stand and stared into the icy sludge. As they pedaled back to the cabin, the whirring of their bicycle chains seemed to Peter the loneliest sound he had ever heard. That was the last thing they did together: Megan didn't want to go hiking, and she didn't want to go rowing. Soon she found Krissa, a girl who was staying at a cabin down the road, and was gone with her much of the day. The only time Peter was certain of seeing her was at dinner, where his projected hearty meals soon devolved into frozen dinners, hot dogs, and grilled cheeses. After eating, Megan returned to Krissa's cabin; her friend never came to theirs.

"Why don't you stay home one evening?" Peter asked her.

"Why? There's nothing to do here."

"You could talk to me. I never see you."

"We're together all the time, anyway," she said.

So in the evenings Peter often sat alone on the porch. Wind bristled the treetops; sometimes a fish leaped and seemed to hang forever before splashing down. He stared through the dark pines into a future as black and deep as the lake, at the end of which was a bare kitchen table where he sat, palms up, expecting nothing. Across the water, he saw lights in other cabins where people sat together—eating, talking, planning—then followed the curve of the shoreline around to the darker regions, where the herons roosted. Often he heard their crying, and sometimes he thought he could see them, even in the dark, as they circled the trees so closely that their wings might have brushed the branches.

He remembered a Japanese folktale Kate had read to Megan when she was little: in it, a fisherman rescues a gull from a net, only to find that it is actually a beautiful princess transformed by an evil magician. Peter smiled and imagined Kate had become one of those lovely herons. The image drifted on his thoughts as a boat drifted on water.

He decided one afternoon to row to the end of the lake where the herons were. At the convenience store he bought a six-pack of beer and a pair of denim gloves. "It'll be a hot one today," the clerk advised, so Peter also bought sunburn cream and a long-billed cap that said GONE FISHIN'. He found the oars in the cellar, pitched them in the boat, and gingerly stepped inside. The boat rocked, then steadied as it accepted his weight. He untied the painter and pushed off. A few yards out he began backrowing.

Peter hadn't rowed for years, and his strokes were choppy. He tried feathering the oars but soon returned to his original stroke. Surprised at how hard he was breathing, he slowed his cadence. After a while, he rested. The sun glared off the water. Except for two fishermen in a distant, hazy boat, the lake was abandoned.

Peter opened a beer and drank deeply, then put the can on the floorboards and continued rowing. His stroke seemed longer now, with more bite and pull. The beer can spilled. Twenty minutes more and he was almost there. His arms and wrists ached; despite the gloves, his palms were chafed. He rubbed his arms and applied more sunburn cream. A gust sent ripples skimming across the lake, and wavelets slapped the side of the boat. Peter scooped up a handful of water. It tasted mossy, sepulchral.

Three herons swooped overhead, startling him. He watched them, and then began rowing toward the point along the shore where they'd disappeared into the trees. Soon he was there, breathing hard, but cleanly. Peter hauled in the oars and allowed himself to drift.

No cabins had been built on this side, and the trees came right to the lake's edge, their roots poking through the loamy soil before plunging into the water. Sunlight scoured the saw grass along the bank. Peter drifted and almost bumped into it before he saw it—the ruin of a small dock, its flooring rotted away. He stuck an oar into the muddy bottom for support and carefully stood up. At first he didn't see the house either: it sat some forty yards from shore, surrounded and sheltered by the tall pines. Peter tied his boat to a log that lay half in the water. By grabbing protruding tree roots, he could scramble up the bank.

The old shingle house, once painted green, had been abandoned for some time. Large sections of tarpaper on the roof had blown away, and one section dipped ominously. Except for several large panes in an upper dormer, most of the windows were surprisingly unbroken. Rows of what had once been a vegetable garden ran along one side; a pie plate still clacked against a wooden stake. A summer chair, its wicker seat fallen out, sat under a tree. Above and around him, herons cried as they flew in and out of their nests.

Peter rattled the front door: it was locked, as were the windows. He peered inside, but could see little through the grime. In back, he found a porch, its screening in tatters, the hook on the outer door long fallen off. A wringer washer sat in one corner; boxes of empty mason jars, a broken broom, two bald tires, and a pile of rusted bolts littered the floor. A woman's once-yellow bonnet, faded and stiff, lay on one of the boxes. Peter expected the inner porch door to be locked also, but it gave way easily.

He entered a kitchen. An old Amana range and ice chest sat heavily along one wall. Dead insects littered the sink. Peter opened the cupboards: except for a sprung mousetrap, they were empty. The kitchen led to a long hallway in whose center a stairway ascended to the second floor. The rooms off the hallway were littered with beer cans and cigarette butts. Peter winced. He went upstairs.

Those rooms were also empty except for more beer cans, an orange crate containing several moldering volumes of a 1911 *Compton's Picture Encyclopedia*, and a pair of men's work boots, the laces still tied, as if their owner had taken ghostly flight. In the last room stood a bureau, its mirror removed from the frame. Peter opened the drawers: he found a baby mouse skeleton and a bag of sachet, dry and faintly fragrant. He gingerly removed the skeleton and threw it out the window. The scent of the sachet seemed to linger in the room. Peter imagined how the summer house must have looked when freshly painted, its starched curtains billowing, the garden musky with vegetables and flowers.

As he left, Peter unlatched a porch window, and locked the kitchen door.

Back at the cabin he found a note from Megan saying that she was staying the night at Krissa's and would return in the morning. He picked up the phone to call her, then dialed Nye instead.

"That's the old Cotter place," Nye said. "Never knew the folks myself. It's been empty for years."

"People have broken into it," Peter said. "I saw beer cans."

"Kids, I expect. They get into foolishness."

"How do you get there by land?" Peter asked.

"Don't really know. That old road is chained off. They don't like folks driving over and pestering the herons."

When Peter awoke the next morning, the idea greeted him like the sun, fully formed and perfect: he would buy the house. He would find out who owned it—surely it still belonged to someone—and buy it. Then he would restore it. He would sand and varnish the floors, straighten the warp of the roof, plaster, and shingle. He would repair the dock, sink new pilings, set in planking. No matter that he knew nothing about construction—he would buy books, Nye would help, he would learn. The garden would come back to life. Peter saw the kitchen dressed in curtains, stocked with food, fragrant with fresh-picked herbs. It would be a place he and Megan could come to in summer and on vacations and holidays. Her room would face the tall pines that almost touched the window; his would be the room of the lady with the sachet. Peter imagined a Megan grown to graceful womanhood bringing her own children to the summer house. He would lift his grandchildren onto his shoulders and show them the nests of the herons.

Impatiently, he awaited Megan's return. He called Krissa's cabin every half hour, but no one answered. He paced the porch. He walked to the dock and looked to the spot on the western shore where the house lay hidden, as if fearful it might vanish. When Megan hadn't come back by lunch, Peter drove over to Krissa's cabin. No one was home. He left a note for Megan to return right away. In mid-afternoon, she did.

"Where've you been?" he asked sharply. "I thought you were coming back this morning."

"We went to a horse show," Megan replied. "Then we all went out for lunch."

"Well, why didn't you call me?"

She shifted uneasily. "Did I have to?"

"Yes, I was worried."

"I'm sorry," she mumbled.

Easy, Peter told himself. *No sense getting angry. Not today.*

"I want to show you something," he said.

"What?"

"A surprise."

She looked at him warily. "What?"

"Let's go to the dock. We have to row there."

"I don't want to row," she said.

"You don't have to. I'll row. You can just sit there like the Queen of Sheba."

"Daddy, I don't want to go."

"Well, you have to," Peter insisted. "It's important. Please."

Megan sighed, but followed him to the boat. Peter pushed them off and jumped in; Megan gripped the gunwales as the boat rocked, then steadied. She sat, chin in hand, staring off the side as Peter rowed. Waterflies danced in anticipation of evening, and once a bass leaped so near that Megan jumped. Somewhere steaks were frying. It was an afternoon you could sing to, Peter thought. His daughter trailed her hand over the side, her fingers delicately lacing the water. Peter searched her face for traces of Kate, yet could find none: her cheeks, once they lost their baby fat, would betray his bones.

"This is the life, huh?" he said as he dipped the oars.

Megan was silent.

Peter hesitated, then said, "I wish your mother were here."

"Kate," Megan said. "Her name was Kate."

Peter pulled the oars deeper.

"Do you miss her?" he asked.

"Why do you keep asking me that?"

"Because you never say anything about her! It's as if she's—"

"She is dead," Megan said. "She died."

"Just answer me—do you miss her?"

"Okay, okay, I miss her! Is that what I'm supposed to say?"

Peter rowed harder, and the boat surged.

"You hate me, don't you?" he said.

She shook her head.

"I didn't kill her, you know."

Megan leaned over the side and began humming.

"Stop that!" he snapped.

She continued humming, louder now.

"Stop it! Look at me."

"What do you want?" she cried. Her face was contorted in rage. "Why are you always bothering me? Why can't you just leave me alone?"

Peter stopped rowing. "Look—"

She began humming again.

He dropped the oars. "You know, I'm tired of you," he said. "I'm sick and tired of you. I'll leave you alone, all right. Maybe you'd like me dead too. Wouldn't you?" She was shaking her head back and forth. "You could really be alone then, right? You little snot!"

"Don't call me names!"

"I'll call you any damn thing I please! I'm your father."

She covered her ears. "Don't yell, don't yell."

"I'll yell all I want!"

"I want to go home," Megan pleaded.

"Well, we're not. We're going where I want to go." Peter picked up the oars and rowed a few fierce strokes, then shoved them over to her. "Here, you row!"

"No!"

"Yes, damn you, you row!"

He grabbed her hands to force the oars into them. "No, no, no," she screamed, clenching her fists. She kicked him. Enraged, he slapped her, then roughly pried open her fingers and closed them around the oars.

"Now—row!" he hissed.

Her chest was heaving, but she wouldn't cry, and she wouldn't row. Peter looked at his daughter across the abyss of the boat. The oars were monstrous in her small hands.

What am I doing? he thought, and was ashamed.

"Here, give them back to me," he said wearily. Megan slumped into her seat, arms tightly folded. Across the lake, a motorboat faded into the wake of its own sound. Peter rowed in silence. When they reached shore, he tied the boat to the log, then helped her up the bank. Megan walked ahead of him, fast, then stopped when she reached the clearing.

"It's just an old house," she said.

No, it's not, Peter thought. But he knew there was nothing he could say about it that she might understand. They would never live here. It had been a madness to think so.

"Why did we come here?" Megan asked.

"I found it yesterday," Peter said. "I—I thought you'd like to see it, that's all."

She wrinkled her nose.

"Let's go around back. We can get in there."

The door that he'd locked the day before was ajar. Someone had been there. Peter pushed it open. "Hello?" he called. The house smelled acrid, coppery, silent.

"Well, let's take a look around." He went into the kitchen, but Megan remained on the porch. "Come on," he urged.

She hesitated, then stepped cautiously into the kitchen.

"Go on," he said. "Look around."

She went down the hall.

"Don't follow me," she said.

"Take a look upstairs," he called after her. "There's a box of old encyclopedias there."

Megan glanced in the side rooms, then went upstairs. Peter listened to the groaning boards as she walked through one room, then another. For one moment more, he imagined the house filled with the scent of wood shavings, varnish, paint. He sneezed, and sneezed again. A pollen was in the air, or dust.

Megan was screaming. Peter ran to the stairwell and almost collided with her as she stumbled down. "Megan—" he cried, but she pushed him away, sliding through his hands like water. He looked up the stairwell. "Who's there?" he yelled. "Who are you?" He hesitated, then went up. From her footsteps, he knew in which room she'd been.

For a moment he thought it was standing there, wings and feet outstretched, miraculously risen as no bird ever could, even as he noted the limp head, the glassed and vacant eye. The heron was dead. Nailed against the wall, it was at once enormous and awkward, and in the gracelessness of death, only pitiful. Its eye held Peter. A breeze through the broken window ruffled its feathers. Peter closed the door and left.

He found Megan sitting in the boat, arms wrapped tightly around her knees. Her breathing was harsh, hurried, and when she saw him, she stiffened and held up her hand to come no closer. He sat on the log across from her.

"I didn't know it was there," he said. "It wasn't there yesterday."

She stared at him, the ghost of hate and anger in her eyes. Something in her seemed to quiver, and then she was crying, shaking her head as if to deny it. Peter didn't know what to do or say. He waited, silence at last seeming wise.

"Who would do that?" she moaned. "Who would want to kill it like that?"

"Kids," he said. "I don't know."

"But there's just no reason for it," she sobbed.

Peter thought for a moment. "No," he said. "No reason at all."

It seemed to calm her. Gradually she grew quiet, and laid her head on her arms. "Why did we come here?" she asked.

"I was thinking about buying it. The house." Megan looked up at him. He grinned. "Bad idea, huh?"

She nodded, and again rested her head on her arms, as if she would sleep. The boat gently bumped against the log. "Megan—" he murmured. He wanted her to raise her head; he wanted to see her face, as if she might vanish.

A cool breeze, sharp as rain, blew across the lake. Peter shivered.

"It's just that I don't know where she went," Megan said, and for a moment Peter didn't know who she meant. "She's got to be somewhere, doesn't she? She can't just be nowhere." Megan clasped her arms around her shoulders and lightly rocked. "Sometimes I—I think I could just— you know—just call her up and say, well, okay, let's go out for a Coke. And she'd come. She'd have to come. I'd tell her, It's just not fair, you at least owe me a Coke."

They sat awhile longer, then pushed off. The ripples that had run toward the shore now seemed to run from it, Peter thought. Or was that his imagination? Did lakes have tides? Could they be charted? He pulled the oars deeply through the water: he wanted them back before dusk.

"I'm cold," Megan said.

Peter had nothing to give her. Instead, he began singing. First he sang "The Skye Boat Song," then "Clementine," Megan looking at him with an old look of scorn and embarrassment, but he would not be silenced now. He grinned at her and kept singing, back to the wind, rowing them across water and time to a place that—for lack of any better word—they would have to call home.

RICHARD KATROVAS

Richard Katrovas was born in Los
Angeles in 1953. The author of
Green Dragons, Snug Harbor,
and *The Public Mirror*, he teaches
at the University of New Orleans.

ALLEY FLOWER

Our Lord has forsaken the poor.
Perhaps because the torn, green eaves
of Canal Street are flapping in the rain,
or because sick Ruthy, filthy sister
of all our alleys and all the flowers
the alley shadows swallow, is squatting
over a grated drain, eyes lifted, singing.
Lord, touch her smudged brow
with your dark, leathery palm
and run your dry tongue through her hair;
she counts the starlings pacing
the cathedral tower and blesses
the warm steam issuing from her body—

blesses this momentary peace
and the sweet angels who even now
are rocketing from the Edge.
Shall we, Lord, measuring this night
against the palpitations
of a cool, urban consciousness,
fetter this sixty-some-odd-year
old virgin, ill-beloved?
Ruthy, no one listens.
Not the polymorphous god you mumble to
on the avenues of twitch;
not the school girls
in their lavender and denim
who trail the scent of forbidden fruit
on Iberville and Royal;
not, Darling, even I who would praise your madness.
For to hear you would be to love you
and to love you would be to go to you
and take your hand and lead you to a room.

W. P. KINSELLA

W. P. Kinsella was born in Edmonton, Alberta, in 1935. His books include two novels, *Shoeless Joe* and *The Iowa Baseball Confederacy*, and eight story collections, including *Dance Me Outside*, *The Thrill of the Grass*, and *The Further Adventures of Slugger McBatt*. He lives in Blaine, Washington.

PRETEND DINNERS

for Barbara Kostynyk

It was Oscar Stick she married. The thing that surprise me most about Oscar and Bonnie getting together is that Oscar be a man who don't really like women, and Bonnie seem to me a woman who need more love than anybody I ever knowed.

She was Bonnie Brightfeathers to start with and a girl who always been into this here Women's Lib stuff. She been three years older than me for as long as I can remember. That age make quite a difference at times. When she was eighteen she don't even talk to a kid like me, but now that she's twenty-three and I'm twenty, it don't seem to make any difference at all.

Bonnie Brightfeathers graduated the grade twelve class at the Residential School with really good report cards. She hold her head up, walk with long steps like she going someplace, and she don't chase around with guys or drink a lot. Her and Bedelia Coyote is friends and they always say they don't need men for nothing.

"A woman without a man be like a fish without a bicycle," Bedelia say all the time. She read that in one of these MS magazines that she subscribe to, and she like to say it to my girlfriend Sadie One-wound when she see us walk along the road have our arms around each other.

After high school Bonnie get a job with one of these night patrol and security companies in Wetaskiwin. Northwest Security and Investigations is the right name. She wear a light brown uniform and carry on her hip in a holster what everybody say is a real gun. She move away from her parents who got more kids than anything else except maybe beer bottles what been throwed through the broke front window of their cabin and lay in the yard like cow chips. She move from the reserve to Wetaskiwin after her first pay cheque. Pretty soon she got her own little yellow car and an apartment in a new building at the end of 51st avenue.

All this before she was even nineteen. It was almost a year later that I got to know her good. A Government looking letter come to the reserve for her and her father ask me to take it up to Wetaskiwin the next time I go. That same night I went in Blind Louis Coyote's pickup truck and Bonnie invite me up to her apartment after I buzzed the talk-back machine in the lobby.

It be an apartment where the living room/bedroom be all one. The kitchen is about as big as most closets but she got the whole place fixed up cheerful: soft cushions all over the place, lamps with colored bulbs, and pretty dishes. She got too a record player and a glass coffee table with chrome legs. The kitchen table be so new that it still smell like the inside of a new car. There are plants too, hang on a wool rope from the ceiling and brush my shoulder when I cross the room to sit on her sofa. Whole apartment ain't big enough to swing a cat in, but it is a soft, warm place to be, like the inside of a sleeping bag.

Bonnie is a real pretty person remind me some of my sister Illianna. She got long hair tied in kind of a pony-tail on each side of her head and dark eyes just a little too big for her face. Her skin is a browny-yellow color like furniture I seen in an antique store window. She is a lot taller than most Indian girls and real slim. She wear cut-off jeans and a scarlet blouse the night I come to see her.

She give me a beer in a tall glass. I don't even get to see the bottle except when she take it out of the fridge. She put out for us some peanuts in a sky-blue colored dish the shape of a heart while she talk to me about how happy she is.

This is about the time that I write down my first stories for Mr. Nichols. Being able to do something that I want to do sit way off in the future like a bird so high in the sky that it be just a speck, but I can understand how proud Bonnie feel to see her life turning out good.

"Someday, Silas, I'm going to have me a whole big house. I babysit one time for people in Wetaskiwin who got a living room bigger than this whole apartment." She pour herself a beer and come sit down beside me.

"You know what they teached us at the Home Economics class in high school? About something called gracious living. Old Miss Lupus, she show us how to set a table for a dinner party of eight. She show us what forks to put where and learned us what kind of wine to serve with what dish."

Bonnie got at the end of her room the top half of a cupboard with doors that are like mirrored sunglasses, all moonlight colored and you can sort of see yourself in them. When she tell me the cupboard is called a hutch I make jokes about how many rabbits she could keep in there.

"I remember Bedelia Coyote saying, 'Hell, we have a dinner party for fifteen every night, but we only got eleven plates so the late ones get to wait for a second setting, if the food don't run out first.'"

After a while Bonnie show me the inside of that cupboard. She got two dinner plates be real white and heavy, two sets of silver knives, spoons, and fat and thin forks, two wine glasses with stems must be six inches long, and four or five bottles of wine and liquor. The bottles be all different colors and shapes.

"Most everybody make fun of that stuff Miss Lupus teach us, but I remember it all good and I'm gonna use it someday. One time Sharon Fence-post asked, 'What kind of wine do you serve with Kraft Dinner?' and Miss Lupus try to give her a straight answer, but everybody laugh so hard we can't hear what she say."

Bonnie take down the bottles from the cabinet to show me. "I buy them because they look pretty. See, I never even crack the seals," and she take out a tall bottle of what could be lemon pop except the label say, *Galliano*. She got too a bottle of dark green with a neck over a foot long and it have a funny name that I have to write down the back of a match book, *Valpolicella*.

"We put on pretend dinners up there at the school. They got real fancy wine glasses, look like a frosted window, and real wine bottles except they got in them only water and food coloring. We joke about how Miss Lupus and Mr. Gortner, the principal, drink up all the real wine before they fill up the bottles for us to pretend with. Vicki Crowchild took a slug out of one of them bottles, then spit it clean across the room and say, 'This wine tastes like shit.' Miss Lupus suspended her for two weeks for that.

"See this one." Bonnie say, and show me a bottle that be both a bottle and a basket, all made of glass and filled with white wine. "Rich people do that," she say, "put out wine bottles in little wood baskets. They sit it up on the table just like a baby lay in a crib."

There is a stone crock of blue and white got funny birds fly around on it, and one that be stocky and square like a bottle of Brut Shaving Lotion, and be full of a bright green drink called *Sciarda*. I'd sure like to taste me that one sometime.

It is like we been friends, Bonnie and me, for a long time, or better than friends, maybe a brother and sister. Bonnie got in her lamp soft colored light bulbs that make the room kind of golden. She put Merle Haggard on the record player and we talk for a long time. Later on, my friends Frank and Rufus give me a bad time 'cause I stay there maybe three hours and leave them wait in the truck. They tease me about what we maybe done up there, but I know we are just friends and what anybody else think don't matter.

"Sit up to the table here, Silas, and I make for you a pretend dinner," Bonnie say. She put that heavy plate, white as new snow, in front of me, and she arrange the knife and other tools in the special way she been taught.

"Put your beer way off to the side there. Beer got no place at pretend dinners," and she set out the tall wine glasses and take the glass bottle and basket and make believe she fill up our glasses. "Know what we having for dinner?"

"Roast moose," I say.

Bonnie laugh pretty at that, but tell me we having chicken or maybe fish 'cause when you having white wine you got to serve only certain things like that with it.

"I remember that, the next time we have a bottle in the bushes outside Blue Quills Hall on Saturday night," I tell her.

Bonnie make me a whole pretend dinner, right from things she say is appetizers to the roast chicken stuffed with rice. "What do you want for dessert?" she ask me. When I say chocolate pudding, she say I should have a fancy one like strawberry shortcake or peaches with brandy. "Might as well have the best when you making believe."

I stick with chocolate pudding. I like the kind that come in a can what is painted white inside.

"Some of this here stuff is meant to be drunk after dinner," Bonnie say, waving the tall yellow bottle that got the picture of an old-fashioned soldier on the label. "I ain't got the right glasses for this yet. Supposed to use tiny ones no bigger than the cap off a whiskey bottle. This time you got to pretend both the bottle and glass. Miss Lupus tell us that people take their after dinner drinks to the living room, have their cigarette there and relax their stomach after a big meal."

I light up Bonnie's cigarette for her and we pretend to relax our stomachs.

"I'm gonna really do all this one day, Silas. I'm gonna get me a man who likes to share real things with me, but one who can make believe too."

"Thought you and Bedelia don't like men?"

"Bedelia's different from me. She really believe what she say, and she's strong enough to follow it through. I believe women should have a choice of what they do, but that other stuff, about hating men, and liking to live all alone, for me at least that just be a front that is all pretend like these here dinners."

She say something awful nice to me then. We talking in Cree and it be a hard language to say beautiful things in. What Bonnie say to me come up because we carried on talking about love. I say I figure most everybody find someone to love at least once or twice.

"How many people you know who is happy in their marriage?" Bonnie say.

"Maybe only one or two," I tell her.

"I don't want no marriage like I seen around here. For me it got to be more. I want somebody to twine my nights and days around, the way roses grow up a wire fence."

When I tell her how pretty I figure that is her face break open in a great smile and the dimples on each side of her mouth wink at me. I wish her luck and tell her how much I enjoy that pretend dinner of hers. Bonnie got a good heart. I hope she find the kind of man she looking for.

That's why it be such a surprise when she marry Oscar Stick.

Oscar is about twenty-five. He is short and stocky with bowed legs. He walk rough, drink hard, and fist-fight anybody who happen to meet his eye. He like to stand on the step of the Hobbema General Store with his thumbs in his belt loops. Oscar can roll a cigarette with only one hand and he always wear a black felt hat that make him look most a foot taller than he really is. He rodeo all summer and do not much in the winter.

Oscar be one of these mean, rough dudes who like to see how many women he can get and then he brag to everybody and tell all about what he done with each one.

"A woman is just a fuck. The quicker you let her know that the better off everybody is." Oscar say that to us guys one night at the pool hall. He is giving me and my friend Frank Fence-post a bad time 'cause we try to be mostly nice to our girlfriends.

"Always let a woman know all you want to do is screw her and get to hell away from her. It turns them on to think you're like that. And every-one thinks they is the one gonna change your mind. You should see how hard they try, and the only way a woman know to change you is to fuck you better . . ." and he laugh, wink at us guys, and light up a cigarette by crack a blue-headed match with his thumbnail.

Guess Bonnie must of thought she could change him.

"Bedelia's never once said 'I told you so' to me. She been a good friend." It is last week already and it is Bonnie Stick talking to me.

Not long after that time three years ago when her and Oscar married, her folks got one of them new houses that the Indian Affairs Department build up on the ridge. After things start going bad for Oscar and Bonnie they move into Brightfeathers' old cabin on the reserve.

"It was Bedelia who got the Welfare for me when Oscar went off to rodeo last summer and never sent home no money."

I met Bonnie just about dusk walking back to her cabin from Hobbema. She carrying a package of tea bags, couple of Kraft Dinner, and a red package of DuMaurier cigarettes. She invite me to her place for tea.

We've seen each other to say hello to once in a while but we never have another good visit like we did in Wetaskiwin. I am just a little bit shy to talk to her 'cause I know about her dreams and I only have to look at her to tell that things turned out pretty bad so far.

She still wear the tan-colored pants from her uniform but by now they is faded, got spots all over them, and one back pocket been ripped off. Bonnie got a tooth gone on her right side top and it make her smile kind of crooked. She got three babies and look like maybe she all set for a fourth by the way her belly bulge. I remember Oscar standing on the steps of the store saying, "A woman's like a rifle: should be kept loaded up and in a corner."

She boil up the tea in a tin pan on the stove. We load it up with canned milk and sugar. Bonnie look over at the babies spread out like dolls been tossed on the bed. The biggest one lay on her stomach with her bum way up in the air. "We got caught the first time we ever done it, Oscar and me," and she make a little laugh as she light up a cigarette. "This here coal-oil lamp ain't as fancy as what I had in the apartment, eh?"

We talk for a while about that apartment.

"I really thought it would be all right with Oscar. I could of stayed working if it weren't for the babies. They took back the car and all my furniture 'cause I couldn't pay for it. At first Oscar loved me so good, again and again, so's I didn't mind living in here like this," and she wave her hand around the dark cabin with the black woodstove and a few pieces of broke furniture. "Then he stopped. He go off to the rodeo for all summer, and when he is around he only hold me when he's drunk and then only long enough to make himself happy.

"I shouldn't be talking to you like this, Silas. Seems like every time I see you I tell you my secrets."

I remind her about those pretty words she said to me about twining around someone. She make a sad laugh. "You can only pretend about things like that . . . they don't really happen," and she make that sad laugh again. "Sometimes I turn away from him first just to show I don't give a care for him either. And sometimes I feel like I'm as empty inside as a meadow all blue with moonlight, and that I'm gonna die if I don't get held . . ."

Bonnie come up to me and put her arms around me then. She fit herself up close and put her head on my chest. She hang on to me so tight, like she was going to fall a long way if she was to let go. I feel my body get interested in her and I guess she can too 'cause we be so close together. I wonder if she is going to raise her face up to me and maybe fit her mouth inside mine the way girls like to do.

But she don't raise her face up. "It ain't like you think," she say into my chest. "I know you got a woman and I got my old man, wherever he is. It's just that sometimes . . ." and her voice trail off.

I kind of rub my lips against the top of her head. Her arms been holding me so long that they started to tremble. "I charge up my batteries with you, Silas. Then I can go along for another while and pretend that everything is going to be okay. Hey, remember the time that I made up the pretend dinner for you? I still got the stuff," she say, and take her arms from around me. From under the bed she bring out a cardboard box say Hoover Vacuum Cleaner on the side, and take out that tall wine bottle, and the heavy white plates, only one been broke and glued back together so it got a scar clean across it.

She clear off a space on the table and set out the plates and wine glasses. One glass got a part broken out of it, a V shape, like the beak of a bird. The wine bottles is dusty and been empty for a long time.

"Oscar drink them up when he first moved in with me, go to sleep with his head on the fancy table of mine," Bonnie say as she tip up the tall bottle. She laugh a little and the dimples show on each side of her mouth.

"I'll take the broke glass," she say, "though I guess it not make much difference if we don't have no wine. If you're hungry, Silas, I make some more tea and there's biscuits and syrup on the counter."

"No thanks," I say. "We don't want to spoil these here pretend dinners by having no food."

MAXINE KUMIN

The 1973 winner of the Pulitzer
Prize for Poetry, Maxine Kumin
was born in Philadelphia in 1925.
Her many books of poetry include
*Our Ground Time Here Will Be
Brief: New and Selected Poems*
and *Nurture*. She has also written
several novels, two essay collec-
tions, and some twenty books for
children. She lives on Hillside
Farm in New Hampshire, where
she and her husband raise horses.

BRUSHING THE AUNTS

Consider Amanda, my sensible strawberry roan,
her face with its broad white blaze
lending an air of constant surprise.
Homely Amanda, colossal and mild.
She evokes those good ghosts of my childhood
Brillo-haired and big-boned,
the freckled maiden aunts.
Though barren like her, they were not petulant.

Peaceable dears, they lay down alone
mute as giraffes in my mother's house,
fed tramps on the back porch
after The Crash,
pantomimed the Charleston
summer nights in the upstairs back bedroom
and dropped apple peels over their shoulders
to spell the name of a marrying man.

Remembering this,
I bring Amanda windfalls.
That season again.
The power of the leaf runs the human brain
raising the dead like lamb clouds in the sky.
The power of the thorn holds the birds' late nests
now strung like laundry from the blackberry canes
where parts of Amanda recur.
Her body fuzz is stickered in the oriole cups.
Copper hairs from her tail hold the packages up.

All fall as I drop to the scalp of sleep
while the raccoons whistle
and the geese cough
and Amanda grows small in my head
the powder streak of her face a blur
seventy pastures off,
the aunts return letting down their hair.
It hangs to the custard of Harriet's lap.
It touches the ridge of Alma's pink girdle
and the dream unwinds like a top.

I am brushing the carrot frizz gone gray
a hundred ritual strokes one way
a hundred ritual strokes the other
in 4/4 time the way it was once.
We dance the old back bedroom dance
till Amanda jitters yanking the tether
her eyes green holes, her blaze gone bright
and the latch flies up on another night.

INTRODUCING THE FATHERS

for Anne Carpenter

Yours lugs shopping bags of sweet corn
via parlor car to enhance the lunches
of his fellow lawyers at the Century Club.
Sundays he sneaks from church to stretch a net
across the Nissequegue River
and catches shad as they swim up to spawn.

Mine locks up the store six nights at seven,
cracks coconuts apart on the brick hearth,
forces lobsters down in the boiling pot.
Sundays he lolls in silk pajamas,
and swaggers out at nightfall to play pinochle.

In our middle age we bring them back, these despots,
mine in shirtsleeves, yours in summer flannels,
whose war cry was: the best of everything!
and place them side by side, inflatable
Macy-daddys ready for the big parade.

We open a friendship between them, sweetly posthumous,
and watch them bulge out twirling Malacca canes
into the simple future of straight losses,
still matching net worths, winning big at blackjack,
our golden warriors rising toward the Big Crash.

ROBERT LACY

Robert Lacy's stories have appeared in *Saturday Evening Post*, *Ploughshares*, and other magazines. "The Natural Father" was reprinted in *Best American Short Stories 1988*. Born in Crockett, Texas, in 1936, he lives in Medicine Lake, Minnesota, and works as a freelance writer, book reviewer, and part-time teacher.

THE NATURAL FATHER

Her name was Laura Goldberg. She had thick black hair and a "bump" in her nose (as she put it), but she dressed well and she had a good figure. She worked as a typist in an abstract office in downtown San Diego, and when Butters first met her in the fall of 1958 they had both just turned nineteen.

They met through a boot camp buddy of his who had gone to high school with her up in San Francisco, where she lived before her parents were divorced. Within a week he was taking her out. Butters was still in radio school at the time and didn't have a car, but Laura did, and she began picking him up several afternoons a week in the parking lot across the highway from the Marine base.

They made love on their third date, on the couch in her mother's apartment out in El Cajon, with the late-afternoon sunlight casting shadow patterns on the walls. It was hurried and not very satisfactory, and Butters was embarrassed by his performance. He felt he ought to apologize or something.

"It's okay," Laura said. "It's okay."

After that, though, they made love nearly every time they were alone together, often in the front seat of her car parked late at night on suburban sidestreets, with the fog rolling up off the bay to conceal them. One night they did it on her bed in the apartment, then had to spend frantic minutes picking white bedspread nap out of his trousers before her mother got home. Another time she met him at the front door, fresh from her shower, wearing nothing but a loose kimono, and they did it right there on the living room carpet, with the sound of the running shower in the background.

Butters was from a little town in eastern Oklahoma and hadn't known many Jewish girls before. In fact, he couldn't think of any. However, Laura's being Jewish didn't matter nearly as much to him as it seemed to matter to her. She was forever making jokes about it, and she liked to point out other Jews to him whenever they came across them, in restaurants or on TV. "Members of the Tribe," she called them, or "M.O.T.s." Butters pretended to share in the humor, but he was never quite sure what he was being let in on. Where he came from, tribes meant Indians.

Still, he was amazed at some of the people she identified as Jewish. Jack Benny, for example. And Frankie Laine. Every time they watched TV together in the apartment the list got longer. One night she even tried to convince him Eddie Fisher was a Jew.

"Bull," he said. "I don't believe it."

"He is, though," she insisted. "Ask Mother when she gets here."

"He's Italian or something," Butters said. "I read it somewhere. Fisher's not his real name."

"Nope. He's a genuine M.O.T."

"Uh-uh."

"He is too, Donnie. Bet you a dollar."

"Make it five."

"You don't have five."

"I can get it."

"All right, Mister Sure-of-Yourself, five then. Shake."

They shook hands.

"How about Debbie Reynolds?" he said. "What's she?"

In March Butters was graduated from radio school and promoted to private first class. Then he transferred to the naval base down at Imperial Beach to begin high-speed radio cryptography school. Imperial Beach was twelve miles due south of San Diego. The base sat out on a narrow point of land. At night you could see the lights of Tijuana across the way.

One night after he had been there about a month Laura picked him up, late, at the main gate, drove back up to a hamburger stand in National City, and told him she was pregnant.

Butters was astounded, of course. This was the sort of thing that happened to other people.

"How do you know?" he said.

"I've missed two periods."

"Jeez. Did you see a doctor?"

"Yes."

"What did he say?"

"He said I was pregnant."

"Yeah, but what did he *say*?"

"He said I was a big, strong, healthy girl, and I was going to have a baby sometime in October. He said I had a good pelvis."

"Is that all?"

"Yes. He gave me some pills."

"For what?"

"One for water retention and one for morning sickness."

"You been sick?"

"Not yet. He says I might be."

"Jeez."

They sat in silence for a while, not looking at each other. Finally he said, "Well, what do you think we should do?"

She spoke slowly and carefully, and he could tell she had given the matter some thought. "I think we ought to get engaged for a month," she said. "Then get married. I know where we can get a deal on a ring."

"What kind of deal?"

"Forty percent off, two years to pay."

"Where?"

"Nathan's. Downtown."

"You already been there?"

"I go by it every day at lunch."

"They give everybody forty percent off?"

"I know the manager. He's a cousin."

On the way back to the base Laura spoke of showers, wedding announcements, honeymoons in Ensenada. She said she thought they ought to sit down with her mother that very weekend, to get that part of it out of the way. Butters, who was hoping to get back on base without further discussion, said he thought he might have guard duty.

"You had guard duty last weekend," she reminded him.

"There's a bug going around," he said. "Lots of guys are in sickbay."

"Come Sunday night," she said. "I'll cook dinner. Elvis is on Ed Sullivan."

"I'll have to see," he said.

"Sunday night," she said.

Sunday was four days away, which gave him plenty of time to think. And the more he thought the more he knew he didn't want to marry Laura Goldberg. He didn't love her, for one thing, and he wasn't ready to get married anyway, even to someone he did love. He was only nineteen years old. He had his whole life in front of him. Besides, he couldn't imagine Laura back home in Oklahoma.

That Sunday evening he caught a ride into San Diego with one of the boys from the base, then took a city bus out to the apartment in El Cajon. Laura met him at the door wearing an apron, a mixing spoon in her hand.

"Hi, hon," she said. "Dinner's almost ready."

Laura's mother, Mrs. Lippman, was seated on the living room sofa smoking a cigarette. She had her shoes off and her stockinged feet up on an ottoman. Mrs. Lippman was a short, heavyset woman with springy gray hair and sharp features. She always looked tired.

"Hello, Donald," she said. "What's with Betty Furness in there? Usually I can't get her to boil water."

"Hello, Mrs. Lippman," Butters said. "How's things at the paint store?"

Mrs. Lippman managed a Sherwin-Williams store down on lower Broadway and complained constantly about the help, most of whom were Mexican-Americans.

"Terrible," she said. "Don't ask. The chilis are stealing me blind."

Laura had fixed beef stroganoff, a favorite of Butters, and when it was ready they ate it off TV trays in the living room while watching Elvis—from the waist up—on "The Ed Sullivan Show." The meal was well prepared. Laura had even made little individual salads for each of them, with chopped walnuts on top and her own special dressing. When they were through eating she put the coffee on, then she and Butters scraped and stacked the dishes in the kitchen while Mrs. Lippman watched the last of the Sullivan show alone in the living room.

"You nervous?" Laura said to him in the kitchen. "You've been awfully quiet since you got here."

"I'm all right," Butters said, scraping a plate.

"Is something *wrong?*"

"No. I'm all right, I told you."

"Well, you certainly don't act like it. You haven't smiled once the whole evening."

Butters didn't say anything. He reached for another plate.

"Look at me," Laura said.

He looked at her.

"It's going to be *okay,*" she said. "We'll just go in there and tell her. What can she say?"

"Nothing much, I guess."

"Do you want to do the talking, or do you want me to?"

"Either way. You decide."

"All right. You do it. That's more traditional anyway."

"What about the other?"

"What other?"

"You know."

"Oh. We don't mention that. Why upset her if we don't have to?"

When the coffee was ready Laura poured out three cups and she and Butters returned to the living room. The show was just ending. Ed Sullivan was onstage, thanking his guests and announcing next week's performers. Laura stood for a moment watching her mother watch the screen, then she set the coffee on her mother's tray.

"Mother," she said, "Don and I have—"

"*Sh!*" Mrs. Lippman said, shooing her out of her line of sight. "I want to hear this."

Onscreen, Ed Sullivan was saying that his guests next week would include a Spanish ventriloquist and a rising young comedian. Headlining the show, he said, would be Steve Lawrence and Eydie Gorme.

"Oh, goodie," Mrs. Lippman said. "Laura, don't let me make plans."

"All right, mother." Laura had taken the wingback chair across the room and was sitting forward in it, her cup and saucer balanced on her knees. She was wearing her pleated wool skirt and a gray sweater, damp at the armpits.

When the Sullivan show at last gave way to a commercial she said, "Mother, Don and I have something to tell you—don't we, Don?"

Butters was seated on the sofa with Mrs. Lippman, the center cushion between them. "Yeah," he said.

Mrs. Lippman looked at Laura, then at Butters. She narrowed her eyes. "What is it?" she said.

"Don?" Laura said.

Butters was studying his coffee. At the sound of his name he looked up and took a deep breath. When he opened his mouth to speak he had no idea what he was going to say, but as soon as the words were out he knew they were the right ones.

"Mrs. Lippman," he said, "your daughter is pregnant."

There was a moment of silence, then Mrs. Lippman brought her hand down, very hard, on the armrest of the sofa. The sound was explosive in the small apartment.

"*I knew it!*" she said. "I knew it, I knew it, I knew it!"

She looked at Laura. "How long?" she said.

Laura was looking at Butters.

"*How long?*"

Laura looked at her mother. "Two months," she said softly.

"Who'd you see? Jack Segal?"

"Yes. Last week."

"I knew it. He won't be able to keep his mouth shut, you know. He'll tell Phyllis. God knows who *she'll* tell. *Look at me.*"

"I didn't know what else to do," Laura said, her voice barely above a whisper.

"You've got a mother, you know."

"Oh, mother."

"Well, you've broken my heart. I want you to know that. You have absolutely broken your mother's heart. And *you*," she said turning on Butters, "you've really done it up brown, haven't you, hotshot? And to think, I took you into my home."

"God," Butters said, "I feel so rotten. I can't tell you how—"

"Oh, shut up," Mrs. Lippman said. "I don't care how rotten you feel. I want to know what you're going to do about it. Look at her. She's knocked up. You couldn't keep it in your pants, and now *she's* knocked up. So tell me: what are you going to do about it?"

Butters didn't say anything.

"Don?" Laura said. "Donnie? Aren't you going to tell her what we decided?"

He looked at Laura. His eyes were round with grief. "I'm sorry, hon," he said. "I really am."

Laura began to cry. Her shoulders shook, and then her whole body, causing her cup and saucer to clatter together in her lap.

"This is going to cost you money, hotshot," Mrs. Lippman said. "You know that, don't you?"

Their first thought was abortion. Mrs. Lippman knew a man there in San Diego who agreed to do it, but after examining Laura he decided it was too risky (something about "enlarged veins"). So Tijuana was suggested; somebody knew a man there. But this time Laura balked. She didn't want any Mexican quack messing around inside her. Then Mrs. Lippman got the idea of hiring a second cousin of Laura's to marry her ("just for the name, you understand"), and she went so far as to get in touch with him—he was a dental student at Stanford—but he turned her down, even at her top price of five hundred dollars. So eventually, as the days slipped away and it became more and more apparent that Laura was going to have to have the baby, they began scouting around for an inexpensive place to send her. What they found was a sort of girls' ranch for unwed mothers over in Arizona. It was Baptist-supported and the lying-in fee was only a hundred dollars a month, meals included.

"What's it like?" Butters asked when Mrs. Lippman told him about it over the phone.

"How do *I* know?" she said. "It's clean. Jack Segal says it's clean."

"Well, that's good, isn't it?" Butters said. "That it's clean?"

"Listen," Mrs. Lippman said. "Spare me your tender solicitude. I don't have time for it. What I need from you is three hundred dollars—your half."

"*Three* hundred?"

"Three hundred. She'll be there six months, counting the postpartum."

"What's that?"

"You don't even need to know. Just get me the three hundred, okay?"

That was in April. In the meantime Butters had washed out of high-speed school and had been sent back to San Diego to await assignment overseas. He was placed in a casual company, with too little to do and too much time on his hands, and it was there that he met, one afternoon in the supply room, a skinny little buck sergeant named Hawkins who rather easily convinced him that maybe he was being had. Happened all the time, Hawkins said. Dago was that kind of town. Why, there were women there who knew a million ways to separate you from your money, and it sounded to him like Butters had fallen for one of the oldest ways of all. Then he asked Butters what his blood type was.

"O positive," Butters said. "Why?"

"Universal donor," Hawkins said. "They can't prove a thing."

The upshot was that two days later, following Hawkins' advice, Butters found himself sitting in the office of one of the two chaplains on base. This chaplain was a freckle-faced young Methodist with captain's bars on his collar and an extremely breezy manner. He tapped his front teeth with a letter opener the whole time Butters was telling his story, and when Butters was done said he thought Butters owed it to himself to ask around a bit, make some inquiries, find out what other boys Laura had been seeing.

"I mean, after all, fella," he said, "if she did it for you, why not someone else?"

And for a few days after that Butters actually considered getting in touch with the boot camp buddy who had introduced him to Laura. He knew where the boy was—up at El Toro, in the NavCad program—all he had to do was call him. In the end, though, he didn't do it. It was just too much trouble. What he did was hole up on base instead. He quit going into town and he quit taking phone calls. He developed the idea that as long as he stayed on base they couldn't touch him. And it worked for a while. He was able to pass several furtive weeks that way, sticking to a tight little universe of barracks, PX, base theater and beer garden. But then one afternoon while he and Hawkins were folding mattress covers in the supply room a runner came in and said the Catholic chaplain wanted to see him. This chaplain's office was at the far end of the grinder, half a mile away, and as he made his way up there Butters tried to occupy his mind with pleasant thoughts. He didn't bother wondering why he was being summoned, and when he entered the office and saw who was sitting there he knew he had been right not to.

"Hello, Miz Lippman," he said. "I figured it might be you."

"You quit answering your phone," she said. "So I came calling. You owe me money."

This chaplain wore tinted glasses and had a stern, no-nonsense air about him. He listened impatiently to Butters' side of the story, then he asked Butters how he, "as a Christian," viewed his responsibilities in the matter. He left little doubt how he himself viewed them.

"You *are* a Christian, aren't you, private?" he said.

"Uh, yes, sir," Butters said.

"Well, what's your obligation here then? Or don't you feel you have one?"

"I don't know, sir. I'm confused."

"Call me father. What do you mean you're 'confused'? Did you agree to pay this woman, or didn't you?"

"Yes, sir. But that was before I talked to the other chaplain."

"What's that got to do with it? Did you agree to pay her? Call me father."

"Yes, sir. Father."

"Did you have intercourse with her daughter?"

Butters blushed. "Yes, sir."

"More than once?"

"Yes, sir."

"Did her daughter get pregnant as a result?"

"Yes, sir. I guess."

"You guess?"

"I guess it was me. But it *could* have been someone else."

Mrs. Lippman bristled. "I resent that," she said. "Laura's not a tramp and you know it."

"Do you *think* it was someone else?" the chaplain said.

"She's not a tramp, father," Mrs. Lippman insisted.

"Do you, private?"

"No, sir," Butters said.

"That's what I thought," the chaplain said. "Now let's get down to business."

So once again it was agreed that Butters would pay half of Laura's lying-in expense, or fifty dollars a month for six months. But this time they drew up a little contract right there in the chaplain's office, which the chaplain's secretary typed and the three of them signed, the chaplain as witness. That night, lying in bed waiting for lights out, Butters thought back over the day's events and decided things had worked out about as well as he could expect. At least he could come out of hiding now.

Just before lights out the charge-of-quarters came in and said there was a phone call for him out in the orderly room. *Jeez*, Butters thought as he got up to follow the CQ, *what now?*

The phone was on the wall just inside the orderly room door. He picked up the dangling receiver and said, "Hello?"

"Hello—Donnie?"

"Laura? Where are you?"

"Arizona. Where do you think?"

"Well. How're you doing?"

"How'm I doing?"

"Yeah. You know: how're you doing?"

"Not too good, Donnie. Not too good."

"You crying?"

"Yeah."

He thought so. "What's the matter, hon?"

"Matter? Oh, nothing. I'm just pregnant, and unmarried, and three hundred miles from home, and scared and lonely. That's all. Nothing to get upset about, right?"

"Don't cry, Laura."

"I can't help it."

"Please?"

"I'm just so miserable, Donnie. You oughta see us. There's about thirty of us, and all we do is sit around all day in our maternity smocks *looking* at each other. Nobody hardly says a word. One of the girls is only fourteen. She sleeps with a big stuffed rabbit."

Butters felt very bad for Laura. She sounded so blue. "Aren't there any horses?" he said.

"What?"

"Horses. Aren't there any horses?"

"*Horses!* God, Donnie, you're worse than a child sometimes. What do you think this is, a dude ranch? You think we sit around a campfire at night singing 'Home on the Range'?"

Butters fingered a place on the back of his neck. "Your mother says it's pretty clean," he ventured.

"Clean?"

"That's what she said."

"When did you talk to her?"

"About that? About a month ago, I guess."

"And she said it was clean?"

"Yeah."

"What else did she say?"

"Nothing. Just that it was clean."

"I see. Well, yes, it's very clean. Spic and span. And the food's good too. We had chicken à la king tonight—my favorite."

"We had meatloaf. It tasted like cardboard."

"Poor you."

"What?"

"I said, 'Poor you.'"

"Oh."

They fell silent, and the silence began to lengthen. Through the orderly room window Butters could see the movie letting out across the grinder. Guys were coming out stretching and lighting up cigarettes.

"Listen," Laura said finally, "I'll let you go. I can tell you don't want to talk to me anyway. I just called to tell you that I've decided to go ahead and have this stupid baby. For a while there I was thinking about killing myself, but I've changed my mind. I'm gonna go through with it, Donnie. I'm gonna do it. But my life will never, ever be the same again, and I just thought you ought to know that."

Then she hung up.

Two weeks later he was on a boat bound for Okinawa.

That was in mid-May. By the time he reached Okinawa, halfway around the world, it was early June. He had made his May payment to Mrs. Lippman the day after the meeting in the chaplain's office, and he mailed her his June payment as soon as he got off the boat. The July payment he mailed her too, but late in the month. The August payment he skipped altogether. And sure enough, not long afterwards, sometime in early September, the company clerk came looking for him one afternoon in the barracks with word that the company commander wanted to see him.

"Did he say what it was about?" Butters asked.

"No," the clerk said. "He don't confide in me much. I think you better chop chop, though."

It was the same old story. The company commander, a major with a good tan, showed him a letter from Mrs. Lippman and asked him what was going on.

Butters told him.

"She claims you owe her money," the major said. "Do you?"

"Yes, sir," Butters said. He was standing at ease in front of the major's desk, looking at the letter in the major's hands. It was on blue stationery.

"How much?"

"A hundred and fifty dollars, sir."

"Well, what do you plan to do about it?"

"Pay her, sir. I guess."

"You guess?"

"Pay her, sir."

"Do you have it?"

"No, sir."

"Where do you plan to get it?"

"I don't know, sir."

"You don't *know*? You think you might just dig it up out of the *ground*, private? Pick it off a *tree*? What do you mean you don't know?"

"I don't know, sir. I guess I'll have to think of something."

"You 'guess.' You 'don't know.' It strikes me, private, that you're just not very sure about anything—are you?"

Butters didn't say anything. A phone rang somewhere.

The major shook his head. "How old are you, son?" he said.

"Nineteen, sir. I'll be twenty next month."

"I see. Well, here's what I want you to do. There's a Navy Relief office over at Camp Hague. I want you to go over there tomorrow morning and take out a loan."

"A loan, sir?"

"A loan."

"They'd *lend* it to me?"

"That's what they're there for, private."

A loan! Now why hadn't he thought of that? Getting it turned out to be remarkably easy too. Oh, he had to answer a few embarrassing questions, and there was a final interview that had him squirming for a while, but when it was all over, in less than two hours, he had a cashier's check for the full amount in his hand, with a full year to repay it and an interest rate of only three percent. He was so elated at the sight of the check that it was all he could do to keep from dancing the woman who gave it to him around the room. Rather than risk temptation he sent the entire one-fifty off to San Diego that same day by registered mail. He considered sticking a little note in with it—something like, "Bet you thought you'd never see this, didn't you?"—but thought better of it at the last minute.

And it was funny, but in the days that followed he felt like a different person. He bounced around the company area with such energy and good humor that people hardly recognized him. One morning he was first in line for chow.

"Jeez, Butters," said the boy serving him his eggs, "what's got into you? You hardly ever even *eat* breakfast."

"Just feed the troops, lad," Butters said. "Feed the troops."

But then it was October, the month the baby was due. Throughout the spring and summer and into the early days of a rainy Okinawan autumn he had done a pretty good job of shutting it out of his mind. He had simply refused to contemplate the fact that what had happened back in February in foggy San Diego was destined, ever, to result in anything so real as a baby. But as October crept in, it got harder. He found he couldn't help thinking about it some nights after lights out, couldn't help wondering, for example, whether it would be a boy or a girl. He hoped it was a boy. Being a boy was easier—girls had it rough. One night he found himself imagining it curled up in Laura's womb, its knees tucked up under its chin, its tiny fingers making tiny fists. And, lying there, he began trying to make out the baby's face. He wanted to know who it looked like, but, try as he might, he couldn't tell. Later that night he dreamed he was swimming underwater somewhere, deep down, and that floating in the water all around him were these large jellyfish, each of which, on closer inspection, appeared to have a baby inside. He couldn't make out these babies' faces either.

But October passed and nothing happened. At least not in his world. Nobody contacted him, by phone or mail or otherwise. Nobody got in touch. And as the days went by and still he heard nothing, slowly he began to believe that maybe it was all over with now, that what had happened was finally history and he could go about his daily business just like everyone else.

He had made friends by then with a boy named Tipton, from Kansas, and the two of them had begun spending their weekends in a tin-roofed shanty outside Chibana with a pair of sisters who worked in a Chibana bar.

One Saturday morning Butters was sitting out on the back steps of the shanty, watching one of the sisters hang laundry in the yard, when Tipton arrived from the base by taxi, bearing beer and groceries and a letter for him.

Butters took the letter and looked at it. There were several cancellations on the envelope, indicating it had been re-routed more than once. He opened it up and took out a single folded sheet of paper. It read:

Dear Don,

The baby is due any day now, they tell me. You should see me. I'm huge. You probably wouldn't even recognize me. I think the baby is a "he." It sure kicks like one anyway. It even keeps me awake some nights with its kicking and rolling around alot.

The nurses say I don't have to see it if I don't want to. They say it's entirely up to me. Sometimes I think I want to and sometimes I think I don't. Silly me, huh? Guess I had better make up my mind pretty soon, though, and quit all this procastinating (sp?).

Don, since I know now I am never going to see you again I guess this will have to be goodbye. I'm not bitter anymore. I was for awhile, I admit, but I'm not now. And I'm still glad I knew you. I just wish things could have turned out better, that's all.

Best always,
Laura

P.S. You owe me $5. (See clipping)

Butters looked inside the envelope again and saw a small folded piece of paper he had missed before. He took it out and unfolded it. It was a photograph clipped from a magazine—*Time* or *Newsweek*, it looked like—and it showed Elizabeth Taylor and Eddie Fisher during their recent wedding ceremony in Beverly Hills. They were standing before a robed man with a dark beard. Both Fisher and the robed man had small black caps perched on the backs of their heads. An arrow had been drawn, in red ink, pointing to the cap on Fisher's head, and along its shaft had been printed, in big block letters, also red, the initials "M.O.T."

Butters sat looking at the clipping for a while. Then he put it and the letter back in the envelope, folded the envelope in half, and stuffed it in his back pocket.

"Your mom?" Tipton said.

"Huh?"

"The letter. Is it from your mom?"

"No. A girl I knew."

"Oh," Tipton said. "You want a beer?"

The legal papers didn't arrive until the first week in December. They were from the office of the county clerk of Maricopa County, Arizona, and they consisted of a form letter, a release document, and an enclosed envelope for which no postage was necessary.

They came on a Friday, as Butters and Tipton were preparing to leave for town.

Butters read the form letter first, sitting on his bunk in his civvies. The letter was very short, just two paragraphs. The first paragraph said that a child had been born on such-and-such a date in the public maternity ward of such-and-such a hospital in Phoenix, Arizona, and that, according to the attending physician, it was free of physical and mental defects. The second paragraph merely asked him to read and then sign the accompanying release. The child was identified, the words typed into a blank space in the middle of the first paragraph, as "Baby Boy Butters, 7 lbs, 6 oz."

When he was finished with the letter Butters set it carefully beside him on the bunk and picked up the release. It was short too, just a single legal-sized page. It asked him to understand what he was doing—waiving all rights and responsibilities in the care and upbringing of the child—and it cited the pertinent sections of Arizona law, which took up most of the rest of the page. Toward the bottom, however, there was a dotted line that caught Butters' eye. He skipped over much of the legal language, but he lingered at the dotted line. "Signature of Natural Father," it was labeled. He looked at it. That was him. He was the natural father. He turned the page over to see if there was anything on the back. There wasn't. It was blank. He turned it back over and looked at the dotted line. Tipton was standing just a few feet away from him, waiting. They had already called their taxi. It was on the way.

He looked up at Tipton. "You got a pen?" he said.

PHILIP LEVINE

Philip Levine was born in Detroit
in 1928. His twelve books include
The Names of the Lost, which won
the Lenore Marshall Prize, *Ashes*,
which won the American Book
Award and the National Book Crit-
ics Circle Award, *Selected Poems*,
and *A Walk with Tom Jefferson*.
He teaches at California State Uni-
versity in Fresno.

NORTH

An empty state train bouncing
on tight track, the rain
streaming the windows.
An old woman, smaller
than a boy of ten, taps
my shoulder and points to
a green clearing bordered
by white fence posts. "Look!"
she commands, "A deer park!"
Her broad hand weighted

with diamonds on each finger.
Seeing I see them, her
tiny wet eyes contract,
and she leans back, squeezing
her black cane's dark head.
She and I are going north. I
for the first time, to find
the ancient coast my fathers
never sailed from. She
perhaps going home or there
already in her dreams, for
now she's sleeping, her head
tilted back, her mouth wide
and gurgling. The train
stops at Humlebaek, and I
step out into the washed air
alone, and take the first road
to the left past a tower
collapsing into a pile
of stones. At last the sun
breaks through, gilding brambles
and wild rose bushes along
the way, which is now only
a footpath. I hear the sea
breaking beyond these woods
of small bent oaks, and then
the trees and bushes give way,
and I descend the little crest
to where it pools on the gray
sand and stones. A northern sea
heaping up huge slow waves
all the way to the sky.
Nothing comes back to me
except the freezing sea spray
and my own voice breaking
on the words, *Farewell, Goodbye,
So Long*, the ones that work.

LARRY LEVIS

Larry Levis is the author of
Wrecking Crew, The Afterlife,
which won the Lamont Prize, *The
Dollmaker's Ghost*, which won the
National Poetry Series Open Com-
petition, and *Winter Stars*. He
was *Crazyhorse's* West Coast Po-
etry Editor in the early seventies.
Born in Fresno, California, in
1946, he teaches at the University
of Utah.

FOR THE COUNTRY

1

One of them undid your blouse, then
used a pocketknife to
cut away your skirt
like he'd take
fur off some limp thing,
or slice up the belly of a fish.

Pools of rainwater shone in the sunlight,
and they took turns.

2

After it was over,
you stared up, maybe,
at the blue sky where the shingles were missing,
the only sounds
pigeons
walking the rafters, their eyes fixed, shining,
the sound of water dripping.
The idiot drool of the cattle. Flies.

3

You are the sweet, pregnant,
teen-age blonde thrown from the speeding car.

You are a dead, clean-shaven astronaut
orbiting perfectly forever.

You are America.
You are nobody.
I made you up.
I take pills and drive a flammable truck
until I drop.

I am the nicest guy in the world,
closing his switchblade and whistling.

4

The plum blossoms have
been driven into a silence all
their own,
as I go on
driving an old red tractor
with a busted seat.
The teeth of its gears
chatter in the faint language
of mad farmwives who have whittled,
and sung tunelessly,
over the dog turds in their front yards,
for the last hundred years.

5

And I will say nothing, anymore, of
my country,
nor of my wife reading about abortions,
nor of the birds that
have circled high over my
head, following me,
for days.

I will close my eyes,
and grit my teeth,
and slump down further in
my chair,
and watch what goes on
behind my eyelids:
stare at the dead horses with flowers stuck in
their mouths—

and that is the end of it.

THE BLUE HATBAND

Sometimes, even in the middle of a conversation
In a bar, even at noon, I turn away.
I stare out at a single brick in a wall,
And a woman without a mouth begins to speak.

I listen, but it is like listening to paper
When a bird walks over it: someone scrapes
Against that brick in a speech that is not human—
And, hearing it, I forget which names I love.

My friends and what I said today mean less
Than a pale blue hatband on a man climbing,
Slowly, the stairs of a building in 1930 . . .
That man arrested Anna Akhmatova's only son.

If she was silenced later, and if she stood
In lines with packages outside each prison,
I hope her anger will become a hollow place
In an elm where lovers hide notes, the snows come,

And the parks are full of skaters. But I think
That Anna Akhmatova has not slept for years,
And now she is awake beyond music, beyond shoes
That button up the sides of each thin ankle,

Beyond her face that lacks teeth, eyes, a mouth—
A face that can stare back, even now, in Ohio,
Until I doze on this train, and let the fields pass,
Their weeds the vague, gray flags of childhood.

❖

But while I sleep I dream St. Petersburg
Out of each book, and they start shooting students
In Ohio, again. Her hair, in each jail, grows whiter.
And when I wake, I have no right to speak.

❖

Anna Akhmatova, watching blood cover the lips
Of horses, remembered her son's skin as snow,
Sky, the shattered porcelain on a roadside—
As the white skins of swans drying over her head,

Once, in a market. Even now, when the dead wake
Inside her blood, she approaches that butcher,
She raises a finger to haggle over such meat,
She stares straight at him, then turns to air.

But the butcher looks up, into his unlit, empty shop.

GARY MARGOLIS

Gary Margolis is the director of
the Center for Counseling and
Human Relations at Middlebury
College. Born in Great Falls,
Montana, in 1945, he has pub-
lished two volumes of poetry, *The
Day We Still Stand Here* and *Fall-
ing Awake*.

BETWEEN US

All I have is these words
   and someone else's story
of Frost talking to his son
   all night, the night before

their words ran out of time.
   I have enough trouble wondering
what it is the world needs to hear,
   let alone if that world was

my son sitting across from me
    tonight. It could be. Already
I have heard him hold his death
    in his own hands, sitting in

front of his loud computer game,
    which he says lets him kill
himself, to push the advancing
    video tanks behind the screen's

blank life. I want to take these
    words out of his mouth, his mind,
and yet I know that is where
    they must live. I can't really

imagine what Frost said and didn't
    say. I've been told he used
to stay up all night naming the stars
    for anyone who couldn't go

to bed either. First I tried to
    say things to get my son between
his covers. Now he does that
    by himself. It's staying in this

world I don't have the words for.
    He will find how the stars, beyond
their facts, stay where they are
    and hold the space between us.

BOBBIE ANN MASON

Bobbie Ann Mason is the author
of two novels, *In Country* and
Spence + Lila, and two story col-
lections, *Shiloh and Other Stories*,
which won the PEN/Hemingway
Award, and *Love Life*. "Murphey's
Pond" was selected for the PEN
Syndicated Fiction Project in
1987. She was born in Mayfield,
Kentucky, in 1940 and now lives in
rural Pennsylvania.

MURPHEY'S POND

Years ago, in high school, Ken Matlock often joked with a girl named
Debbie Watson about going to Murphey's Pond. It was a dare between
them. They were chemistry lab partners—buddies, never sweethearts.
Ken had imagined that if he had gone with her there, she would have
loved him. But they never went. They weren't sure how to find it, and
people got lost there, returning with tales about the snakes they had seen.
It was even said that boa constrictors and alligators were there. Now the
university has built a boardwalk out onto the swamp and graveled a road
leading to it. And at last Ken is going with Debbie to Murphey's Pond.

It has been ten years since they saw each other, and both have been divorced. Ken ran into Debbie at the K-Mart. He was buying a tube of caulking and she was buying flashlight batteries. She was home from Lexington, visiting her parents. She had on a wool cap with reindeer on it. Her cowboy boots made her taller, and she was better-looking than Ken remembered. They had hardly exchanged greetings when she said, mischievously, looking him straight in the eye, "I dare you to go with me to Murphey's Pond."

"That snaky swamp?" he said, grinning. It was strange that he had put Murphey's Pond out of his mind, though he had often thought of Debbie. He had imagined her in other settings. He thought of her on a beach, running in the sand.

She laughed at him. "Don't be silly. The snakes are hibernating this time of year."

She explained that she had returned to school. She was getting a master's degree in wildlife biology at the University of Kentucky. It was a relief to be divorced, she said. "Thank goodness I didn't have any kids."

"I've got two little girls," Ken said. "They live with my ex-wife and her husband in Paducah, but I get to see them."

"What are their names?"

"Shayla and Christi. Six and four."

"Those are cute names." Debbie paid for her flashlight batteries and put the change in her jacket pocket. Then she said, laughing, "I like that hair, Ken."

Ken had a permanent in his hair. Although everyone seemed to like it, he suddenly knew when Debbie commented on it that it was entirely wrong. He felt ashamed. After they had made arrangements to go to Murphey's Pond, Ken went to his car and sat there for a moment, his face burning. He peered in the rear-view mirror and saw how silly his hair looked. On the radio, someone was singing a dumb song about radioactivity. Ken shifted gears and shot out of the parking lot, as though he were late for something.

In high school, Debbie was a cheerleader and an A student. She went steady with a linebacker named Chuck, and she always wore his gold-and-blue letter sweater. Ken worked after school in a grocery store and drove a junky Chevy. Debbie rode in it once. She was always leading him on, teasing him, and she begged him for a ride home from the grocery store. He almost stripped the gears at a traffic light. In chemistry lab, Debbie sometimes gave him her homework, saving him from failing the course. When she sneaked him her notes once during a test, he was so impressed by her boldness that he felt there was a possibility for something to develop between them. But it never did, even after she broke up with Chuck. After she went away to college, Ken went to work for his father, building houses, and later he married Betty Stairs, a quiet, conventional girl who belonged to a homemakers' club, taught a Sunday School class, and held down a full-time job at the telephone company. But Betty shocked him by running off to Cairo, Illinois, with a cemetery plot salesman. In a way, Ken was glad. It saved him from asking any serious questions about his marriage, which he realized later was pointless, if there was supposed to be a point to marriage, other than children. From time to time while he was with Betty, the memory of Debbie surfaced in the middle of the night, the way a realization that one is going to die someday will sometimes strike at odd moments. He realized Debbie was a central fact of his life. But he would not have been at all surprised if she had not recognized him that day in the K-Mart.

Debbie's mother Erlene is their guide to Murphey's Pond. She drives them there in her husband's pickup truck on a sunny, cold afternoon. Erlene, a farm woman, is fat and unpretentious, with a hearty laugh like Debbie's. For several miles, she talks about snakes. She tells a story about a man who had been bitten by a snake at Murphey's Pond. When his friend returned with help, they could not find the man at first. He was so covered with mosquitoes that he was camouflaged, appearing to be a log.

"But the mosquitoes drawed out the poison," Erlene says. "They saved his life." She downshifts as they turn onto a dirt road. "Snakes are the most dangerous in the spring, when the fish start sponding."

"She means spawning," Debbie says to Ken, who is sitting on the narrow seat behind her. Debbie pats her mother's shoulder affectionately, but Ken is disappointed that she is along. He admires the truck, a Dodge Ram Charger with a topper. His head bumps against a Remington 12-gauge shotgun on a gun rack behind him. It occurs to him that he has not been hunting in more than six years.

"Cottonmouths will come right after you," says Erlene. "I had one come out on a log at me when I was fishing. They crawl *at* you." She makes a curvy, swimming gesture with her arm. "They just keep a-coming.

In the spring, about the time the grass is up, that's when you have to watch out for them."

"I don't guess we have to worry about that today," says Ken.

It is a bright, cold day, well below freezing. The sky is blue and clear. Ken should have dressed more warmly. Debbie is wearing her reindeer cap pulled down over her ears. Her hair falls around her face the way Sissy Spacek's hair did in *Coal Miner's Daughter.*

On the way, Debbie tells him about the old house in Lexington she is renovating. "It's so neat," she says. "It has this old brickwork in the kitchen that I exposed, two stone fireplaces, and a lot of good oak paneling in the dining room. It's a terrific house."

"It's a awful big house to keep up," says Erlene.

"I like it. I feel comfortable there."

"She's got a living room you could roller-skate in," says Erlene.

When Debbie says she had siding put on the house last summer, Ken demands to know all the details—what kind, the price, the installation. He has a siding business now.

"Damn," he says. "I wish I'd known. I could have saved you a lot of money. I could have given it to you at cost."

"Well, it wasn't aluminum siding," says Debbie. "It was Masonite."

"You have to paint Masonite. I could have gotten you vinyl steel. That's big now. We're doing more of that than aluminum."

"Well, I didn't know."

"I could have saved you a hundred dollars, I bet."

"Too late now!" she says. She tugs at her cap and looks out the window.

After driving up a bumpy dirt road, Erlene finally jolts to a stop in a graveled clearing. She opens the door and as she gets out of the truck, she yells, "Oh, not another one!" Debbie scoots behind the wheel and helps her mother step down to the ground.

"She has a charley-horse in her leg," Debbie explains to Ken.

"You're not supposed to rub a charley-horse," says Erlene, grimacing with pain. "But you can pat it." She touches her calf and tries slowly to stretch out her leg.

"Why can't you rub it?" asks Ken.

"You might work a blood clot loose, and it would go to your brain."

After Erlene's charley-horse subsides, they walk down a path to the pond. Trees and small islands are scattered throughout the water, giving the impression that the pond is shallow. The surface is rough. It has frozen, thawed and refrozen, and hunks of ice stick up from below. The weeds and dried stalks embedded in the ice are like the objects Ken's wife had on the coffee table—flowers and seeds captured in clear plastic. Ken's leather shoes crunch on the bog. Then he steps in some mud.

"Look how the sun's shining," says Erlene. "It's liable to draw snakes out."

"If you see a snake, it'll be so sluggish, you could probably pet it on the head." Debbie points to a yellow, diamond-shaped sign that has had its lettering obliterated by bullet holes. "That sign probably said 'No hunting,'" she says sarcastically.

She skips out onto the boardwalk, which makes a roughly drawn semicircle out over the edge of the swamp. Ken takes Erlene's elbow when he sees her hesitate. She smiles at him, and they walk out behind Debbie. It occurs to Ken that in the summertime the long leafy arms of the cypress trees will be stretching in a canopy over the boardwalk.

"Everybody said I was crazy to come here," Ken says with an awkward laugh. He is thinking of snakes dropping from the cypress limbs.

"I wish we could see a Great Blue Heron," says Debbie, leaning over the railing. "It's an incredible sight. It's a deep, dusky blue all over and it looks like a stork."

"That would be something," Ken agrees. He imagines a giant blue bird carrying a baby.

"They're white when they're young and turn blue when they mature. The young ones are sometimes confused with egrets."

"Where'd you learn so much?"

She shrugs and walks away. Ken sees a bird in a tree.

"There's a blue bird over there," he says, pointing.

"That's just a bluejay."

The jay squawks, flaps its wings, and flies to another tree.

Erlene shivers and tightens her thin headscarf. Leaning against the railing, she says, "That time the snake chased me, Patricia Williams was with me, and she just stood there. I asked her later, 'Why didn't you help me?' and she said, 'I couldn't. I just froze.' That snake was after this bullfrog. The bullfrog came jumping along, and after it this big snake humping along like this—it had these humps in it like the Loch Ness Monster? That thing was six or seven feet long and as big around as both fists. Patricia got in the car, but I was afraid to get in because the snake was on my side. Then it crawled under the car."

"Why didn't Patricia drive the car away?" Debbie asks.

"Oh, she can't drive. She sat in the car, and I walked down to a house and got some men to drive the car away for us. Then we tore the car apart to see if the snake had got in through a hole or something."

Ken thinks of a snake story of his own to tell. He tells about two guys he heard of who were fishing in the swamp in a boat when a snake fell out of a tree into the boat. "One of them grabbed his shotgun and blasted out the bottom of the boat trying to get at that snake!" Ken cries, laughing. "And then they sat there and looked at one another while they sank!"

Erlene laughs appreciatively, but Debbie seems to be studying a patch of bark on a tree. She breaks off a piece and studies it.

"Let me take your picture," says Erlene. She has brought a camera.

She poses Debbie and Ken on the boardwalk. They lean against the railing, side by side, not touching. Some of the railing has fallen down, and parts of the walk are broken, the wood splintered. Ken has been imagining men in hipboots building the boardwalk, sinking four-by-sixes into the snaky swamp. Beside him, Debbie shifts position. Her arm brushes his.

The picture pops out of Erlene's camera, and in sixty seconds a solemn, pasty-faced couple appears, frozen against the railing. The icy pond is a gray blur behind them. Debbie looks at the picture for a moment, laughs, then hands it to her mother. Erlene pockets the picture.

Debbie has ducked under the railing, and she is walking on the ice. Both Ken and Erlene cry out warnings, but Debbie stomps the heel of her boot on the ice. "Look how thick it is. Don't worry."

"I see cracks," says Erlene.

"I wish we could go skating," says Debbie. She slides in her cowboy boots to a cypress tree. The tree has knobs protruding around its base, like knuckles sticking up through the ice. Ken thinks of the tree as a gigantic arm from outer space, its hand clutching something horrible under the water, and its knuckles emerging raw and bleached.

"This place is great," says Debbie, sliding a little. "Murphey's Pond is one of the most unspoiled places around, and it's got a greater variety of reptiles and amphibians than just about anywhere in Kentucky. I want to camp out here in the spring. I'm doing a paper on a certain turtle, and I'd love to collect the data here."

"You could study study alligators," says Ken. "I've heard there are alligators here."

"There couldn't be alligators here. That's ridiculous."

"That story about the alligator is true," Erlene says matter-of-factly. "But I bet it was one of those baby ones from Florida that people buy and then let loose. But if there was hot springs down under the pond, alligators could live here." She shivers. "I'm freezing."

"I wish I had worn a hat," says Ken.

Debbie slides back to the walk and ducks under the railing. "I told you I liked your hair," she says, smiling.

Debbie and Ken are walking alone together, down the woods trail, while Erlene waits in the pickup with the heater on. The trail is barely visible through the thicket. It zigzags through a patch of cypress knobs, roots extending through the swamp.

"They look like little tombstones," he says.

"No, little sea creatures," she says. "Like something I saw once in a surrealist painting."

She kicks at a log and stoops to study the dirt beneath it. Ken thinks of the snakes hiding in the logs, or in their burrows, or wherever they hibernate. He says, awkwardly, "Well, we finally made it to Murphey's Pond."

She laughs and walks ahead of him.

"Are you really studying turtles?" he asks when he catches up with her. "I saw big sea turtles on a special once. Those things grow as big as the side of a barn."

She nods. "Those sea turtles are endangered. Did you know they weep when they lay their eggs?"

"It must be an awful big effort."

"It must hurt like hell." She rolls over another small log. She says, "And they sleep in the bottom of the sea, for hours, without breathing. But when they swim, they have to come up for air."

"I think they said that on that TV show, but it's hard to remember. I can't remember things like that. Why is that?"

She walks on, then stops at a cypress tree and looks hard at him. "So how is your life, Ken? How did you turn out?"

He shrugs. "Okay. I've got a nice house—down near Lone Oak. On weekends I take my little girls to my mother's and get some home cooking, but most of the time I eat out. The business is good. It pays the bills." He laughs nervously. "Nowadays, that's saying something."

"Still playing golf?"

"Uh-huh. I played in the Boots Randolph Open last year."

She is still scrutinizing him. She is seeing an overweight guy with inappropriate shoes and a permanent. He knows how this is going to end. He is going to say, "Well, if you ever need any siding, look me up." And she will say, "Sure. Call me if you ever get to Lexington." That simple and that flat.

"I could have moved out of this area, the way you did," he says apologetically. "But it's what I know." His shoe scrapes a cypress knob. "And what about you?" he asks. "How's it going for you?"

Hesitating a moment, she says then, "I've made a lot of mistakes." She bends her knee and rests her foot behind her on a tree. She says, "But I guess I learned something about myself through it all, though."

"Don't we all. That's life."

"I married this guy and dropped out of college, which I should never have done."

"You were too young," Ken says. "So was I."

"I had a rotten marriage. He was a beast. He used to *beat* me."

At Ken's intake of breath, she says, "Oh, I know that sounds melodramatic. I didn't end up in the hospital or anything. The horrible part is that I was somehow brainwashed into thinking it was funny. For the longest time, I really believed that when we had these fights we were just playing. That's the way it would start out, a friendly tussle, but then I'd get bruises all over from his fists. And then later I would tell a friend or somebody, 'You just don't know how hilarious it was, us going at each other like cats.' I mean, can you *believe* I could have been so stupid? Me, the big brain in chemistry class?"

"I can't even imagine that happening to you," says Ken. "It makes me mad! I'd like to whip that guy."

"But I let it happen. That's what's so scary." She lowers her foot and puts her fists into her jeans pockets. "Somehow I always confused cruelty and humor. That's why it embarrasses me to see you. I was always like that with you, making a big joke out of everything. I know I mistreated you. I feel I should apologize."

She leads the way down the trail again. She says, "If he ever laid a hand on me again, I'd sue him for all he's got."

"If he lived that long," says Ken, following her. "He wouldn't if I heard about it."

"If I come back to western Kentucky in the spring, would you come with me to the pond?" she asks without looking at him.

Ken can't tell if she is teasing. He says, "Sure. You mean when the snakes are falling out of the trees?"

His heart is racing; his excitement is like the feeling of being jarred awake by a telephone call in the night. The dare is still on. With everything frozen now, nothing counts. Everything is too safe—the boardwalk, the leafless trees, the ice. The real question is whether they can come here in the spring, when the grass is up.

They are losing the trail, and she suggests turning back. They are both shivering. The pond is somewhere beyond the trees, out of sight. The trail is hard to find, because of the carpet of brown cypress needles, and as they retrace their steps, Ken imagines getting lost with Debbie. He is pursuing her through the twisting paths in the frozen swamp. They stop and wait, perhaps build a fire, send smoke signals to Erlene. Ken can see why it makes sense to slow down, to wait, like the water creatures sleeping, until it is time to come up for air.

WILLIAM MATTHEWS

A professor at the City College of
New York, William Matthews was
born in Cincinnati in 1942. His ten
books include the poetry collec-
tions *A Happy Childhood*, *Fore
seeable Futures* and *Blues If You
Want* and a collection of essays,
Curiosities.

*DRIVING ALONGSIDE
THE HOUSATONIC RIVER
ALONE ON A RAINY APRIL NIGHT*

I remember asking
where does my shadow go at night?
I thought it went home,
it grew so sleek at dusk.
They said, you just don't
notice it, the way you don't tell yourself
how to walk or hear
a noise that doesn't stop.

But one wrong wobble
in the socket and inside the knee
chalk is falling, school
is over.
As if the ground were a rung
suddenly gone from a ladder,
the self, the shoulders bunched
against the road's each bump, the penis
with its stupid grin,
the whole rank slum of cells
collapses.
I feel the steering wheel
tug a little, testing.
For as long as that takes
the car is a sack of kittens
weighed down by stones.
The headlights chase a dark ripple
across some birch trunks.
I know it's there, water
hurrying over the shadow of water.

KINGSTON

No photograph does justice, etc.,
but what does a photograph care
for justice? It wants to be clear,
the way an angel need not mean,
but be, duty enough for an angel.

No angels here. Hovels seen from far
enough away they look picturesque.
The blatant blue sky so cool in pictures
is gritty with heat. The long day stings.
We squint at the lens. Though the lines

in our faces are engraved by the acids
of muscle-habits, not by tears.
Sympathy we have to learn. Here's
a family of three living in a dead car.
The guidebooks warned us away

from this, and so we came,
ungainly, spreading
our understandings of sorrow like wet wings.
We turn and turn, but everywhere is here,
a blurred circle of wingscuffs.

AN ELEGY FOR BOB MARLEY

In an elegy for a musician,
one talks a lot about music,
which is a way to think about time
instead of death or Marley,

and isn't poetry itself about time?
But death is about death and not time.
Surely the real fuel for elegy
is anger to be mortal.

No wonder Marley sang so often
of an ever-arriving future, that verb tense
invented by religion and political rage.
Soon come. Readiness is all,

and not enough. From the urinous
dust and sodden torpor
of Trenchtown, from the fruitpeels
and imprecations, from cunning,

from truculence, from the luck
to be alive, however cruelly,
Marley made a brave music—
a rebel music, he called it,

though music calls us together,
however briefly—and a fortune.
One is supposed to praise the dead
in elegies for leaving us their songs,

though they had no choice; nor could
the dead bury the dead if we could pay
them to. This is something else we can't
control, another loss, which is, as someone

said in hope of consolation,
only temporary, though the same phrase
could be used of our lives and bodies
and all that we hope survives them.

THOMAS MCGRATH

Thomas McGrath, the founder and
first editor of *Crazyhorse*, was
born on a farm in North Dakota in
1916. A Rhodes scholar, he
worked as a scriptwriter until he
was blacklisted for his political
convictions in the 1950's. His
many books include *Letter to an
Imaginary Friend, Passages to-
ward the Dark, Echoes inside the
Labyrinth*, and, most recently, *Se-
lected Poems, 1938–1988*, which
won the Lenore Marshall Prize.

PROLETARIAN IN ABSTRACT LIGHT

Now on the great stage a silence falls.
In the long shudder toward collapse and birth,
There enters, singing, the muffled shape of a future.
He has no face; his hands are bloody;
He is for himself; he is not to please you.

You have stolen my labor
You have stolen my name
You have stolen my mystery
You have stolen the moon

The coldness of song goes on in his barbarous tongue.
The hours condense like snow. The marble weight
Of his dream, like a heavy cloud, leans on your glass houses.
Expropriated of time, he begins himself in *his* name;
He stamps his null on your day; the future collapses toward him:

I do not want your clocks
I do not want your God
I do not want your statues
I do not want your love

GONE AWAY BLUES

Sirs, when you are in your last extremity,
When your admirals are drowning in the grass-green sea,
When your generals are preparing the total catastrophe—
I just want you to know how you can *not* count on me.

    I have ridden to hounds through my ancestral hall,
    I have picked the eternal crocus on the ultimate hill,
    I have fallen through the window of the highest room,
    But don't ask me to help you 'cause I never will.

Sirs, when you move that map-pin how many souls must dance?
I don't think all those soldiers have died by happenstance.
The inscrutable look on your scrutable face I can read at a glance—
And I'm cutting out of here at the first chance.

    I have been wounded climbing the second stair,
    I have crossed the ocean in the hull of a live wire,
    I have eaten the asphodel of the dark side of the moon,
    But you can call me all day and I just won't hear.

O patriotic mister with your big ear to the ground,
Sweet old curly scientist wiring the birds for sound,
O lady with the Steuben glass heart and your heels so rich and round—
I'll send you a picture postcard from somewhere I can't be found.

    I have discovered the grammar of the Public Good,
    I have invented a language that *can* be understood,
    I have found the map of where the body is hid,
    And I won't be caught dead in *your* neighborhood.

O hygienic inventor of the bomb that's so clean,
O lily white Senator from East Turnip Green,
O celestial mechanic of the money machine—
I'm going someplace where *nobody* makes your scene.

Thomas McGrath   321

Good-by, good-by, good-by,
Adios, Au 'voir, so long,
Sayonara, Dosvedanya, ciao,
By-by, by-by, by-by.

SANDRA MCPHERSON

Born in 1943 in San Jose, Califor-
nia, Sandra McPherson directs the
creative writing program at the
University of California at Davis.
Her five collections include *The
Year of Our Birth*, *Patron Hap-
piness*, and *Streamers*.

PICKETING OUR ANTI-CHOICE SENATOR AT REED COLLEGE, SEPTEMBER 1982

Our organizers hiss
A raised hope of helium.
I tie off balloons

Until my hands dye rose.
Some slip away,
Escalate through the arms

Of a cold silver fir.
Our feet sound wet
By the time sun comes out. It all

Makes the Senator, too,
Come out
To talk with us.

We hold up our stakes,
The backward
Coathangers.

Staying in procession, crossing
The picketline,
Passing

In his long lurid robe and mortarboard:
My priestly old
Married lover,

Who wouldn't have wanted my child.

DAVID MURA

David Mura's book of poems,
After We Lost Our Way, was a Na-
tional Poetry Series selection. He
is also the author of two works of
nonfiction, *A Male Grief: Notes on
Pornography and Addiction* and
Turning Japanese. He was born in
1952 in Great Lakes, Illinois, and
now lives in Minneapolis.

THE EMERGENCY ROOM

Note. Stab. *(long a) is short for* stabilization

You were just a med student then,
and as evenings grew dark and scattered with stars,
you'd return from the County coiled tight, straight
from the trenches, drugged by the lack of sleep:
"At ten a stab. case came in. The woman was moaning
(she'd been found behind the 7-Eleven).
David, half of her skull had been crushed in,
her whole left side paralyzed. She
was naked from the waist down . . .
No, they didn't catch him. And no one knows
who she is. I just hope she wasn't conscious.

They thrust tubes down her throat, her nose,
IV's in her body, and left her stripped, exposed
on the table, while the doctors and nurses gathered
their instruments. It was like another assault.
I sat there and wrote it down, instrument by
instrument, procedure by procedure, cut by cut
. . . Now? If she's lucky, she won't wake up . . ."

Later, down in Arkansas, they picked him up,
brought him back for trial. Barely
literate, a black ex-con. On TV, in a brief clip,
his face looked hollowed, haggard, his teeth
gapped and twisted, his eyes dead. It was as if
he'd become a thing like stones or dust,
sand or salt, his soul a net full of shadows.
I felt unnerved, fatuous, somehow responsible . . .

And the victim? Beneath the covers, shivering
almost unconsciously, you left her for another,
her story spilling out—
                    "That wasn't all. At two
a woman came in with her blouse torn open,
her skirt in shreds. She was in shock.
Gradually I got her story out: From the age
of before she could remember, she had been raped
by her father. David, I couldn't believe it:
She was thirty-four . . . Finally, she moved
across the river, came to the city only for therapy.
This time her father was waiting. He chased her down 94,
forced her to the side of the road and walked her
into the woods and tied her to a tree . . ."

Silence. You sat up, pulled your knees to your chest.
Asked for water.
                    "He tried again and again. He kept
holding his limp penis, pressing it against her.
In rage, he began to stuff mud up her vagina,
at the same time, whipping her thighs with a pine branch.

This went on from late afternoon to long after sunset . . .
After she finished, I didn't know what to say. I just cried.
She, she seemed startled. Relieved . . ."

Susan, what can I say? Some part of me
knows that man? What *do* I know? Even then
I knew I'd never comprehend how the rapist,
the incestuous father, his almost inhuman rage,
that could crush so endlessly his will to love,
enters, like a messenger, a woman's existence.
And yet—God, is this why I'm telling this?—
I felt jealous. You had witnessed these stories . . .

It's years later. A friend tells me of writing on the Holocaust,
spending night after night in the office of Himmler,
in visions of ash and the crystals of gas: how the desire arose
to rub each entrenched, lime-drenched body against the reader's
psyche and skin. And then on a trip to Dachau,
she was there, shaking, holding her palm to the brick
of the ovens, feeling the weight of those voices, those faces,
those spirits push against her, enfold her, a presence
as palpable as a violent wind; and yet it was only when
she walked through those gates—"Work Sets You Free"—emblazoned
    above,
and walked down the hill to a small sapling,
surrounded by pink, blushing petunias, only then
was she able to sit and rest and let it out,
the only answer annealed to that earthly beauty—
"I knew that I couldn't write it with just Himmler, the camps,
the corpses, there had to be more, these moments of release"—
a clarity of tears, sunlight; the aimless, unfolding
hills; a sapling, petunias, bending in the breeze.

LISTENING

And from that village, steaming with mist, riddled with rain,
from the fishermen in the bay hauling up nets of silver flecks;
from the droning of the Buddhist priest in the morning,

incense thickening his voice, a bit other-wordly, almost sickly;
from the oysters ripped from the sea bottom by half-naked women,
their skin darker than the bark in the woods, their lungs

as endless as some cave where a demon dwells
(soon their harvest will be split open by a blade, moist
meaty flesh, drenched in the smell of sea bracken, the tidal winds);

from the *torrii* halfway up the mountain
and the steps to the temple where the gong shimmers
with echoes of bright metallic sound;

from the waterfall streaming, hovering in the eye, and in illusion,
rising; from the cedars that have nothing to do with time;
from the small mud-cramped streets of rice shops and fishmongers;

from the pebbles on the riverbed, the aquamarine stream
floating pine-trunks, felled upstream
by men with *hamachi* tied round their foreheads

and grunts of *o-sha* I remember from my father in childhood;
from this mythical land of the empty sign and a thousand-thousand
     manners,
on the tip of this peninsula, far from Kyoto, the Shogun's palace,

in a house of *shoji* and clean cut pine, crawling onto a straw futon,
one of my ancestors laid his head as I do now on a woman's belly
and felt an imperceptible bump like the bow of a boat hitting a swell

and wondered how anything so tiny could cause such rocking
     unbroken joy.

328   *David Mura*

JACK MYERS

Jack Myers is the author of four
books of poems, including *The
Family War*, which won the
Elliston Book Award, and *As Long
as You're Happy*, which was a se-
lection in the National Poetry Se-
ries. He was born in Lynn,
Massachusetts, in 1941 and
teaches at Southern Methodist
University.

THE ENERGY IT TAKES TO PASS THROUGH SOLID OBJECTS

for my son, Jacob

My son with food on his face
is banging on his highchair like a prisoner
who lost the ability to speak.

He would like to grab the cat
who has slipped by like the fieldmouse
fleeing her mind. His demands rise and disperse
like night off the skull of morning.

Last night we let him sleep between us
and he thrashed around wrestling sorrows
his own size. Then he sat up quietly

in the dark like a miniature alien,
my own exposed heart, calmly weighing
the critical mass of stillness between us.

My son with food on his face,
food oozing through his fists,
screams his life is like no other.
He is being pulled straight out of his seat
by the long black fur of his imagination
and all I can do, he screams, is nothing.

I try to remember but I can't sing
the song my mother sang to me
which made a solid object out of feeling.
I open my mouth and with the energy it takes
to pass through solid objects, I arrive
silently at that place from which all feeling comes.

It will take a long time to make him civil
before he can unstrap himself from the raucous
taste of peas, the wheels of orange carrots
and leave this house. He will have to loop
on wider and wider journeys, joining his circle
to ours, until the food he orders is exotic,
and inside the elusive feel of soft black fur
is the woman he will marry and the raggle-taggle
parade of cats and family.

He cries and his cries float up, joining ours,
the ones we don't notice. I show my son the rain
and he shrieks and shrieks delightedly.
This is how it is for him inside all day,
rain from one moment to the next, all day
falling down through exclamation points.

There is no toy for this. Only sleep.
And so I stay with him caught halfway in between
the desire to be someone else and his stuffed animal,
mouth sewn shut, eyes pasted wide open, arms flung out.

WILLIAM OLSEN

William Olsen was born in Omaha
in 1954 and teaches at Western
Michigan University. His first col-
lection, *The Hand of God and a
Few Bright Flowers,* won the Na-
tional Poetry Series Open Compe-
tition in 1988.

THE UNICORN TAPESTRIES

The things we leave behind must, for those
who find them flattened, scentless inside books
or in a gesture they make that isn't theirs,
be very much like the desk I found in the alley
one night, coming out of one way down another,

when I couldn't sleep or write letters, and walked.
The desk had lost a leg, and couldn't get away.
Some initials cut through oak had outlasted love.

Turning over the drawer to interpret
The contents, I thought of the farmer centuries ago
and the stack of "curtains" he found in a chest.
All the crazy things he couldn't understand:

the unicorn, Christ reborn; the seductive
damsel, Mary, who lured Him into the circular fence,
Her dress lifted ever so slightly, Her glance askew,
His smiling as if all the world centered on Him,
a field of lilies, violets, passionate roses
and periwinkles, "joy of the ground"—

he took them to the barn to cover the potatoes.
Little worked that winter. The potatoes darkened
the light that hid inside them. They grew eyes
until they were nothing but vision drained of life:
the unicorn bleeding and braying all winter
as the farmer lifted it and saw his work

ruined, for all his efforts.

STEVE ORLEN

Born in Holyoke, Massachusetts,
in 1942, Steve Orlen is the direc-
tor of the creative writing program
at the University of Arizona. His
collections of poetry include *Per-
mission to Speak* and *A Place at
the Table*.

BAGATELLES

My father who forgets that yesterday
   He saw a bird the color of sky not slate,
Who argues with the endless irritation
   Of the elderly, remembers which leg
He broke at soccer, not the year but the sharp
   Blueing bone escaping through his skin.
He phones to tell me the past comes to visit
   When he sits listening in his room alone,
And the simple accumulation of years,
   Like a jigsaw puzzle pieced together
In an afternoon, tells him all he needs to know.

I told this to a woman. We were dancing
At our 20th highschool reunion, her thigh
   A presence against my own. I could barely
Remember who she was. I didn't remember
   Telling her, "Pretty soon boys will be chasing
After you," though she did, and how solemn
   I'd looked, how she planned her future then.
Years later, standing before a mirror
   Brushing her hair, the memory shuddered
Through her like music through an empty room.

On the night of my 40th birthday,
Far from home, I stayed up late and lonely.
   Snow fell on a city in the valley,
Lights in the windows went off, roofs blended
   Evenly with snow, evergreens with snow
Until the whole white valley dissolved.
   I could vaguely remember women I'd loved,
Flake by flake snowing down, the courtesies,
   Undressing slowly, pleasure given, pleasure taken,
The nerves barely inquiring of each other.

Not memory, but ellipsis. Not the consciousness
Of afternoons, but gray light falling, Beethoven
   From the next room, the *Bagatelles* he wrote,
Not to be remembered by, but to be played
   Practice afternoons. On top of the piano,
Some bric-a-brac given me by friends, a brass
   Whale paperclip, an ivory elephant no bigger
Than a child's lost tooth, and a globe
   With two polar bears seesawing in the snow.
When I turn it over, I see us years from now,
   Talking on the phone. One says, *Remember this?*
And the other, rising white on white, *Remember that?*

STANLEY PLUMLY

Stanley Plumly was born in Barns-
ville, Ohio, in 1939. His books in-
clude *Out-of-the-Body Travel*,
Summer Celestial, and *Boy on the
Step*. The recipient of the Delmore
Schwartz Memorial Poetry Prize
and other honors, he lives in Balti-
more, where he teaches at the
University of Maryland.

AMERICAN ASH

The day is late enough you could stand
within the time it takes a door to drift
back shut and watch half a tree go dark,
the other half still green with the afternoon.
I have in mind the big one down the street,
west of the house, the light so stacked and split
it bottles up, brilliant at the top.
Downing going the other way is shade.
Upstairs the light is candle-in-a-shell.
Someone is getting ready to go to bed.

The house is rich with camphor, mint, and oil
of wintergreen, and on the dining table
roses in a bowl.
                    I think it is nineteen
forty-five. Sepia will never get
quite right the year in color, my mother's
dress, for instance, red and yellow daisies
on a regimental blue to end the war,
nor my father home from work to work his garden.
He has a lantern. It is almost May,
the streetlights coming on, one to a corner.
If it is true the soul is other people,
then the antique finish of the thing
is how we love the past, how the aging
of a photograph becomes, like leaves, deciduous.
At the head of the stairs my mother's
mother's bedroom and beside hers the mahogany
and cedar of her father's . . . For a hundred years
the sun has set against the high side of the house.
I could climb those stairs, I could sleep and be
filled with the dead odors of moths and wools
and silks, with the sweet addictions of the flesh.
I could float a little lifetime above the kitchen talk,
branch, green, the sudden burden of the leaves.

WITH STEPHEN IN MAINE

The huge mammalian rocks in front of the lawn,
domestic between the grass and the low tide—
Stephen has set his boat in one of the pools,
his hand the little god that makes it move.
It is cold, the sky the rough wool and gaberdine
of pictures someone almost talented has painted.
Off and on the sun, then Stephen is wading . . .

Yesterday we saw two gulls shot out of the sky.
One of them drifted into shore, broken, half-eaten,
green with the sea. When I found it this morning
all I could think to do was throw it back. One wing.
Its thin blood spread enough that Stephen is finger-
printed and painted with washing and wiping dry.
Even his boat, at the watermark, is stained.

I lift him, put him up on top of my shoulders.
From here he can watch the deep water pile, turn over.
He says, with wonder, that it looks like the ocean
killing itself. He wants to throw stones, he wants
to see how far his boat can sail, will float.
The mile or more from here to there is an order of color,
pitched white and black and dove- or green-gray, blue,

but far and hurt from where he is seeing.

DAVID RIVARD

David Rivard's first collection of
poems, *Torque*, won the Agnes
Lynch Starrett Prize. Born in 1953
in Fall River, Massachusetts, he
currently teaches at Tufts.

THE VENICE OF THE NORTH

I used to walk for two or three hours
each day along the canals in Gamla Stan.
The barges with white hulls moved past.
Early winter, cobble-stone turned into snow.
One morning as flurries swept down I watched

students protest near a government building,
chanting their demands, a small bunch.
There was a tourist hotel in a square
where three prostitutes huddled drinking tea,
cold, breath rising, two of them arm in arm,

as anonymous as anyone could desire.
From a distance the tall one with bright
cheeks flicked her eyes over my face, why
should I be all alone? The whole city seemed
to ask something, just as each feeling

would turn into a question I asked myself.
And if there are cities I won't see again,
who can prove my answers back then were lies?
Not lies, really, but things I should have said
that went unsaid. The snow had ways of

falling or, blown by wind, rising, through
lighted rows of high apartment windows.
I knew a woman living in a place like those.
I could imagine what she was doing at home,
how she switched off the radio, got up

from the couch, and sorted her clothes into
piles of laundry. She'd peer at a button,
brass pressed with a shape—an anchor?
or was it crossed swords?—then toss it
into a waste basket and slam the door

as she left the room. Her name was Vera
and she was slowly going blind. She did
some sort of work at a little restaurant
near the start of the suburbs: behind it
the sea froze and you could walk on the water

any time in winter. Once, waiting for
the end of her shift, I headed out to
a channel marker. Looking back toward
a hill outlined by bare maple, I remembered
the morning newspaper, pictures of a new

work-camp, how carefully the chain-link fence
had been hid behind a grove of trees.
When she told me she quit her job, I had
almost asked what she would do then.
She said that going blind was like a trial

for political crimes, drawn out so the
citizenry may learn from your example.
A guard brings out two needles, light pink
with fluid, pricks you, and you think you're dead.
Later on, you wake, the cell is dark,

a voice is asking, *Now will you behave yourself?*
I never told her I loved her. I thought
it was a lie, though of course there is
a lie inside my memory of this
and I did love her but was afraid.

I walked all day for three days. Tuesday,
I went by her flat for the last time,
past the row of porno shops, and the Swedish word
for *punishment* made me think of a photo
of two people lying across each other in a bed.

In the window, among all the contraptions
of love, I was staring back. Down an alley
were stores peddling shoes, wood and leather clogs
hung in place on the brick and tile fronts.
A whole wall of them rose into the sky,

a way of walking, vanishing, snow-like,
above the islanded city of Stockholm,
the Venice of the North, the third Venice
being memory, the punishment for all questions.

VERN RUTSALA

Vern Rutsala is the author of *Back-tracking, Ruined Cities, Selected Poems,* and other collections of poetry. A professor at Lewis and Clark College, he was born in 1934 in McCall, Idaho.

THIS LIFE, THIS DAY

It is this: the Spanish rice we had
for dinner, the movies we
saw—*Badlands, Days of Heaven*—
and the cat now sleeping
on the box of old pictures, my photo
at twenty-four on top, SP4 in khaki
so long ago. Does anyone
remember Charley Starkweather

and peace-time armies?
All days reach back and forth—
all radios squawk and spit,
old teams run on fields
in ghost stadiums, old
thunder booms and snaps
over Iowa and Bavaria, over
Minneapolis and London as this day

343

reaches back and forth, here and there,
now and then. This day
was Spanish rice and movies,
memory and sadness, the films
telling us how those brown album pictures
of my father may have been, the music
teaching us a lesson we almost
learned before it stopped.

But we are here with the huge
insignificance of this day—
see us return from the movies,
see the small red car nudge
against the curb, hear the dog bark
his accusatorial greeting, see us walk under
the leaves to the door. What
we saw is behind us now—the pictures

we paid to see and those we
didn't: dark buses returning to the barn,
leaves flying and falling in streetlights,
clouds against the moon.
See us now drink glasses of juice
or milk, see us drink beer
or wine in this quiet sacrament
of the return. We carried our lives

out with us like canteens and brought
them back to be refilled.
We're not asked to believe this.
We don't know what it means.
It is here as we are here now
in this house and need no
camera to confirm our presence.
We move at ease through these rooms

that we've never seen before.

PETER SACKS

Peter Sacks was born in 1950 in
Port Elizabeth, South Africa, and
now lives in Baltimore, where he
teaches at Johns Hopkins. He is
the author of two poetry collec-
tions, *In These Mountains* and
Promised Lands, and a critical
book, *The English Elegy: Studies
in the Genre from Spenser to
Yeats*, for which he received the
Christian Gauss Award.

VALERIE

You've joined those
who cross the ocean after me,
arriving under dark,
the mute ones, visiting.

I understand the others,
tangled in the heart's own fear,
but you stood always
on the margin,

345

our vacation-aunt each
winter down the coast,
the small-town doctor's wife,
Aunt Val, or Aunty V,

ferrying us each day
from beach to tennis club—
the road through canefields
out of town.

One year, dazzled
by a motorcycle parked
outside the house,
all chrome and sunlight,

I, just ten, leaned up
to touch its handlebars,
and as I peered at the speedometer,
the yellow figures under glass,

90, 100, 110,
the bright exhaust pipe
burned into my leg for seconds
before I knew enough to tear away.

For days the massive blister
oozing through the gauze
was no match for your patience.
In the garden,

wild banana trees,
their wide leaves white
under the coastal salt,
the weak papaya branches

awkward in the wind,
a bougainvillea's
brilliant splash of crimson
over the chicken run,

I'm watching you unwind
another roll of gauze,
the scissors in your right hand,
safety pin between your lips.

Is it the manner of your death
that brings you back
these nights, your son beside you
at the wheel, the drunk accelerating

on a blind rise
coming at you with a violence
nothing in your life
had led you to suppose?

Once, though, as we drove home
from the beach, a cane-press worker
flagged us down, held up
the bloody ruin of his arm.

I remember your voice
seemed to shield us
from the raw pulp of the hand
held to the car window,

blood on the lowering glass,
the shattered bone laid
bare under the flesh.
You were speaking Zulu,

"Let me wrap your hand,
come with us to the hospital,
the doctor's there." It seems now
we were always frightened in that country.

I still turn to it with a child's fear.
—Valerie, if you could hear,
I'd say watch over us.
Watch over the dark coast.

IRA SADOFF

Born in 1945, Ira Sadoff is the au-
thor of five collections of poetry,
including *Settling Down, Palm
Reading in Winter,* and *Emotional
Traffic,* and a novel, *Uncoupling.*
He teaches at Colby College.

AT THE HALF-NOTE CAFE

for Gene Ammons

Once I heard him play
"Willow Weep for Me,"
in a tone so full and sentimental,
I felt a gap between my ribs
and lungs, a dearth of air
sorrow soon enough would fill.
I found the blues unfair to boys
like me who came to bars unprepared
for grief that wasn't strictly personal.

I told my girl I knew everything
of suffering and love, but when
I heard a woman, drunk, cry out
in front of everyone, "Don't go, Jug—
I'll give you all of what you want,"
my face went blank and limp
as an infant when a stranger shakes
a rattle in his face. Later, when he
hit bottom, the last broken chorus
of "Body and Soul," I collapsed
in my girl's arms, my composure
crushed by a simple saxophone.
I couldn't think of what to tell her.
What the hell did she know anyhow?
We both came from the same suburban town.

It was a brittle winter night in New York.
We had nowhere to go except her
parents' house, so we drifted down
Greenwich Ave. hand in hand. I'd never seen
streets so crowded after dark—with drunks,
half-dead, and kids who should have been
in bed. I'm surprised we made it out alive.
I know if I'd seen my stupid grin
of confidence, that wide-eyed stare,
my gaping face, I would have smashed it
just for the experience. We were lucky
though we didn't know it then. We ended up
parking in my mother's car. We kissed,
a mindless ritual of courtship, then I
took off her blouse, grabbed her breast,
put her stiffened nipple in my mouth.
I gasped for air, couldn't get enough of it.

DENNIS SCHMITZ

Born in Dubuque, Iowa, in 1937,
Dennis Schmitz has published six
volumes of poetry, most recently
String, Singing, and *Eden.* The
recipient of a Shelley Memorial
Award and other honors, he
teaches at California State Uni-
versity in Sacramento.

TO RAYMOND ROSELIEP

man dozes while God designs sleep
the eighth day of creation.
angels' wings lick the commercial

weather of Paradise—
even the fib, buck-toothed,
is beautiful. but only enough sleep

is left over to make a single
corpse—so it is we enter heaven
one by one. even though lovers

would sleepwalk
each other's bodies, our dreams
can repeat only the duplicity

of the senses. the poet's work
is to whittle blue
sky out of the high forks of the florid

maple, to make night from one
owl. & with his own nightsweat wash
enough talk to wake each of us

the other side of sleep.

SHEILA SCHWARTZ

Sheila Schwartz was born in Phila-
delphia in 1952. Her stories have
appeared in *The Atlantic, Mss,*
and other magazines, and "Mutatis
Mutandis" was reprinted in *The
Pushcart Prize XIV: Best of the
Small Presses 1989–1990.* Her first
collection, *Imagine a Great White
Light,* won the 1990 Editors' Book
Award.

MUTATIS MUTANDIS

(Love)

There was evening and there was morning the sixth day, and for what? So
that she, Miriam, could walk alone to her bunk every night while the
others groped and rustled in the dark, so that her only friend, Renee,
could ditch her just like that for a creep named Harvey Haas, so that
Chaim Picker could torment her ceaselessly, interminably, with his ob-
scure, a priori liking?

Everyone else that summer got smoke in his eyes, got satisfaction, got
do-wa-diddy-diddy-dum-diddy-do. Not her. Not mutatis (though not yet
mutandis) Miriam. All she got was, "Nu, Miriam?" All she got was the

353

correct answer every time she raised her hand. All she got was taller and taller. (Five feet ten and who knew when it would stop? Tall like a *model*, her mother always said. An attractive girl. Only thirteen years old and so shapely. Wait!)

But there was no end in sight. Too big, too smart, and on top of all this—the teacher's pet (a real *drip* in other words). It was a simple concept with a simple proof: Chaim Picker was a real drip. Chaim Picker liked her. Ergo, *she* was a real drip.

And so the proofs of *his* drippiness, clear and manifold.

For one thing, he spoke way too many languages all of which were queer. According to the others, his Hebrew was queer, his Yiddish was queer, his English was *totally* queer. (What was all that "Omnipresence" stuff, anyway?) To make things even worse, he wore the exact same thing every single day—a creepy black suit, black shoes, black yarmulke, and tsitsit (the *epitome* of queerness). When he lectured the tsitsit swayed with him, back and forth, back and forth, Baruch HaShem Amen V'Amen! As far as anyone knew, these fringes were the only things he had ever kissed, in the morning when he put them on, and in the evening when he lay himself down to sleep.

Miriam saw him differently. He wasn't really a drip, just an "anachronism" (as she had discovered in one of her recent forays through the dictionary). For Chaim, it was clear, reminders of God and his commandments were everywhere, not only in the ceremonial fringes he wore, but in the whoosh of pine trees, in the birds flying overhead, even in his tea glass, spoon handle pointing upward like the metal finger of God, admonishing.

A bachelor, born circa 1930, he had a propensity for closed spaces and esoteric questions. Witness the inordinate amount of time spent in his tiny cabin. Witness the thick curtains on his windows, the hours spent in the library studying. Witness (they had no choice) his probing technique in class.

They groaned. Good Lord, more questions! He was going to kill them with all his questions. At every damned word he had to stop and wonder: who what where when and why, and sometimes why again. WHY does it say "in the beginning"? Hasn't everything always been here forever and eternally? So where did this "beginning" come from? And how could God precede it?

And furthermore. What is meant by "the face of the deep"? Wasn't this "face" covered by darkness? And wasn't it also empty and formless, but still visible in the "darkness"? (If it was *truly* darkness.) And how could this "darkness" *and* the spirit of God move upon the waters or whatever they were at the same time and in the same place and did this imply identity? And if so then what is meant by "in the beginning"? Miriam? Good, Miriam. *Correct.* For him, nothing in the stupid book was just simply what it was. Nothing in the whole damned world.

It was true, Miriam thought. Everything had its layers, its surfaces, its unexpected depths, even the riddle he asked them every day at the start of class: "Nu, children. What is the meaning of 'peel'?" Even the answer Barry Sternberg gave for the twenty-fifth straight day, "Miriam" instead of the true meaning "elephant." (Though it might seem otherwise, Chaim explained to her one day after class, Barry really was a good boy, he meant no harm by his remarks. "He's a sick boy," Chaim had said, "a boy with many problems. He needs people to pay attention, and not just *you*. Whom do you think has been scribbling on the walls all summer long? And other pranks I am not at liberty to mention. Just try to ignore him, Mireleh. The more any of us pays attention, the more he'll keep on doing it.")

Barry popped up and took a bow.

"Sternberg," Chaim said.

"What?"

Chaim pointed to the bench.

"Who *me?*" Barry pretended to be astonished. He spread his arms wide to capture his amazement. "What did I do? What in the 'H' did I do?" he asked the class.

"Please sit down."

"Why?"

"Sternberg. You may leave or you may sit down. *Choose.*" Chaim placed both palms flat on the table.

Barry pointed. "The right one," he said.

"Sternberg!"

"The left?"

"OK OK OK," Chaim told him. "That was an interesting exercise. You have made for us a good variation on the state of innocence and on the meaning of will. But now, *we* will go on." He clasped his hands behind his back. "Nu, children?" He turned toward the class. "And vus is 'peel'?" His smile was hopeful. He waited.

"Oy!" Barry flopped back onto the bench. "Oy oy oy!" He shook his head. "These Jews. These Jews! They are *just never* SATISFIED." Then he went into his act. He made his eyes blink, made his jaws click-clack together. "Nu, Meereyum." His voice came out slow and underwater. "Why don't youuuuu tell us vussss." As though drowning in precision, he sank to another octave. "Cumpute it for him, Meeeeer-ee-yummmmm."

They burst out laughing.

"Sternberg, *leave.*"

"Shtarenbeerg, *liv!*" Barry flapped his hands. Shoo! His grin implied a cheering crowd. He made no move to leave.

"OK OK. My accent is very funny; it's very funny indeed, I agree. There's truth in everything," Chaim said. "So, therefore, one more chance, Sternberg. This is Erev Shabbat and I'm giving you the benefit. Now what is 'peel-pool'?" He bent forward and nodded as if nudging him the correct answer.

Which gathered on Barry's face into a big, knowing grin. "An elephant pool—where Miriam swims." He sprang up from the table. "Shtarenbeerg—*LIV!*"

They laughed.

Miriam tried to ignore them, she tried to ignore Barry as Chaim had asked her to. After class he had repeated what he'd said before, "No matter how disturbing these events seem, we must pretend we don't notice. He's a child crying just to hear the sound of his own voice, a sad boy, a very very unhappy human being." And when she hadn't been convinced ("But why does he always pick on *me*?") he had added, "Listen, Mireleh. You are my best student. It's a shame that he spoils your concentration so I'll tell you a secret—for your ears alone, fashtays-tu?" When she'd nodded, he took hold of her hand, as if to prevent her from running in horror when she heard the truth. "Barry is an orphan," he whispered. "*Both* his parents at once—a terrible misfortune. He lives with his aunt. She's been very generous, but he has never gotten used to his fate. For this reason he sees a psychiatrist. A *psychiatrist*," he repeated. "You understand what this means? It's crucial for us to set a good example."

She tried, but it was difficult. Every day Barry sat down next to her. "Sha-loom, Meereyum." Winking to the class, he sprawled himself out until he was so close she could feel his tanned arms and legs glistening against her own pale ones, rubbing sweat. Everytime she moved over, he moved over too until there was no place on the bench to sit. She tried to ignore him. She remembered what Chaim had said: "It is better to be persecuted than to persecute others." She tried to believe him. She stared at her hands, and at the trees, and at the big heart carved into the wooden table.

RANDY & JOSH IN '63.

That was the way the summer went; this was the pattern of love. Someone looked at you in services, in class, at dinner. Three times (a holy number). His friends noticed. They kidded him and giggled. *Your* friends heard about it and they told *you*. You blushed and shrugged your shoulders, not yes, not no. Sometime later (after a movie, or lunch, or Friday night dancing on the tennis courts) you heard footsteps on the path behind you, a voice which leapt to life in your ear, "Wanna take a walk?" Sometime later, the ID bracelet, a binding silver promise on your wrist. (Or was it the ID first and *then* the walk?)

That was the way it went and it happened to these people: David Stein and Leslie Gold. Yitzi Feinberg and Shira Oster. Josh Blum and Karen Bregman. Bennet Twersky and Susan Gould. The boys from Bunk 3 and the girls from Bunk 19. The kitchen help and Gladys Ticknor. Stacy Plisky and everyone. Once it almost happened to her, but it was only Norman Levine, the boy with the slide rule.

Still, even love with a slide rule was permissible in certain cases. According to the Talmud there were many faces to love—some smiling, some weeping. Love could be a wind, a deep well; it could be a tiger waiting to spring.

That was all well and good, but *this* was nothing of the kind. According to Leo Goelman, the camp director, love was one thing, *neetzool* was another. He gave them a long lecture about it the morning that this sign was discovered painted on the library wall:

Suzy Creamcheese—What's Got into You?

Whoever had done this, Leo Goelman shouted, had no idea what love meant, not a clue. Real love was sacred. It was not something to joke about. What this prankster had in mind was something else—"neetzool" he reiterated. "Neetzool" meant *exploitation*, a lack of respect, a lack of individuality. "Neetzool" was what you felt like doing with anyone at all.

His interpretation discouraged no one.

Every night there was the same rush for the woods, the same giggling in the bathrooms afterwards. Every night Miriam listened to Shira and Renee whispering about what they had done (always, just loud enough for her to hear, just soft enough to make her feel that she was eavesdropping).

"We went to second. What did you guys do?"

"Only first."

Everything was euphemism. First base. Second base. Making out. Popping flies. Once Shira looked at her and laughed. "You don't know what we're talking about, do you?"

When they got between the rough, white camp sheets, instead of saying their prayers, they thought of what they had done, of what they might do tomorrow. They dreamed of scratchy bark against their backs, and later, eventually, of their names carved into that bark.

Miriam saw things differently:

They would meet somewhere, in a park, in a cafe, in the rain. He would be wearing a long coat, military style, black, but not as black as his hair which was blue-black, seething with midnight. He would smoke thin cigars and know everything there was to know about poetry and film. Whatever he stared at, he would stare at intently. "Ah! A reader," he would say. "That's good. A woman who thinks." His eyes would linger on her face.

She would hand him her copy of *Steppenwolf* and he would turn the pages slowly, his unnaturally delicate fingers slipping beneath the paper. He would pause to read some comment in the margin. "Coffee somewhere?" he would murmur.

Rain would fall. Time would pass slowly. They would go on and on.

Or it might happen like this:

They'd have something in common (a love of nature or justice). Both of them, hard workers, diligent believers in a cause. People with principles! (Civil rights, maybe? disarmament?) Whatever their protest, they would run from the tear gas together, find shelter in a burned-out basement, wrap their wounds, never come out.

Or it might be like this: Before she even spoke, he would love her.

Other girls got letters from their boyfriends back home: "Are you still stuck in that dopey Bible camp? When are you coming home? I have a great tan from hanging around the club. The women adore me. Ha. Ha."

And they wrote back, a big pink kiss on the outside flap: SWAK.

Miriam got letters from her mother every day. "My darling, Miriam," or "Dearest Miriam," or "My darling, little Miriam," they began. She hoped that Miriam was having a profitable summer, that the other girls were nice, that Miriam was wearing all her nice, new outfits.

And as if that weren't enough. "P.S." she said. "You're a wonderful girl. I miss you."

Another week passed and they were still crawling through Genesis. God had made light and plenty of it shining down on every corner of the field, making the air hum, making the horizon, through the waves of heat, seem to curl up into the sky. The grove where they had dragged their benches and table was no better. It was too hot to think. It was too hot to answer. Only Chaim, in his eternal black wool suit, was moving.

They had been over and over the Garden of Eden. Chaim had delineated it for them in graphic detail, had made them sweat blood over it. The fragrance! The fruit trees! The making of each creature—how splendid! The perfection of the whole thing. Now they were stuck on Adam's rib (a difficult passage).

Why was it that Eve had been made from Adam's rib and not from dust, as Adam had been? God could do anything, correct? So why then from a rib?

Shelley Katz did not know.

Danny Goldfarb did not know.

Barry Sternberg did not give two hoots.

"*Think*, children."

"To make them fit?" As soon as she'd asked it she blushed. The heat of her mistake began to rise through her, to swell inside of her, to do something, at any rate, totally awful.

"Nothing would fit *you*," Barry said. "Not even *this*." He showed her with his hands.

"I didn't mean—!" But it was too late. They were too hot to answer, but not too hot to laugh. She wondered what the Talmud had to say on the subject of laughter. It could be a wind? A deep well? A tiger waiting to spring?

Chaim bent forward to block their amusement. "Don't be a clown, Sternberg. Do you never learn? Of course Miriam didn't mean this literally," he said. Then he frowned at them. "You meant it *figuratively*, didn't you, Mireleh? A metaphor? Something for something else, wasn't that your intention?"

She nodded faintly. Something else—oh sure. The road was a ribbon of moonlight. My love is a red, red rose. That was what she had meant—some other perfect fit. "I guess so," she said.

"Correct, Mireleh. That's very good." Chaim patted the table in front of him as though it were her hand. "Very good indeed." He held up his Bible, print outward, and pointed to the passage. "You see, we have here, class, a metaphor—a lesson we can read between the lines—"

"Between the what?"

"Between the LINES, Sternberg." He tapped the page. "Beneath what is said literally, children, we have a second, more important—"

"Beneath *who*?"

Chaim sighed. "Beneath what is said *literally*, a second truth, as Miriam has pointed out—what is good is often hidden."

"You can say *that* again!"

Chaim set down the book. "Please, Mireleh. Please tell us simply and QUICKLY and in what manner, *figuratively*, these two fit."

"Yeah," Barry whispered. "Give us all the figures!"

The blush crept through her, literally, figuratively, fittingly and otherwise. However she had meant it she didn't know and didn't care. All around her they were grinning. Barry was grinning; he was coursing with possibilities (loose? tight? dry? deep?). Barry nudged her with his leg. "Nu, Mireleh—so tell us already."

She tried to slide away from him and when she did, her legs lifting from the bench made a slurping sound.

"Correct!" Barry exclaimed.

"That *is* correct," Chaim said as though she had answered. His eyes told her: "Bear with him. Ignore him. Be brave." As if to demonstrate how suffrance like this was achieved, he ignored Barry and the sound and their laughter. He ignored everything he could possibly ignore. He clasped his hands together and squeezed. God made Eve from Adam's rib, he told them as he started to sway, to insure a perfect match, to make a coupling of the right and left halves so that no part should be omitted, no part lacking. It was a union perfect as the Garden, a union fragrant as a citron, alive with light. "We're talking about the crown of creation—*you understand me, class?*"

Sure. They understood.

On Friday nights it was standing room only in the woods. She could hear them in there hugging and kissing, fondling and caressing, zipping and unzipping, rubbing, pushing, their desire shredding fabric. She could hear them giggling and whispering and groaning, an ocean of sound that described each touch, that rose like steam through the woods.

(The Library)

No one knew as much about that library as she did, except perhaps the librarian himself, and even *he* didn't know it in the same way.

She knew that the wood smelled in the morning, and the dust, of years of thought—resinous. She knew that the sun lit the letters on the bindings, gold. She knew which books had pictures, which ones had tiny, unreadable print. She knew who came there, at what hour, and for what purpose.

Chaim was there every afternoon from lunchtime until dusk poring over commentaries on the Bible. He didn't lean on one elbow like the others, but held his arms stiffly at his sides and swayed back and forth over the text as though he might dive into it. Sometimes he closed his eyes. She could watch him for hours and he never noticed her. Even when he lifted his head for air, his eyes shone with a blank, unseeing light.

Often, after he'd gone, Miriam would slip into his chair. She would pick up the book which still lay open on the table awaiting his return, and she would try to read what *he* had read that afternoon. There were reams of words, some in Hebrew, some in Aramaic, all without vowels, mysterious, impossible. She could only read the very large print—the phrase, or word, that was the subject of all that commentary: IN THE BEGINNING. DARK AND UNFORMED. She sat with the dictionary and puzzled out words. She wrote down translations, verbatim, awkward, but no matter what she did, she found nothing. The words were just words. Chaim still remained a mystery.

Then, eventually, she discovered that the words didn't matter. Maybe she couldn't understand them, but she didn't have to because it was just as pleasant simply to sit in the dark and pretend, to slide her fingers over the page, (occasionally, to sway a little), to skim the elusive grains of sense, silently, as though reading. She imagined that was what mystics did when they meditated. They chose some words, they shut their eyes, they rocked themselves to sleep. Every day she did this a little longer—a half hour, forty-five minutes, an hour—when she should have been playing basketball, or making lanyards, when she saw Barry coming towards her, over the hill.

As for Chaim—. One evening she hovered over the book he had left behind until it was almost dark. The librarian had gone home to his cabin. Dusk had thickened around her and she had let it, had liked it, the feeling of darkness melting into her, the way the words melted into her fingertips and her fingertips melted into the pages, the way the pages melted back into the darkness, slowly, very slowly, and the darkness melted back into her. She was dreaming that the letters had become figures, tall and thin, in long dark cloaks, broad black hats. They had all joined hands and were dancing in a circle around her making the room quake with joy. Faster and faster they whirled until the walls fell away, the sky became a blur—stars, moon, night thrashed against the galaxy; she couldn't catch her breath.

Wood creaked.

She opened her eyes.

A dark figure was coming towards her. Tall. Twisting. A shadow that bent. Unfolded. Bent again as though searching for a path through the twilight.

"Who's there?" she whispered.

The figure stopped. "Vus?"

Not the spirit of a letter, but Chaim. She had conjured him, complete, in his long black coat, his round black hat. "Vus machst tu, Mireleh?" he inquired.

Still not seeing clearly, she blinked. The hat he wore cast shadows on his face making from his features, shapes—caves and crags. "Ah," he said softly. "You're reading. Please don't let me disturb you," as though this were the most natural thing in the world, to be sitting in the dark with a book. She glanced down. She must have fallen asleep right on top of it. The pages were all crinkled and there were spots of saliva. She thought she smelled the oil from her hair. Ashamed, she closed the cover. "I wasn't really reading," she sighed.

But he didn't answer. Instead, a white hand leapt to his beard and began stroking it, thoughtfully, gently, as though this were a demonstration of how to treat the world. Something about this puzzled her. Not the motion, but the whiteness of his hand. Her own hands were obscured by darkness, but his shone pale as though lit up from inside. She thought of miracles that she'd studied—the Hannukah candle that burned for eight days; the bush in the desert exploding into flames. She thought it might be some strange effect from the Ner Tamid, the Eternal Light, that burned above the Ark against the wall. Or, she might have lapsed back into her dream, lulled by his silence.

"Mireleh?"

He was asking her something. One hand soared to his hat brim where it hovered as though waiting for an answer.

"What?"

"Pirkei Avot. The Ethics of the Fathers, you remember? It says there: 'On three things the world depends—on Torah, on work, and on the performance of good deeds.' Do you believe this?" He gestured. His hand swooped towards her like a dove, plummeting down.

Another magic trick? She pushed the book away. "I guess so." Why had he come back this late? Why hadn't he turned on the light? Did he come here to hide the way she did?

He did not help to make things clearer. Folding himself into the chair across from her, he said, "May I sit down for a minute?" Then the conversation began, a long conversation which made no sense, that seemed like words weaving through the darkness, occasionally surfacing, then dipping, then floating up again making strange ripples through all that had gone before.

"So how are you liking it thus far?"

"Liking what—the class?"

"The class. Anything."

"Not bad," she said.

"Ah, I see," he said sadly. His hat bobbed agreement. "At your age life is merely 'not bad.' I suppose God thinks you should be grateful for this. Well. Let's put Him aside for the moment." There was another long silence much more than just a moment, during which pause she wondered, was this really Chaim sitting across from her saying: *Let's put God aside?* She could feel him staring at her, his gaze like the hour after midnight, a mournful, naked look that made her lose her balance, made her fall slowly towards the center of the earth.

Finally, he sighed. "You know what is my favorite poem in the English language?" He recited it for her: "Sonnet number 73," he announced, as though it were a psalm. "Bare ruined choirs where late the sweet birds sang'—that's Shakespeare. Isn't it sad?"

"I guess so." She didn't understand at all, really. Shakespeare. The Torah. Sweet birds and ruined choirs. What did he want from her?

He didn't explain. Instead, he wished her a good evening as he stood up, then drifted from the room. "You'd better go too, Mireleh. Your counselor will be worried."

But he came back again, the next night. Again, he settled himself into the chair across from hers and began speaking as though no time at all had intervened. Perhaps it hadn't. Whatever was on his mind was still there, pressing him, tugging at logic, winding good sense up into a ball—that came unravelled as soon as he opened his mouth to speak: "Do you know 'Ode to a Nightingale'?" he asked her. "Do you know this one by Hopkins?" Again he recited to her, his voice trembling as though *he* were the poet falling over the edge of the world into discovery. She knew this must be another secret he was telling her; something else he believed in besides God and good deeds and the Talmud Torah, a secret she must not divulge to anyone. The verses frightened her. In bed, after lights out, she chanted to herself all of the lines she could remember: "All is changed, changed utterly . . ." . . . "Though worlds of wanwood leafmeal lie . . ." . . . "I have been half in love with easeful death . . ."—lines that went against what they prayed for each morning: "Blessed art Thou O Lord, King of the Universe who removest sleep from mine eyes and slumber from mine eyelids, who restorest life to mortal creatures . . ." It was as though she'd seen Chaim wandering through a new landscape—a shadowy glen drenched with mist, moss-covered, hopeless.

By the third night, she was waiting for him, for the conversation that made such confusion, that made her grasp the arms of the chair she sat in, so solid, so wooden. He didn't greet her this time, just picked up the threads of their last talk and began braiding them, rocking back and forth as though praying, as though fevered. He spoke until the dark became as thick as a trance, until she leaned into this, waiting, bending towards him so that their knees brushed under the table, his rough and woolen, hers bare and tender, very warm. She wanted him to say something that would break the spell, something ordinary: "That's fine, Mireleh," as he would have done in class, "You're a good girl, my *best* student . . ." But he didn't say a word, and what he didn't say gathered between them.

She tried to think of a question to ask him, a polite question to engage his interest, but the only ones that occurred to her pertained, oddly enough, to his legs. What were they like beneath the fabric of his trousers? Pale? Calloused? Were they as white as his hands? As smooth?

Suddenly, he leaned forward as if he had been speaking to her all this time. "And you know what they say? They say that the Torah was written by men."

"What?" She was still thinking of his legs, white as paper, the black curling hairs.

"By *men*," Chaim repeated. His words rushed through her. He was looking at her earnestly. For a minute she imagined he had heard what she was thinking, that this was the way scholars made passes, by a reference, that he would reach across the table and draw her to him; they would kiss across the table, only the outstretched Talmud between them. Then she realized he wasn't looking at her at all. He was staring the way he did when he was unable to pry himself loose from his holy books and go back into the world. "That's what they think!" he exclaimed. "Can you believe it? By men and not God. That there isn't any absolute and, therefore, no suffering. It's as simple as that." He laughed, incredulous. "There are no *real* laws. Only *human* laws. Is that ridiculous? We should think like the others, they say. The Chinese. The Hindus. They think it's better to meditate, that it's all right to leave the suffering of this world behind, while we Jews, we *real* Jews," he shook his head, "*we* stay and suffer, throwing our souls into the fire and groaning when we are burned. And then we think we know." He slapped the table. "And then we think we have done our part!" His fist came down.

She tried to make sense of it later. For several days, she added up the evidence, subtracted what didn't fit at all, and divided by what was obscure. On the one hand, there was the lateness of the hour each time they talked; there was his prolonged stay, the personal nature of his questions, his lingering over the poems, his knees brushing hers. On the other hand, there was his unexpected leap to the Hindus, his discussion of suffering, and after his fist struck the table, his apology: "Never mind," he had told her. "It's late and I've probably driven you crazy with all this nonsense. I keep forgetting you're only thirteen. Thirteen in America is an easier age."

Than what? she wondered.

She began to dream of him at night, a dream bathed in different lights. Gold. Dark green. Over and over.

In her dream it was a Sabbath afternoon, dry as ashes, like a day held under a magnifying glass to start a fire. Everyone was resting, tired, quiescent, in their cabins, reading newspapers, or poems or love letters: "My darling, my dearest, sweetheart . . ."

Except her.

She had been walking for hours looking for something, her eyes were fixed on the road. Whatever it was, she had lost it. A bracelet? An earring? She was looking for a glimmer in the road as the sun beat down against her back pasting her yellow shirt to her skin with sweat. It was hot. It was so very hot. The road was a dusty glare—empty, forlorn, forever.

Suddenly, she looked up. There were woods! From nowhere, green rushed out to welcome her. On both sides of the road, deep green, the trickling of running water, branches waving. Leaves. Meadows of thriving grass—Queen Anne's lace and wild timothy.

Someone touched her arm. A tall figure dissolving into shadows in the woods. She followed though she couldn't see, could only feel the deep cool breath of the forest soothing her. She walked for hours, until the setting sun came through the trees in threads—orange, green, yellow sprays of light that dazzled her.

Against this light, she saw Chaim. In black as always, long coat, velvet yarmulke, clasping in one hand his Bible, the special one from Israel with its silver cover beaten to the shape of tablets, a turquoise stone inset for each commandment. In his other hand, a bunch of flowers, white, which he handed to her, then kissed her cheek. A warm, moist kiss. "I like big girls," he whispered.

They lay down together.

He began to kiss her. Lips to her mouth, lips to her hair, to the hollow of her neck, to her lips again until she shivered though his lips were warm like cinnamon or cloves, and smooth as the wood of a spice box. Then stinging. Then sweet. Over and over, his lips, until his hands moved over her too, touching her and stroking her, unbuttoning clothes, sliding them over her skin as swift as angels, (she was naked; he was naked), reading her body with his fingertips, skimming her arms, her legs, her breasts, with hands that were lighter than whispers, than blessings, until light poured over both of them, into them; they were inside it. He was rocking her back and forth; she was curling herself around him.

By day what remained of her dream? He was naked; she was naked. Nakedness in all its conjugations. I was naked, she thought. *We* were naked. Had been naked. Would be. Might.

She watched him in class as he bent over his text and she didn't see his black clothes, she saw his skin, white and smooth and glowing. When he said her name, she could hardly answer. When he moved his fingers over the pages, she flinched. And when he started to sway she felt her body swaying with him; she couldn't bear to look.

(Hunger)

Precedents for such romances: David and Abishag, Abraham and Keturah, Isaac (he was over forty) and Rebecca, Esau and Judith, Joseph and Potiphar's wife (sort of), Pablo Picasso and what was her name? his latest wife, someone slim, exquisite; at any rate—a woman to be proud of.

She imagined how it would feel to look like that, as thin and graceful as a lulav—the wand made of palm fronds and myrtle and willow that the men waved on Sukkot, the harvest festival. She pictured herself that way, and then Chaim, taking her by the hand, introducing her proudly: "This is Miriam. She's not only a great reader, she's also very lovely—don't you think?" He would bow to his own words, dazzled, faithful. In private he would touch her as he had in the dream. "I'll tell you a secret, Miriam—for your ears alone. I'll tell you all of my secrets . . ."

But it wasn't just for Chaim she had decided to do this; there were the others as well. How wonderful, she thought, to leap and twirl and float right past them, to rise above their laughter like a wisp of smoke. How wonderful never to hear Barry say again, "Here she comes—THUMP! THUMP!" She would be thin as a switch, that's what she'd be. She'd lash the world with her beauty, make them all run before her—awed, delighted.

If not, then she'd disappear.

She had already given up lunch and sometimes even dinner; it was nothing to give up the rest. The first day she didn't even feel hungry, and whenever she did she drank a cup of tea.

Strangely enough, she seemed to have more energy, not less. Instead of going to meals and activities, she took long walks around the countryside. She hiked through the woods and trekked across pastures so that she could climb to the tops of hills rough with brambles, boulders. She searched for waterfalls, a far-off rushing sound. She made her way through marshes where only algae grew or the stumps of trees pointing upward for no reason.

Each day she dared herself to go a little farther. Once it was a walk to the next camp five miles down the road. The following day she went into town, then another five miles past an abandoned church with a cemetery plot, untended, crooked crosses scattered everywhere as wayward as weeds. On Wednesday it rained and still she hiked all the way to the lake at Equinunk. Because it was pouring no one was there, so she took off her clothes and swam. That was beautiful, floating in the lake, rain washing down through the trees, rattling in the leaves, drenching her face. The sky was iron gray, a ceiling of clouds descending.

But then, everything was more beautiful, she found. No matter what she looked at it seemed clearer, as though it lit up under her gaze and announced itself: I am water. A maple tree. The sky. I am stone.

When she grew tired of just walking she began another kind of journey. She watched Chaim. A man mysterious. A man apart.

His curtains were always drawn, but she found some holes in the plank-ing that allowed her to see different parts of the room, though never very much at once. There was the floorboard view and the closet view. There was the view of the bookcase, the view between the bottles and jars in the medicine cabinet. There was a complete view of the ceiling from under-neath the bunk, but this required hardships that made it not worthwhile.

She settled for glimpses.

From various angles at various times, she saw his feet in socks, in slip-pers. She saw a glass of water placed on a chair next to the bed. She saw a handkerchief dropped, a handkerchief plucked up again. A bag of laundry set down in a corner. Often, a broom swept balls of lint and hair into a pile. Pantslegs! Coatsleeves! All of a sudden—his face! as he leaned over to collect the dirt into a dustpan, as beatific as though he were gathering manna in the desert.

What she hoped to discover, she couldn't say precisely, but every day she made her pilgrimage. Every day she knelt, hidden behind the walls of his cabin, trying her best to peer in.

Some days were more rewarding than others.

On Friday afternoons, for instance, he always polished his shoes so that they would be bright and new for the Sabbath. First he removed the laces, gingerly, as though they were made of silk. Then he took a whisk broom and brushed off all the loose dirt. With a nail file he scraped mud from the welt of the shoe, then poked a pin into all of the perforations. When the shoe was finally ready, he shook the bottle thoroughly, a lurch-ing sound, heavy, like medicine being mixed, then removed the ap-plicator and began painting—first the sides, then the tongues, then the heels. Last, he let them dry for half an hour, then rubbed them with a cloth until they shone.

Another ritual was the preparation of tea which he drank, without fail, at 4:30 in the afternoon. He had a small electric kettle stationed above the bookcase, a silver spoon, a china cup.

At night, instead of turning on the overhead light, he burned candles. Miriam could barely see anything then, but the flicker of shadows was enough to intrigue her, the occasional hiss and snap of flame made her shiver.

She shivered, too, the time she spied his slender hand lift a bar of soap from the shelf in the bathroom. As he removed the wrapper her heart leapt up, for had he not closed the cabinet door just then, she would have seen his robe removed as well, would have seen him stepping into the shower.

She never actually discovered anything she hadn't already observed just by sitting on her bench in class with others. He was meticulous. He was thoughtful. He worshipped the acts of ordinary life the same way he worshipped knowledge. Nothing new.

But here, alone and unguarded in his cabin, he was framed in mystery. From her vantage point, each hint of flesh loomed statuesque. Each gesture swelled with meaning. The smallest act became a revelation.

Her devotion turned boundless. From his morning ablutions to his nighttime prayers, she scrutinized every motion. She was his prophet. In a thick notebook she wrote down all he did, printing the words in straight, careful lines as though they were already gospel:

"At dawn, he wakes . . ."

"Late afternoon: he groans and stirs—too much study in one position? . . ."

"Evening: Walks to the window and stares into the woods . . . He sighs . . . Eventually, he lets the curtain fall . . ."

"Later: Night has come. He waits for sleep . . ."

She studied these notes daily, searching for patterns. She asked herself questions: which had more significance—the order of his actions or the spirit in which they were performed? Could she estimate that spirit? Could she guess the exact nature of the intention that informed each action?

No more than she could understand Barry, who daily grew more bold in his troublemaking. She wasn't his only victim anymore. Perhaps because the end of summer was approaching he began to expand his horizons. From simple pranks like graffiti and pool dunkings, he leapfrogged to more elaborate crimes—putting paint in the windshield washer of the camp bus, hiding all the canoe paddles the night before the big trip down the Delaware, making streamers of the underwear he pirated from the girls' bunks and draping them in the trees. He stole cake from the baker's closet—poppy seed strudel and cream puffs and chocolate éclairs, the spoils of the camp director and the rabbinical staff always kept locked up against just this kind of invasion. During Saturday morning services he let loose a collection of live crickets that rasped and whirred like a demented congregation. He ordered subscriptions to the library from Crusade for Christ, from the American Nazi Party.

Everyone assumed it was Barry. It had to be him. Who else would have had the nerve? Miriam, herself, saw him one night at the camp junkyard breaking windows with one of the missing canoe paddles. The junkyard was a clearing in the woods at the end of a narrow, rutted road. It was the place where they piled all the ruined furniture—the mildewed mattresses and ravaged sofas, the crippled chairs and tables, as well as things like martyred pianos, mirrors that were cracked, embittered.

Over this ruined kingdom, Barry reigned, forcing homage with beatings, breaking spirits that were already broken. He pounded and whacked and hammered and when he'd shattered every window into a thousand frightened splinters, he began ranting aimlessly, "Take *that* you bastard! Take *that* you bitch!" flailing and thrashing and smiting all of the unfortunate subjects in his path.

If his behavior in class was any measure of his loss of self-control then this was to be expected. Late in the season, he and Chaim had learned a new kind of dance—contorted, ugly. It drove away all peace and quiet, all possibility of reconciliation. By that time, it was just the two of them. As though Miriam were a shade that had been lifted to reveal his true enemy, Barry no longer bothered to tease her. Chaim was the target now, a willing target who bent to receive the arrows.

Each morning Barry strolled in an hour late: "Did I miss anything? Are we still on chapter two? That dumb old stuff? Lord! Will this ever be over?"

Each morning he pushed Chaim a little bit further: "Excuse me, dear teacher, Moreleh, Your Highness, I mean. That just doesn't make any sense to me. Is that really the translation? Are you certain this is the answer?"

"Why do we have to study this boring garbage anyway?"

"Well, that's a silly law if I ever heard one!"

He would goad and bully and impugn and just as Chaim was about to lose his temper, as his face began to redden and his voice began to shake, he would pull back: "Hey. Don't get excited, man. Take it easy, will you? I'm just an ignoramus, a clown, a boy who likes to sow his nasty oats—what do you care? Look. Don't pay any attention to me. I don't mean anything, you know. Not really."

Chaim appeared determined to endure. It was as if by yielding to his anger he would prove himself a liar; he would have to admit that Barry was not a "good boy," someone to "bear with." Setting an example was all that seemed to matter. Ignoring the price, he continued to sidestep these challenges and affronts, to pretend that they were merely bursts of high spirits. Kindling.

She was walking in circles. That's all she knew. She was further than ever from understanding him, from understanding anything. Further still the night she saw this, something so strange she was not convinced afterwards that she had seen anything at all.

She had been fasting for a week, for two weeks, more. She had been living on tea and water and water and tea. Many times she had seen things that weren't there. Flocks of birds when she bent over, swarms of ants, dark fountains spouting from the ground. She saw afterimages of what she had just seen on top of what she saw a second later—trees on top of buildings, rocks on top of heads.

At night she couldn't sleep. She closed her eyes and had visions (she couldn't think of another name for what she witnessed). Big dots. Masses of color. Parades of geometric shapes. All the parts of the body, in parts: huge eyes, knees, foreheads, ribs. She saw lines, flashes of lightning; as before—letters from all of the alphabets dancing together without shame.

Still. Even this made a certain kind of sense. What she saw in Chaim's cabin—no sense at all.

First his feet walked over to the bookcase. They walked back to the bed and paused. She heard the sound of sheets of paper being ripped from a book, from many books. This went on for several minutes during which time the feet returned to the bookcase, presumably, to remove more books. Then she saw knees, hands, a pile of paper.

A coat was thrown to the floor, then a shirt. One set of ceremonial fringes. And just when her heart began to pound thinking she would see him at last, she saw, instead, a pair of hands strike a match, reach forward to the paper; and when it was on fire (blazing in fierce darts of color) he muttered something in Hebrew, the hands came down; she saw him lay himself down, back first, on top of the flames.

What would it have meant provided she had actually seen it? After she awoke from her faint she thought of several possibilities. He had a rare skin disease that was held in check, though not cured, by daily doses of charcoal and extreme heat. He had decided to become a Hindu mystic. He was a magician. A pyromaniac. She was crazy.

She knew she should stop fasting. She told herself that every day. She was becoming very light. Much lighter than anyone else. Invisible. A wraith. It was true. She had found the trick. She could pass right through other people and they didn't even notice her. In turn, the words they spoke passed back through her and on into the night as if through ether. What they meant no longer sank into her flesh and lay there trapped.

But it wasn't only that. It was the strength she had achieved, the concentration. It was feeling that once she gave in, once she gave up just a little bit, she gave it all up; she gave up forever herself. It was feeling that she might see again the flames in Chaim's cabin, and, like a ledge or a bridge, some wide open space between heights where she might fall, it was daring to see those flames again, wanting to see them rise through his back.

(Chaos)

But that was cool, wasn't it? Barry had asked the morning they finally finished reading chapter three. Wasn't screwing on the Sabbath a double mitzvah? a double good deed? Wasn't that the law—double your pleasure double your fun? So why did Adam and Eve get the boot? What was wrong with one little screw?

Smoke hissed from the torches. Her insides hissed with hunger. It was the evening of Tisha B'Av, a fast to commemorate the destruction of the

Temple, the precedent (as Chaim called it) for all the two thousand years of suffering that came after.

They were sitting on the floor reading "Lamentations." By the waters of Babylon, remembering Zion.

He was standing, a man apart, a man mysterious, in a corner by the door, swaying as though he had been swaying for days and days and couldn't stop. The torchlight swayed with him, and the congregation, sitting in the long shadows on the floor, chanted: "From above he hath sent fire into my bones, and it prevaileth against them. He hath spread a net for my feet, he hath turned me back: He hath made me desolate and faint all day . . ."

Barry had disappeared. Three days ago. "Who needs your stupid class?" he had said. "Who needs your fucking Torah?" He had stalked off into the woods and they hadn't seen him since.

At first they thought he was just going in there to sulk, to make a scene. "You were right," they told Chaim. "He was really being a jerk"; and Chaim, still furious, still clutching his Bible, had called after him only faintly: "Sternberg, wait."

He hadn't appeared on the baseball field later that afternoon when they were scheduled to practice, nor had he shown up for dinner; and by the time "lights out" had rolled around, they knew he wasn't fooling. They knew they had to look for him.

But, by then, it was too dark to find anyone. The woods had filled with fog.

They were swaying together and the room was hot. They were packed together on the floor, sitting cross-legged, swaying back and forth, voices rising with the smoke. "I am the man that hath seen affliction by the rod of his wrath. He hath led me and brought me into darkness, but not into light . . ."

"Fool!" At Barry's question, Chaim had banged his book down on the desk. "For *this* you suddenly come alive? For *this* you are suddenly familiar with the text? For *this* you open your foolish mouth?"

Whatever had gotten into Barry had gotten into him as well. He was more than just angry. He was a pillar of smoke, an avenging cloud. "How many times have I asked you, children, and nobody knows? How many times and no one has even bothered to ask me themselves or to look? What's wrong with you? Can't you think? All summer long I ask you questions. All summer long, you sit there like death!"

But this was not the worst. He had slammed his Bible down on the desk—a vast sacrilege; in the old days, a sin almost equal to murder. When he saw what he had done, how he had crushed the pages and broken the binding, he cried: "Ah, look! Look! Look what you made me do. This is what comes of 'peel-pool'!"

But he hadn't explained.

Instead, he had picked up the broken book and cradled it in his hands, turning the pages gently, slowly. Then, sighing a cold, deep sigh, as though he had found an irreparable injury, he had hugged it to his chest and started swaying back and forth chanting in Hebrew, "Forgive me, forgive me, forgive me . . ."

It was the evening of Tisha B'Av, the start of a fast to commemorate the destruction, the suffering, the marching in of armies, the marching out of hope. The fast had begun at sundown, would continue until sundown, twenty-four hours. They would pray tonight and all day tomorrow sitting on the floor and fasting, praying, sighing.

Barry had disappeared. Three days ago. "Who needs your stupid class?" he had said. "Who needs your fucking Torah?" He had stalked off into the woods and they hadn't seen him since.

The next morning they had thought they'd find him crouched behind the door of the bunk waiting for the right moment to spring out at them. "Ha! Ha! Fooled you assholes. You gave me up for dead, didn't you? Well, I'll tell you the truth now. I had a superb night. On the town, of course." (Though his clothing might be crumpled, though bits of leaves might cling to his hair.) He had done this twice before, they said. Each time, they had called his aunt. Each time, they had called his psychiatrist. "It's just a manipulation," the psychiatrist said. "His version of suicide." And the aunt had said, "It's true. He runs away all the time. He hides in some safe place. He makes everyone suffer."

"But thou hast utterly rejected us; Thou art very much wroth against us."

Now they were finished with "Lamentations." They were beginning the long litany of suffering. Leo Goelman stepped to the podium. "Two specialties, we have," he said. "Suffering. Memory. Of these we have made an art."

They were lighting candles—one for each phase of history, one for each hallmark of the art. The First Temple and the Second Temple. The exile in Babylon and the exile in Persia. The Greek occupation and the Roman. The Inquisition and the Dark Ages. The pogroms and the Cossacks. Treblinka and Auschwitz and Dachau . . .

Barry had disappeared, but he couldn't have gone very far. The evidence was clear. There were signs of him everywhere. Books pulled from their shelves. Benches overturned in the classrooms. Messages on the library wall.

And Chaim had not been in his cabin, had not been there for three days. There had been no shoes on the floor, no fringes, no pale, white hand reaching towards her in the cabinet. She had waited for him and waited, had hoped he might be sitting there in the dark, within the curtains, clutching a pile of paper, maybe singing softly or muttering or clasping his hands together and curling himself up in prayer.

Barry had disappeared, but there were signs of him everywhere. In the prayer books that were stolen, in the candlesticks that had fallen down, in the pages torn from books and scattered in the grass, in the things that were missing—scarves, rings, bracelets (handed back, lost somewhere). Some even said in the weeping at night in the cabins (from the upper bunks, from the lower).

Even here, there were signs. The torches burned brightly. They swayed. She was hungry.

She had waited until after dark, herself, curled up amid the pine needles, the weeds and dry sticks, hungry and thirsty, until finally, when the first damp fog of evening began to seep into her skin, she felt she couldn't wait another minute longer. She had crept up the stairs, had nudged the door open, found a room completely empty. There had been no clothes in the closet, no books on the shelves, and, except for an old brown suitcase which stood by the door, there was only a dustpan propped against one wall, the faint smell of something burnt.

Smoke rose. Shadows rose. She could feel herself rising with them, lighter than air, so faint she felt like vapor.

Barry had disappeared. Chaim had gone after him. She had gone after Chaim.

All day long, on the hottest day of summer, she had walked. Through pine forests, through stands of maple, through shrubs matted with vines and creepers. There was no path, but she kept on going, drifting along in a cloud of hunger. Every time she moved, a trail of sound and light churned inside her, turning to heat and dust, a dry aching thirst that caked her throat, that made her lean against a tree and gasp.

But even this was not the worst, that she had walked until late afternoon, until her thirst was so great that it pushed her through the underbrush to a stream where she drank and drank and drank. Even this was not the worst, that when her thirst had stopped, when the roaring had stopped in her ears, she had heard weeping, had looked up and seen a man in black sprawled on the ground weeping and weeping and weeping. Nor even this. She hadn't gone to him and caressed him. She hadn't knelt and kissed him; nor had he, in his turn, kissed her, had not said "I like big girls," had not held her until the sun came through the trees in threads: orange yellow green sprays of light.

It was this—what he *did* say. "You know what is 'peel-pool, Mireleh? I'll tell you what it really is. Not just the dictionary definition—*casuistry*, the athletic misinterpretation of words, in a quiet room filled with dusty old books . . ."

He had made her sit down beside him. He had held her hand.

"Listen. It was many years ago, not here, but in a village far away. There was a boy just about your age. It was going to be his Bar Mitzvah. He was coming of age. He was going to know what there was to know— about the world, about himself, and his family was very happy, very excited; or they would have been excited. But this was a bad time. A bad place. There was no Torah then. It was forbidden, strictly forbidden.

"The boy's father was a rabbi, the head of a yeshiva until they closed them down. After that, he was a rabbi in secret. He had hidden the Torahs, every single one of them. The penalty for this was death. For being a Jew. They were burning all the Torahs, burning the yeshivot; they were marching us all away.

"Every day whoever wanted to, whoever was brave enough, whoever was left, would slip out of their houses, go to this secret place to pray."

"And the Bar Mitzvah?" she had asked, though she already knew the answer. "Did he have it?"

He shook his head. "When they found the Torahs they would burn them. In a heap they would pile them in the street along with other holy books, law books, whatever they found that looked sacred. They would pour kerosene on top and set them on fire, let them burn into ashes. There were some Jews who tried to rescue them. There were some who believed in Kiddush HaShem, the commandment of martyrdom for God, for His word, a commandment outweighing all the others, but *never* to be invoked, some said. Others, like my father, threw themselves onto the flames."

"But did you—"

"I, Mireleh? Not I. Not then."

And that was not the worst. It was not only that, but this: Barry never knew when to stop. "Sure," he had said as Chaim rocked back and forth with the ruined book. "Sure, man!" He had raised his arms and held out both hands in benediction. "We forgive you—no problem. No fucking problem. Forgiveness, *free and complete*. Don't give it another thought."

Chaim had stopped swaying. He had set the book down on the table carefully, very accurately, had set it down in some precise diagram that only he could see of a Bible set down in anger. Then, as if it were also part of the same diagram, one which told him how to convert thought into motion, rage into sound, he had slapped Barry across the face, had shouted:

"*You* forgive *me*? *You* forgive *me*? To whom do you think you're speaking? To some goniff? To the devil? Get out of here you little bastard!"

And this. Finally there was this: "Bergen Belsen, Madanek, Theresienstadt . . ." They were still listing, matching up the horrors with the lights. Barry still hadn't come back. She was still hungry. In his corner, Chaim was still swaying, back and forth, back and forth, Baruch HaShem, Amen V'Amen.

Behind him, the torches swayed, glowing. And for a moment, as he bent over his text, she didn't see clothes, but flesh, saw the pale skin of his back, on either side of his spine, saw letters (the ten commandments? the ten plagues?); she saw the torches burning behind all of them, saw all of them, like Barry, alone in the woods in the dark.

CHARLES SIMIC

Charles Simic was born in
Yugoslavia in 1938. The most
recent of his thirteen collections
of poetry are *Selected Poems
1963–1983, Unending Blues,* and
The World Doesn't End. A pro
fessor at the University of New
Hampshire, he has won numerous
awards, including a MacArthur
Fellowship and the 1990 Pulitzer
Prize, and was a finalist for the
Pulitzer Prize in both 1986 and
1987.

BROOMS

for Tomaz, Susan and George

1

Only brooms
Know the devil
Still exists,

That the snow grows whiter
After a crow has flown over it,

381

That a dark dusty corner
Is the place of dreamers and children,

That a broom is also a tree
In the orchard of the poor,
That a hanging roach there
Is a mute dove.

    2

Brooms appear in dreambooks
As omens of approaching death.
This is their secret life.
In public, they act like flat-chested old maids
Preaching temperance.

They are sworn enemies of lyric poetry.
In prison they accompany the jailer,
Enter cells to hear confessions.
Their short-end comes down
When you least expect it.

Left alone behind a door
Of a condemned tenement,
They mutter to no one in particular,
Words like *virgin wind moon-eclipse*,
And that most sacred of all names:
Hieronymous Bosch.

    3

In this and in no other manner
Was the first ancestral broom made:
Namely, they plucked all the arrows
From the bent back of Saint Sebastian.

They tied them with a rope
On which Judas hung himself.
Stuck in the stilt
On which Copernicus
Touched the morning star . . .

Then the broom was ready
To leave the monastery.
The dust welcomed it—
That great pornographer
Immediately wanted to
Look under its skirt.

4

The secret teaching of brooms
Excludes optimism, the consolation
Of laziness, the astonishing wonders
Of a glass of aged moonshine.

It says: the bones end up under the table.
Bread-crumbs have a mind of their own.
The milk is you-know-who's semen.
The mice have the last squeal.

As for the famous business
Of levitation, I suggest remembering:
There is only one God
And his prophet is Mohammed.

5

And then finally there's your grandmother
Sweeping the dust of the nineteenth century

Into the twentieth, and your grandfather plucking
A straw out of the broom to pick his teeth.

Long winter nights.
Dawns a thousand years deep.
Kitchen windows like heads
Bandaged for toothache.

The broom beyond them sweeping,
Tucking in the lucent grains of dust
Into neat pyramids,
That have tombs in them,

Already sacked by robbers,
Once, long ago.

GRAVITY

I'd like to see it sometime
As it loads up,
As it throws another shovelful
On the congregation.

Ooooh! That's what the choir
Of the First Baptist Church says,
And the birches as they bend low
In observance:

Sunday evening service,
Where it wants everybody
Hunchbacked,
Everybody kissing the earth.

And later—like the beasts
Of burden—heavily
In its bit and harness
Over the freshly fallen snow.

LOUIS SIMPSON

Louis Simpson was born in
Jamaica, British West Indies, in
1923 and emigrated to the United
States in 1940. His books include
At the End of the Open Road,
which won the Pulitzer Prize, and
Collected Poems. He has also pub-
lished three works of criticism,
most recently *A Company of
Poets*. Since 1967 he has been on
the faculty at the State University
of New York at Stony Brook.

AKHMATOVA'S HUSBAND

for Vera Dunham

Akhmatova's husband, Gumilev,
was a poet and an explorer.
He wrote poems about wild animals
and had fantastic ideas:
a red bird with the head of a girl
and a lost tram that goes wandering . . .

shedding fire "like a storm with dark wings,"
passing over bridges,
by a house with three windows
where a woman that he loved once lived,
and, rushing toward him,
two raised hooves and an iron glove.

Gumilev fought in the Great War
with almost incredible valor,
twice winning the Cross of Saint George.
He envisioned a little old man
forging the bullet that would kill him.

It wasn't a German bullet, it was Russian.
Gumilev was killed by his own countrymen
as poets in Russia frequently are.

Everyone talks about Akhmatova
but no one talks about Gumilev.
That wouldn't have mattered to Gumilev.
When the man from the government came to kill him,
"Just give me a cigarette," said Gumilev,
"and let's get it over with."

ARTHUR SMITH

Arthur Smith is the author of *El-
egy on Independence Day*, which
received the Agnes Lynch Starrett
Prize and the Norma Farber First
Book Award. Born in Stockton,
California, in 1948, he teaches at
the University of Tennessee in
Knoxville.

A LITTLE DEATH

Anyone almost anywhere on the walkway could have
    heard it—I did—
That boom-like, intermittent grunting
    pained with effort, resonating suddenly like a foghorn
Through the late-summer, Sunday afternoon drowse
    of the Knoxville City Zoo.

Here, I thought, was an animal
    so overwhelmed
The most it could hope for was to bellow into being
    that intensity—those waves mounting, even then

Bearing it away. A group already ringed
    the tortoise pen,

Where earlier, leaning over a barrier of logs, patting,
    and then more boldly
Stroking the larger of the two, his fatherly, reptilian neck
    craning—distended, really, upward,
Tolerantly, it seemed—I had reckoned
    him old,

So old, in fact, that crowding
    back around the pen,
I expected to find him dead or, worse, still living,
    convulsed
With those horribly irreversible last spasms for air.

He was "dying," to be sure, clambered up
    and balanced—to say the least—precariously on
The other's high-humped shell,
    his stump-like front feet extended forward,
Grasping, as they were able, the other's weathered carapace,
    for leverage,

His own neck dangling, gaze floating
    vacantly downward,
And his mouth agape, saliva
    swaying on short, thick threads only inches
From the other's bony face. And,
    all along,

The noise. It wasn't pretty
Though it was soon over—
This "little death" referred to in our youth,
    snickeringly,

As "makin' bacon," back when all knowledge
Belonged, by fiat, to the young, but here witnessed
    in the frank

Generation of matter, all amenities
        beside the fact—

The male beached on his own bulk, panting, less than
        tolerant, now,
Of the heavy-handed petting,
And the female, unencumbered again,
        scooting rather

Indifferently toward the mud-bracketed pond
        tattered with froth-pads
Of algae, immersing herself as far as the shallow water
Would allow.

DAVE SMITH

Born in Portsmouth, Virginia, in
1942, Dave Smith has published
many volumes of poetry, including
*The Roundhouse Voices: Poems
1970–1985* and *Cuba Night*. He
has also published a novel,
Onliness, and edited *The Pure
Clear Word: Essays on the Poetry
of James Wright*. He teaches at
Virginia Commonwealth
University.

SUNDAY MORNING: CELIA'S FATHER

The man stops in his labor to sweep at his forehead
with a glove stiffened to a claw, leaves
at his feet not yet lit but already
smoldering with the light of death.

I see him take off his hat to the passing children,
the bright, uncomprehending belief on them,
leaving their arms well laden
with hymnbooks and unalterable words.

For him what is real is dying Summer, the hot clutter
that comes and weaves in the maples
now gone to more than gold . . .
but when a few small faces

fold against the unexpected rattling gusts, tears
whipped along the edges of their eyes,
often he finds himself kneeling,
scratching with stiffened arms

to reclaim each unfired cheek of green wind remembers
and skids past the circle of his keeping.
Often I see him pause and rise,
tall, as if a chill digs in.

Some mornings he calls the strange children to him.
They gather fists of pine cones and feed
his fire. He knows this is forbidden,
but the cold, hours of leaves overwhelm him.

When that yellow smoke rises like a daughter's hair,
he rakes, dances with small caps and coats.
They ride him like an old stick risen
and he beats them into laughter, helplessly.

KEN SMITH

Ken Smith was born in Silver City,
New Mexico, in 1944. He is the
author of *Decoys and Other
Stories*. His stories have appeared
in *The Atlantic*, *TriQuarterly*, and
other magazines. He teaches at
the University of Tennessee at
Chattanooga.

THE NICEST MAN

Every year Mr. O'Simmons would lend me and Vern mules so we could
go up to Amador Springs and hunt. We'd stay until we killed three deer,
one for each of us and one we would give to whoever was staying at the
main ranch house. Mr. O'Simmons was pretty much of a big shot around
there. He was on the county board of commissioners and he owned the
Mule Shoe Cattle Company. Vern was his nephew. He was an idiot.

It wasn't like he went around slobbering or talking stupid all the time.
Fact is, he never said much when he was around people. He'd just stare at
you with his head pushed forward and this pinched look on his face, like
he had been studying you so hard he'd given himself a headache. He had
big buck teeth and big eyes and big ears that stood out from his head and

bent forward a little. But if you'd seen him when he wasn't in one of his staring moods, you'd have thought he was as normal as anybody. Just quiet and ugly.

Then too, if he was around women a lot, he'd play with himself. I know that's why Mr. O'Simmons' sister kept him locked up in the house whenever he was in town.

They'd let him come out to the Mule Shoe if someone was around to watch him. Mostly that someone was me. Even from the first I could handle Vern. If he got to fussing, I'd just sit down and start doing something, like whittling, and Vern, he'd pull out his knife, find himself a stick, and whittle right along with me. As long as I'd sit there and whittle so would he. Usually whatever mood he was in that had made him so nervous would be gone when we finished.

Mr. O'Simmons and his sister were always marvelling about how I could take care of Vern, and I think they'd have left him out to the ranch permanent if I'd been around. But I was too young to spend all my time doctoring cows, so I'd work in town for a time, then out to Mr. O'Simmons' for a while. Two or three months in each place. And Mr. O'Simmons didn't seem to mind much, though he always acted a little uneasy whenever I'd tell him it was time for my town stretch.

"This work will wait," he'd say. "You do what you got to, Tate." He never got mad. You know how ranching is, the hard work's mostly seasonal. And I'd always be back with him during both roundups and in the summer screwworm season.

And every fall, just before roundup, Mr. O'Simmons would come out from town and say it was time for venison, and he'd tell me to get the horses and mules and take Vern on up to Amador Springs.

The Amador line shack is up in high country, where the juniper and oak are just giving over to spruce and pine. Vern would always be so enthused about going that it'd rub off on me. He could handle a rifle just fine, and he always wanted to do all the gutting and skinning. If I'd let him do that, he'd do whatever else I told him to. Not like Mr. O'Simmons who'd send Vern away whenever we were butchering a steer, not like his mom who'd slap his hands whenever he'd start messing with himself. I'd let him do most things, within limits, of course. You could see sometimes he just needed to be let alone. It wasn't all of him was an idiot, wasn't all of him ten years old.

But sometimes he did give me the jeebies. The worst thing he did, the thing that got me the most, was that he'd talk to dead things, talk away just like they could hear. The first time he did it, he nearly drove me crazy, but I don't know, after I'd seen him do it several times, it stopped bothering me. It just seemed natural for Vern.

There were times, even, when it was funny, Vern talking to something dead. One year, the year I did the stupid thing, though I never meant any of it to hurt Vern, we shot a spike buck that ran a ways before he died. He got down into the bottom of a narrow, rocky creek, and even afoot we had hell getting to him.

After Vern gutted the deer, we had to lift him up over a high wall of rocks to a little flat spot I figured we could get the mule down to. I walked back up the trail to where we'd tied the horses and mule, and as I led the mule back down, I could hear Vern talking his head off to that little spike. "Ain't nothing to worry about," he was saying. "Don't be scared cause there's nothing to get scared about."

Of course we had Mr. O'Simmons' white mule, and of course that mule decided he wasn't going to stand still for us to load the deer. He'd side-step or back off or kick, and no matter how hard either Vern or I tried to hold him, that damn mule would move. He'd stand there fine until we almost got the deer loaded, then he'd cut up and the buck would come crashing down.

At the time I was fuming. But looking back, it must have been about the funniest sight you'd ever see. Here I am, after our fourth try, holding the mule's hackamore tight, my fist right up under his chin, cussing and promising that if he doesn't stand still, I'm going to pigtie him and throw him down. And all this time, me ranting at that damn mule, Vern is standing spraddle-legged over the dead deer, his hands on his hips, saying, "I told you, dammit, I ain't telling you again. Get up on that mule."

We finally got the little spike loaded, and since that finished our hunt and it was still early in the day, we headed for the main ranch house. Mr. O'Simmons was there when we got in, and the first thing I said was that I'd pay him two hundred dollars for that white mule.

Mr. O'Simmons looked kind of surprised. "He ain't that much to pack," he said.

"I know," I said.

"He's old. He ain't worth that much."

"To me he is," I said. "It'd give me two hundred dollars' worth of pleasure just to shoot the son-of-a-bitch."

Mr. O'Simmons got a kick out of that. He laughs real high and Vern is laughing too. And all evening Vern seems in such good spirits. Later, while I'm out at the corral graining the mules and the night horse, he comes out all smiles and asks if I'm going to shoot the white mule in the morning.

I tell him no, it was only a joke.

Vern seems kind of let down. "Well, I wish you would," he says. "I got a couple things I'd like to say to him."

You see, he was an idiot, but he was likeable. And left to himself, he was harmless as a new, wobbly-legged colt. I never meant any of it to happen.

Vern must have been close to thirty that last year we hunted, the year he wanted me to shoot Mr. O'Simmons' white mule. After our hunting and just as we were about to wind up the fall branding, Mr. O'Simmons brought this old drunk named George out to stay at the Mule Shoe. He was always bringing someone like George around to dry out. The old man was really all right. He'd tend the chickens and any livestock we had up, and if he was there in the spring, he'd put us in a little garden. Maybe he was just an old drunk, but he could grow anything.

George never paid much attention to Vern. But every evening he'd talk my ears off, always bragging about this big family he had back in Texas, and since we'd stayed together at the ranch before, it was mostly stuff I'd already heard. Usually I didn't listen. I always figured if he really had a family, he'd have gone back to them and tried to straighten himself out.

All that fall he talked about a niece of his named Rita, about how the family was thinking of sending her out to him because she'd gotten in some kind of trouble back home. I never believed much of it, though. I figured it was just the whiskey working its way out of his brain.

And I kept thinking that way until one winter evening when Vern and I were sitting on the porch while George cleaned up after supper, and right out of the blue Mr. O'Simmons drives up to the house with a pickup load of groceries and furniture and baby toys and this dark-haired woman named Rita. And her baby boy.

We all got to work that evening, making one of the back rooms suitable. Mr. O'Simmons was something. If I hadn't realized it before, I did then. There wasn't anything he wouldn't do for you if he knew you and your family. George, of course, was beaming. He'd coo over that baby, and he was always going on about how pretty Rita was, though I couldn't see anything special about her. Not that she was ugly—by no means am I saying that.

She was thin and small, and her hair never looked good, kind of stringy and straight. She had a poor complexion, but real pretty eyes, dark and big, and she had this way of looking at you like whatever you were saying was just about the most important thing she'd ever heard. And she had all the parts a woman should. When she got into Levis or something else tight, she could make a man notice.

Vern took to her right away, but she seemed quiet and a little scared of him. Then after a few days, she got just like George. Now I had two of them talking me silly. Then her boy cried some, like all babies, and I got to missing the quiet times when Vern and I had the place to ourselves.

One evening after Vern and I had been out in a dry camp for two or three days mending fence and I was in a bad mood, I said something that upset her. I can't remember exactly what, but it had something to do with the supper she had made. I was trying to pay her a compliment, but it didn't turn out that way. She acted hurt most of the evening, and I felt bad about whatever it was I had said. When George went in to bed, I tried my best to apologize, but she wouldn't hear of it.

She said she felt like she was barging in on us, and she could understand how her being here with the baby and all could cause problems.

Then I really felt bad. I sat with her on the porch and tried over and over to tell her that she wasn't in the way.

All this time we were talking, Vern had been out to the corral doing something or other. When he came back he sat at the top of the porch steps and stared at Rita, which got me nervous. Then suddenly, sure enough, Vern starts messing with himself, right there in front of her.

I tried to make Vern go to bed, but he wouldn't budge. If Rita noticed what he was up to, she didn't let on, she just sat there talking, trying to change the subject from whatever it was I'd said about her cooking. Finally I couldn't stand it any more, so I asked if she wouldn't like a little walk to settle her food.

As we got up from our chairs, I told Vern to stay put, that if he didn't mind me, it was the end of our hunting. He took his hand away from his pants and waved at me. He stuck out his bottom lip and frowned, then made a hissing noise through his buck teeth.

Rita and I walked down to the corral. I was trying to figure how to explain about Vern. I knew there was a way to tell her, but I couldn't seem to get started.

"Sometimes he gets funny," I said finally.

Rita just looked at me.

"Sometimes it's best to let him alone."

"Yes," she said.

"Sometimes he sort of . . ."

"Tate," she said. She stepped closer to me and touched my arm. "I'm a mother. I know about men."

Something in the way she said that last word got to me. In the dark, with only the kitchen light on, we could just make out the outline of the porch. I couldn't see Vern, but I could tell by the sounds he made that he was still at it.

Rita was quiet, leaning a little toward the house, like she was listening too. I asked if she didn't want to walk a ways farther.

She said no, she'd like to sit on the top rail of the corral. "Will you help me up?" she asked.

I lifted her. In a while we heard Vern stand up and go into the house.

"The poor boy," Rita said.

"He don't know any better," I told her.

A little wind came up against our backs. As Rita shifted on the rail, her knee brushed against my arm. "It must be hard," she said. "A grown man like that."

"Yes," I said.

"It must be hard for any man out here alone."

I said it wasn't so bad. Then her leg pushed harder against my arm.

"Tate," she said, "why don't you take me into the tack room."

I stayed in the tack room for half an hour after she'd gone, leaning against a saddle, smelling the horse sweat and saddle soap and her smell, and I knew already I didn't like her, not that way. I'm not saying I like a woman who lays back and chews gum while you do it, but this Rita, she was just too crazy. She kept saying she wanted it to hurt, and while we were doing it, she used words I didn't even know women knew. Before I walked out of there, I had decided it was time to tell Mr. O'Simmons that I was ready for my town stint.

I snuck into the dark house. Vern was breathing heavy as I stepped into our room. I knew he wasn't asleep, but I played like he was. I undressed and went to bed. In a few minutes I heard him turn over. In the dark I could tell he was looking at me.

"Tate," he said, "she's your friend, ain't she?"

"Yes," I told him. "Kind of."

"She likes you, don't she?"

"I don't know, Vern. Go to sleep."

"Especial, I mean."

"I don't think so," I said.

He sighed and turned again in bed. I heard him mumble something, then he said, "I just wish . . ." But he went quiet after that. In a few minutes I said his name, but he didn't answer. I wanted to tell him that she probably liked us both the same.

And that night, lying there after Vern had dropped off, lying there thinking thoughts too big for me, was when I came up with the worst idea I ever had.

It took me a few days to get up the nerve to ask her. We'd been to the tack room twice more. Like I said, I really didn't like her especially. She was too fast a woman for me, always too ready, but I was young and she was there, and it seemed like it would hurt her feelings less to do it than for me to say no.

This particular night, after we were finished, as I stumbled around in the dark trying to get my pants on, she took hold of me again.

"I can't get enough of you," she said.

That's when I asked her.

She was quiet for a long time. Then she got up and started easing her dress down over her head. "You don't even like me, do you?" she asked.

"I do," I said.

"Then why do you want me to do it with him?"

I said I didn't know, not for sure.

"Because you like him more than me?"

"You're the one said you feel so sorry for him and all," I said. "You're the one said he needed someone."

"But I want you."

The tack room was quiet and dark. I wanted to say I was sorry, but I didn't. I felt like a damn fool for even asking, but part of me still wanted bad for her to say yes, she'd do it. It seemed important to me, really important, that Vern, just this once, have that feeling.

I was just starting to say something when I felt her hand on my shoulder. "Tate," she said. I tried to see her face, but there wasn't enough light. "Oh, Tate," she said, then she walked out the door.

Early the next morning I was saddling my horse when Rita came down to the corral. She had hardly looked at me at breakfast, hadn't spoken two words to anyone.

"If I do it," she said, "will you know I'm doing it because you asked?"

"Yes," I said.

"He's never . . . ?"

"No," I said. "Never."

She said, "God," and she made a funny noise, a kind of wheeze. She walked away a few steps, then came back. "He's so ugly," she said.

"In lots of ways he ain't," I said. "Most ways he's just another man."

She smiled then. "And you think with me another man, more or less, won't make any difference?"

"I never said that."

"No, I did. You were thinking it, though."

I looked at her for a long time, then got on my horse. "Really, I'm sorry," I said. I wanted to tell her how good it would be for Vern, but I didn't.

As I started off, she called me back. She reached both hands up and rested them on the pommel of my saddle. She leaned heavy into the horse's side. "Tate," she said. "Tate, I can't help it. I just can't keep from doing it. Damn you, can't you understand?"

I said I thought I did.

She asked about whiskey then and I told her where I kept a bottle hidden in a boot box in my closet. She nodded and looked up at me. She backed away from the horse and put her hand up to shield her eyes from the sun. I reined the horse around so the brightest part of the sky was at her back.

"Don't let George know about the whiskey," I said.

"I won't. I'll send him down to the neighbors for something or other."

"I'll see you this evening," I said.

She looked up at the house. George was walking out back toward the chicken coop. Vern was nowhere in sight. "Get down a minute," she said. We walked around to the back side of the corral. She told me to hold my horse between us and the house. She unbuttoned her Levis, then took my hand and put it between her legs. "Kiss me," she said. "Hard. Get me started good before you go."

All that day, as I was riding up to the rim to dynamite a spring that clogged up every winter, I felt good for Vern. And I felt good about Rita too. She was a chippy, she'd admitted that herself, but she was a good one. She understood that everybody, even an idiot, deserves to have it at least once in his life.

That evening when I came back to the ranch, I could tell as soon as I saw Vern that they'd done it. He was standing out behind the house, throwing rocks over into the big wash. Usually, if I'd been gone all day, he'd have been at the corral even before I got unsaddled. But today he wasn't, he just kept pitching those rocks.

When I was finished at the corral, I walked part of the way to the house and yelled at him. He turned and waved, but he didn't come pup-running, nearly wagging, like he usually did.

"Hey, Tate," he yelled.

"Hey, yourself. What are you doing?"

"Throwing rocks," he said. "Until supper."

"You fix that eaten-out place in the corral?"

"Yep," he said. "Me and my friend. We been doing stuff all day."

I waved at him again and went into the house. George was drinking coffee in the front room. He told me he'd brought back a stray from the neighbors. It was the same old cow that broke out about once a month, he said, and the neighbor had her penned up when he rode down there to borrow some milk.

I told him I'd take her way up toward the rim in a few days and see if she wouldn't behave herself up there.

"I doubt it," he said. "Some cows you can't never do nothing with."

I heard Rita in the kitchen, so I went in. She came over to me, smiling kind of fake-like, and kissed my cheek.

I pushed her back. "Jesus," I told her, "George is right out there."

"I know," she said. "He can't hear."

My hands were around her skinny upper arms. I looked at her for a minute, trying to think of the right thing to say. Finally, I leaned close to her and whispered, "Thanks."

She seemed to flinch. She studied me for a long time, then she began toying with a scab on the top of my right hand. Still looking down, she said, "We won't be going to the tack room anymore, will we?"

I didn't answer and in a minute she looked up. I could tell she knew. And it was funny because right then I wanted so much to hug her, to just wrap her up and tell her she didn't need to feel like anyone was better than her. Nobody. But instead, I dropped her arms. Hugging her would only get the whole thing started again.

In a few seconds her eyes got teary. "I'm glad I did it," she said. "Whatever anyone else would say, I'm glad. Whether for you or for him or for pity, I'm glad."

I couldn't say anything. I got myself a cup of coffee and went out to watch Vern throw rocks.

Vern was good for two days, then it happened. There's no one to blame for it but me. After all, I knew he was an idiot, and I should never have let it get started.

The thud was what woke me. Then Rita's baby started bawling. I must have known, even then, because I didn't bother to light the kerosene lamp. I grabbed the flashlight, pushed the switch, and saw that Vern's bed was empty.

I found him on top of Rita. He was naked, and he'd worked her nightgown up. She was pushing at him quietly, trying not to cause a ruckus and wake up George.

"Help me," she whispered, when she saw my light.

I grabbed Vern from behind, but he struggled loose and socked me. I had to hit him twice with the handle of the flashlight before he'd settle down. Luckily, I got him back to his own bed without waking George. And Rita finally got her baby quieted down.

Back in our room I tried to tell Vern that he couldn't just go in there and take her whenever he wanted, that he had to wait until she invited him to the tack room or someplace. I talked and talked, but I couldn't get through to him. There's some things you just can't explain to an idiot. He kept calling her his friend, shaking his head, and messing with himself.

"Vern, I'll conk you again, you don't stop that and listen," I told him.

"My friend," he said, and poked his chest.

I picked up the flashlight and pretended I was going to hit him again. "I mean it, Vern," I said.

In a while he calmed down. I got him dressed and we went out to the porch.

"We can still go hunting, Tate?" Vern shook his head. "I'm good at hunting."

"You hit me," I told him. "You don't mind me anymore."

"I'll mind," he said.

"Okay," I said. "You mind me right now because we're going to town." He put his hand to his chin, then breathed heavy and started moving his eyes around. He raised his shoulders and tucked his head down between them. "Now you mind," I said. "You promised."

"We can still go hunting and do stuff?" he asked.

I told him yes, but that now I needed to go to town, that we'd come back in a few days. "You want to see your mom, don't you?"

Vern nodded his head yes, but I knew it was a lie. We packed our gear and loaded it, as quietly as we could, into my old Plymouth. I sent Vern to the tack room for my saddle, and while he was out there, I snuck into the house and into Rita's room to tell her we were leaving.

"Make up something to tell George," I said.

"What?"

"I don't know. Something."

"You'll be back?"

"Couple of days," I said, knowing that I was going to tell Mr. O'Simmons that things at the ranch were fine and that it was time for my town jag. As it happened, I never saw her again.

On the way into town I reminded Vern that he'd promised to be good. Then I told him not to say anything about Rita, not about anything they'd done in the tack room, not about anything that had happened tonight. "Just don't say anything at all about her," I said.

"She gave me whiskey," he said. "She drank some too."

"Okay, Vern. Just be quiet about it from now on."

He eased back in the car seat and clamped his hands together behind his head. "Sure, Tate," he said. He looked at me for a minute, then out into the dark. "She likes us a lot, huh?"

"Yes, Vern. Now just forget it."

"I'll mind you, Tate," he said. He let out a sigh and wiggled down deeper into the seat. "Damn straight," he said.

We stopped at the lake to kill some time so we wouldn't get into town until the next morning. The wind was up and we parked near the shore, leaning against the old Plymouth, smoking cigarettes, and listening to little waves plop against the rocks. It was a peaceful couple of hours, but it didn't do me much good. I kept thinking about Rita fighting quiet under Vern. She'd have let him do whatever he wanted before she woke up George. I kept thinking about Vern and how I'd had to hit him to make him mind. I kept thinking about me being so scared.

Early that morning I dropped Vern off at his mother's, then went over to see Mr. O'Simmons. Like usual, he was nice about me quitting him for a while. He asked if I'd found a job in town.

"Not yet," I said.

He smiled then, like he was asking when I was going to grow up, but kindly, too, like he was doing his best to understand. He bought me breakfast in a little cafe. Then he gave me ten dollars more than my wages worked out to and said he'd be glad to see me come spring. He was a fine man, and I don't blame him a bit.

It was two days after they'd gelded Vern that I found out about it. His mom had locked him in the house and went out for a while, but Vern managed to sneak out. The witnesses, people I talked to myself, said it didn't seem Vern meant the little girl any harm. He just chased after her and grabbed her up and hugged her. They said he didn't try to undress her or anything like that. Everyone said he was just hugging her like a doll. She was only thirteen and, of course, it scared her silly.

The two men who grabbed Vern and took him home said he didn't put up any kind of fight. The little girl's folks caused a ruckus, though, and in the end Mr. O'Simmons and his sister thought there was only one thing to do.

You've got to know how I felt when I heard. For a few minutes I tried to blame Rita, but that was no good. She didn't even know Vern, and it was me that was supposed to be watching out for him. For a whole day I kept asking myself how I was going to get on in this world if I couldn't even watch out for an idiot, a good, well-behaved idiot at that.

The morning I left town there were only two people I wanted to see— Vern and Mr. O'Simmons. And I'd like to be able to say that I confessed everything but, of course, I didn't.

Vern's mother met me at the door, and I told her I was leaving and that I'd like to say goodbye to him. She studied me for a long time, then hugged me and told me thanks for all the things I'd done for Vern. She was crying a little.

"Tate," she said, "I don't know how we'll ever find another young man to take care of him the way you did. To take him places. Hunting and all."

I sort of shrugged and asked where Vern was. The house smelled clean. My head started to hurt and the notion only then came to me that I didn't know how to tell Vern goodbye.

Vern's mother nodded toward a closed door. She said Vern was in there, but she'd rather he didn't have any company for a few days.

"But I'm leaving," I said. "This morning. Right now."

She patted my arm. "It's all right," she said. "Later I'll tell him you came by."

"I got to see him," I told her.

She took hold of my arm hard. "He's bad right now. He wouldn't want to see you." She let go of me and folded her hands in front of her waist. She looked toward the closed door of Vern's room, then back at me. "We had to tie his hands," she said. "He keeps trying to take off the bandages."

"Damn," I said. Then I whirled and started for Vern's door.

"Tate!" she screamed. She moved to block my way and I stopped. Then I started cussing her, the first and only time I ever did that to a woman. Man, I looked right at her face and I cussed like a sailor.

She didn't even flinch. "We had to, Tate," she said. "You know we did." Her voice was calm now, and quiet.

When my feet hit the sidewalk outside I knew, even in the state I was in, that it was myself I was cussing.

I found Mr. O'Simmons at Ramsey's Feed Store. He was in the office, visiting with old man Ramsey and a couple other ranchers. He knew something was up because when I first walked in, he looked up like he'd been expecting me and said, "You want to talk to me, Tate?"

I nodded.

Mr. O'Simmons stood and put his coffee cup on the counter. "Thanks, Bob," he said to old man Ramsey. Then, just before we got to the door, he turned and flicked his hand at the three men. "See you fellas," he said.

We walked out back to the holding pens, and Mr. O'Simmons lit a cigar and gave me one. I took it and looked down at the cellophane wrapper.

"I hear you're leaving us," he said.

"I got to," I said. I wondered how he had known.

He put his foot up on the bottom rail of the pen and looked at two fat cows lying in the dirt, chewing their cuds. One had a blind eye. "You ever come back and want a job, Tate, you got one," he said.

"Thanks," I said. I looked out into the pen and told him I was sorry to hear about Vern.

"I know," he said.

"Why?" I asked. "From everything I heard, it didn't seem like he hurt the little girl any." It was the first time I'd even come close to calling him on anything, but I could tell that he wasn't surprised. He turned and looked right at me. "It's hard to figure, ain't it," he said. He put his foot back up on the fence.

"He didn't mean nothing by it," I said.

"We talked to doctors, Tate. Experts." Mr. O'Simmons took off his hat and wiped his forehead with his sleeve. "It was done on their advice. They said once something like this gets started . . ." His voice trailed off. He put his hat back on. "I had my own doubts," he began again. "But his mother, it was her decision, it's what she felt was best." He reached over and put his big hand on my shoulder. Then he sighed and shook his head slow. "It's a bad thing all right," he said. The cow with the blind eye struggled up out of the dust and looked at us.

I told him goodbye and started for the Plymouth. Mr. O'Simmons walked a ways with me. Before we got to the car, I said I was just as sorry as hell. He looked at me and said I shouldn't take it so bad. "You realize," he said, "that Vern'll be okay." He was sure of that, I know. And I know he did feel awful bad about everything. He smiled, then, and shook my hand. His grip felt strong and sure. He was the nicest man I ever knew.

GARY SOTO

Gary Soto was born in 1952 in
Fresno, California, and teaches at
the University of California at
Berkeley. He is the author of *The
Tale of Sunlight*, *Where Sparrows
Work Hard*, *Black Hair*, and other
books of poems, and in 1985 he re-
ceived the American Book Award
for his collection of prose reminis-
cences, *Living Up the Street*.

HEAVEN

Scott and I bent
To the radio, legs
Twitching to The Stones,
Faces wet, arms rising
And falling as if
Trying to get out
Or crawl the air,
Thick with our toweled
Smells.

It's 1964,
And our locked room
And its shaft of dust,
Turning, is all
There is—though momma
Says there's the car
To wash, the weeds,
The grass and garbage
Tilting on the backsteps.
"Yeh, Yeh," we scream
Behind the closed door,
And boost the radio
To "10" and begin
Bouncing on the bed,
Singing, making up
Words about this girl,
That car, tears,
Lipstick, handjives
In alleys—bouncing
Hard, legs split, arms
Open for the Lord,
Until Scott can't stand
It and crashes through
The screened window,
Tumbling into a bush,
His shoulders locked
Between branches,
His forehead scratched
But still singing,
"Baby, baby, O baby."

WILLIAM STAFFORD

William Stafford was born in
Hutchinson, Kansas, in 1914. Dur-
ing World War II he served four
years in labor camps for conscien-
tious objection, an experience re-
corded in his memoir *Down in My
Heart*. His numerous books of po-
etry include *Traveling through the
Dark*, which received the National
Book Award, *Stories That Could
Be True: New and Collected Poems*
and *An Oregon Message*. He lives
in Portland, Oregon.

THE EARTH

When the earth doesn't shake, when the sky
is still, we feel something under the earth:
a shock of steadiness. When the storm is gone,
when the air passes, we feel our own
shudder—the terror of having such a great
friend, undeserved. Sometimes we wake
in the night: the millions better than we

who had to crawl away! We borrow their
breath, and the breath of the numberless
who never were born.

We know the motions of this great friend,
all resolved into one move, our stillness.
Why is no one on the hills where they
graze, the sun and the stars, no one
clamoring north, running as we would
run to belong to the earth? We come, we
celebrate with our breath, we join on the curve
of our street, never lost, the surge of the land
all around us that always is ours,
the beginning of the world and the end.

THE COLOR THAT REALLY IS

The color that really is comes over a desert
after the sun goes down: blue, lavender,
purple. . . . What if you saw all this in the day?
And the sun itself, those rays our eyes jump through
on their way to light, what swords come out of that globe
and slice—life, death, disguise—through space!

Once I was going along and met in Reno
by a table a woman with a terrible face: I saw it
under a lamp that revealed what a desert was
if you lived there the way it is. She had found
what was left in her life after the sun went down.

Since then I pause every day to bow my head
and know, as well as I can, the light, and behind
that light the other glow that waits to shine
for those who survive past noon and by luck are saved
for a while from those rays that could find anyone any time.

BY A RIVER IN THE OSAGE COUNTRY

They called it "Neosho," meaning
"a river made muddy by buffalo."
You don't need many words if you
already know what you're talking about,
and they did. But later there was
nothing they knew that made any difference.

I am thinking of those people—say one
of them looks at you; for an instant you see
a soul like your own, and you are both
lost: what the spirit has given
you to do is unworthy: two kinds of
dirt, you look at each other.

But still, I have waded that river
and looked into the eyes of buffalo
that were standing and gazing far:
no soul I have met knew the source
that well, or where the Neosho
went when it was clear.

MAURA STANTON

Maura Stanton was born in Evan-
ston, Illinois, in 1946 and grew up
in Peoria and Minneapolis. She
has published three collections of
poetry, most recently *Tales of the
Supernatural;* a novel, *Molly
Companion;* and a story collection,
The Country I Come From. She
teaches at Indiana University.

GOOD PEOPLE

The sight of all these people in the street
Heading a dozen directions, in puffy coats,
Icelandic hats, in boots or rubber shoes,
All walking stiffly on the melting ice,
Necks bent against the wind, makes me giddy.
If we could hear each other think, the noise
Would shatter glass, break the best hearts.
A businessman in a camel overcoat
Passes a red-haired girl with a yellow scarf,
And neither will ever see each other again

Or see me standing outside the florist's.
I'm buying flowers for my mother, who lies
In the hospital with a blood clot in her vein,
Almost recovered. I saw her yesterday
And through the doors of other rooms I glimpsed
Face after face I didn't recognize,
Twisting on wet pillows, or watching TV.
How accidental my existence seemed—
I might have sat beside some other bed,
I might have loved that man in blue pajamas

Or kissed the silent child in the metal crib
Receiving a transfusion, as I did once,
Thirty years ago to save my life.
Then a car honks. A woman jostles me.
I stare in wonder down the crowded street.
I could be a part of one of these strangers
Breathing hard in the cold, Kentucky air,
That tall man with gnarled, shaky hands
Or that heavy woman, or part of someone dead
Who thought that life was choice, not accident.

OZ

The barometer dropped. The light dimmed to a funny yellow. Massive clouds shifted and reshifted above the city. Everyone knew it meant tornados.

It was after supper. I sat on the back step, my elbows propped on my knees. For a while the heavy trees did not move. Every leaf appeared to be weighted by the atmosphere. The birds sounded shrill, and the two cardinals who lived in the yard kept flying back and forth between the gutter and the neighbor's elm. The woodpecker, who so irritated my father, landed on the TV aerial, pecked at the metal pole, and sent a moaning vibration through the house.

My mother appeared at the screen door. "Do you want some coffee?"

"No thanks," I said.

My mother came out onto the steps with her blue mug. I made room for her to sit down.

"Where is everybody?"

"The girls are sewing in the basement. The others are upstairs playing a game. I don't know where Pat disappeared to."

"I saw him go down the alley with his basketball," I said. I glanced covertly at my mother, who had not smiled for three days, ever since my brother Joe had flown off to basic training in Louisiana. He had been drafted. His birthday had been the third date drawn on the television lottery, and everyone knew that he was destined for Vietnam. It made me feel strange inside when I considered that Joe was a year younger than I was.

"I called Danny at work," my mother said. "We're out of sugar."

"I hope he gets home before it pours. Did he ride his bike?"

My mother nodded. "I closed all the windows."

"I hate this kind of weather," I said. "It makes knots in my stomach."

My mother sipped her coffee, looking up at the sky. A breeze had sprung up, lifting a strand of her dark brown hair, which had once been as light as mine. That was before her first pregnancy, I knew. I had marveled at the old photographs.

"Did Dad call?"

She nodded. "He's in Rapid City. He'll be back Friday."

Suddenly the siren blared from the schoolyard three blocks away. We both jumped.

"They've sighted one." My mother stood up to scan the moving sky. "We'd better all get to the basement."

"I'll go get Pat," I said.

I ran down the backyard sidewalk. The wind took me by surprise in the alley. The trees heaved above me, and dark green leaves spun through the air. Neighbors were hurriedly folding up their lawn furniture.

"Pat!" I shouted. My voice seemed to stream back over my shoulder.

I spotted him at the end of the alley, dribbling his basketball as he walked home. Big drops of rain began to fall. I ran back to the house and stood under the awning outside the door. Pat continued to move slowly, still dribbling his basketball which grew increasingly hard for him to control in the wind.

"Hurry!" I shouted. "What's the matter with you?" I looked up at the roiling, black sky, then down at the peonies, whose heavy, pink heads had been blown almost flat.

The basketball rolled out of Pat's reach, and he had to chase it. The rain plastered his hair to his scalp. When I saw that he had finally reached the yard, I darted inside and ran down the basement stairs. I could hear the shrill, excited voice of the disc jockey on the top forty station that my sisters liked to listen to while they sewed. I went into the big room that was paneled halfway up with knotty pine. It was part playroom, part storeroom, and recently my father had moved down his desk and some of his books.

"They've sighted two tornados," my mother said. "Out near Lake Minnetonka. One of them touched down."

I sat on the old, flowered couch next to my mother. The little kids, who had brought down a Chinese checkers game, had scattered the marbles across the floor and were chasing each other around and around the ping-pong table. One of my sisters was hemming a jumper in the corner. Another had spread out a paper dress pattern on one end of the ping-pong table and was cutting some brown corduroy with pinking shears.

One of the little kids, Sonia, started to sing. "London Bridge is falling down, falling down!" she shouted at the top of her voice. She ran faster and faster, passing her brother.

"Hush!" I said. "We're listening to the radio. This is important."

Sonia sang to herself. Her lips moved as she kept running. Finally she collapsed in a heap by the desk. The radio began to play an announcement from the National Weather Service, explaining where to take shelter.

"Are we in the right part of the basement?" my little brother asked. He hoisted himself up on the bar, where the Christmas ornaments were stored. "Which way is north?"

"This is the right part," I said.

I could hear hail beating at the windows. I looked at the distracted face of my mother and wondered if she was worrying about tornados or thinking about Joe in the army.

"Where's Pat?" my mother asked in a moment. "Didn't he come in?"

"He must be upstairs," I said. "I'll go see."

I ran up the basement stairs before my mother could get up. The kitchen was dark but lit by flashes of lightning. Pat was standing on the back steps, under the awning.

"Are you crazy?" I said. "They spotted some tornados. Get downstairs before you worry Mother sick."

Pat shook his head. "I'm teaching myself not to be afraid," he said. "Just in case."

"In case what?"

He shrugged.

"Please don't talk about enlisting anymore," I said. "You're only sixteen. Mother is upset enough as it is about Joe."

Pat stared out at the rain, saying nothing.

I returned to the basement. "He's just at the top of the stairs," I said, to reassure my mother. "It's raining pretty hard." I sat down on the floor next to Sonia.

The disc jockey, whose voice was almost hysterical, began announcing more tornado sightings. There were unconfirmed rumors of a destroyed trailer court in North Minneapolis. Someone had called to report a tornado in St. Louis Park.

"Should we go to the work room?" asked one of my sisters. "Aren't you supposed to stand against an inner wall, or under a door frame?"

"I'll go," said Sonia. She took my hand. Her skin felt clammy.

"That's only if you don't have a basement," I said. "We're all right here."

The lights flickered. Pat came down the stairs at last. There were water drops on his face. "Danny just called," he said. "He's going to stay at the store until this is over."

"Good," my mother said. "I hoped he'd have sense enough."

Pat flung himself into our father's desk chair. "What's worse," he said to Mother, "tornados or buzz bombs?"

She glanced at him speculatively. She had been an army nurse in London during World War II. "As long as you heard the buzz bomb coming, you felt safe," she said. "When you couldn't hear it, that meant it was about to fall."

"Did one ever fall near you?"

"All around me. But the hospital was never hit, thank God."

"Were you afraid?" Pat asked, his eyes lowered.

"I got used to being afraid, I guess."

"But you weren't afraid in France, were you?" I asked. "At the chateau?"

"That was towards the end of the war."

"Tell us about it again," one of my sisters asked as she knotted her thread.

We had all seen pictures of the chateau with its mansard roof, turrets, gatehouse and formal gardens. I loved the picture of my mother standing in front of a lake on which three swans floated. There was another picture of my mother and her friend, Lucy, in their winter uniforms at the top of a long avenue of snowcovered topiary trees.

"It was huge," my mother said. "When our unit was first stationed there, we slept in bedrooms with enormous gilt ceilings and French windows opening onto balconies. Later, after the patients arrived, we nurses moved up to the old servants' quarters, but those rooms were large, too. It was funny," she said, half closing her eyes, her voice husky as she tried to remember. "We got water from a big canvas Lister bag which was kept at the top of the grand staircase. The Germans were supposed to have poisoned the well before they retreated."

"Was the staircase marble?" I asked.

My mother nodded.

"Did you get to know any of the patients?" asked Pat.

"Some of them. There were a couple of boys from New Jersey who used to kid me about my Southern accent. Then there was a little skinny fellow who'd been shot in the chest but was almost recovered. He did card tricks for us. We called him Ginger because he had red hair. And later on I got to know a boy named Glenn from Morehead, Kentucky—not too far from where I grew up. We used to talk about home. He was in love—" she stopped, biting her lip.

"With you?" I asked awkwardly. Everyone was looking at her. Only Pat had swiveled the desk chair to face a bookcase and seemed to be reading the titles of the books. Sheets of water covered the basement windows. I imagined that I was in a boat.

"Not with me. With my friend from Boston, Lucy Baxter."

"Did she love him?" I blurted out. Then I felt embarrassed, and coughed to cover myself.

"She was wild about him." My mother took a deep breath, and I knew she was about to tell a story that she had never told us before. "She used to wheel Glenn down to the nurses' lounge when nobody was using it, and play records for him. We had an old wind-up Victrola, and the Red Cross had given us a lot of old records. Lucy and I used to dance together."

"Together?" asked one of my sisters, raising her eyebrows.

Mother laughed. "All the nurses danced with each other."

"What kind of dances?" I leaned forward.

"Oh, fox trots and tangos. But mostly waltzes. Our favorite records were *Begin the Beguine* and part of something by Tchaikovsky called *Serenade for Strings*. That was Lucy's favorite. But she could play the piano, too. I remember one night—it was past midnight—when I'd left my book in the lounge. I went downstairs in my bathrobe and when I got to the door, I heard her playing something that she called a barcarole. The door was partly open. Glenn had been wheeled up beside her at the grand piano, and she kept looking at him as she played. Her face was radiant. I was about to turn around and go back to bed when she heard me. 'Frances,' she called. 'Come here a minute.' I went in. She ran up and hugged me. 'Glenn and I are going to be married!' I congratulated both of them. They kept smiling and holding hands. I wanted to leave them alone, but Lucy insisted on playing the Tchaikovsky record. Glenn wasn't supposed to stand yet, so she made me dance with her all around the room. She was still in uniform, but I was in my long, maroon bathrobe. Glenn laughed and laughed. Lucy had a bottle of champagne in her room, and she ran up to fetch it. Glenn talked on and on about how he and Lucy would show up at his mother's door in Morehead and eat biscuits and chicken. Then Lucy was going to take him for a ride in a swan boat in Boston and buy him a lobster. Lucy came back with the champagne. We toasted. We vowed we'd all be friends forever."

"And did they get married?" I asked.

Mother frowned. She pushed a lock of hair back from her forehead. "Glenn recovered. He recovered too quickly. He was sent back to the front and died in one of the last battles of the war."

"How awful!" I swallowed. "It sounds like a movie."

Mother looked at me sharply. She seemed about to say something, but she only shook her head. I flushed, and realized that I had misunderstood her story.

"What did Lucy do?" I asked after a pause.

"We had both been transferred to other hospitals by then. I wrote to her from Paris when I heard about Glenn, but she never replied. I wrote to her in Boston, too."

"You never heard from her again?"

"Never. That was so many years ago. We were so close. We used to go for long walks together on our days off. We told each other everything." My mother's voice shook. "And then, it was as if she were dead. Blown away. As if I only dreamed her."

A loud clap of thunder made me gasp. The lights flickered again.

"I think there's a flashlight in the middle drawer of the desk," my mother said, and I was relieved at the firmness that had come back into her tone. "We'd better keep it ready."

Pat fumbled in the drawer.

My little brother began swinging his legs and kicking his heels against the bar. "I wish we had a TV down here," he said. "Who wants to play Crazy Eights?"

Nobody answered him, for the lights went out suddenly. Sonia gave a strangled scream. Pat, who had found the flashlight, turned it on and swung the beam around the basement. It was hardly necessary, for lightning flared almost continuously at the windows. From across the room I watched my mother, whose face kept flashing into view. I thought about Lucy Baxter. She and my mother had gone to Paris on a pass once and had eaten army rations while they rode around in a horse-drawn carriage. They had both taken French lessons from a charwoman in wooden clogs who worked at the chateau, and later they discovered that she spoke some kind of dialect. Nobody could understand a word of their French. My mother had always spoken of Lucy in great detail and with deep affection. And now here was the ending of the story, which my mother had always known, which changed and darkened all the scenes before, and was still capable, after all these years, of disturbing the even pitch of my mother's voice. She had always spared us this ending.

"I think they just said Lake Harriet!" one of my sisters cried nervously as a clap of thunder drowned out the radio. "Someone's sighted a tornado over Lake Harriet!"

"That's only two miles from here," my mother said.

In the silence that followed the thunder, we all listened to a report from a mobile news unit which had reached the trailer court in North Minneapolis. We heard descriptions of uprooted trees and twisted metal. Roofs had been ripped off some trailers, and others were overturned. The reporter began to interview a sobbing woman who could not find her husband.

"I'm afraid," Sonia said. She moved closer to me.

"What a horrible night," one of my sisters said in a tight voice.

"Get further back from the window," Mother said to Pat. "I hope Danny's all right."

"The store has a basement," Pat said. He slid his chair to the center of the room.

"Oh, no," Sonia groaned. "The cat! Where's Fluffy?"

"She'll be fine," I said. "She can see in the dark."

"She's upstairs." Sonia's voice trembled and rose. "She was on my bed. She'll be blown away!"

"No, she won't."

"I've got to get her." Sonia struggled to her feet. "We can't let her die up there."

"Hush, Sonia," mother said. "Cats can take care of themselves."

"Not Fluffy."

"I'll get her," I said. "Go sit on the couch, Sonia. Stop crying, I'll get her."

Before Mother could stop me, I ran up the basement stairs. The lightning flared rapidly and garishly at the kitchen windows. I felt as if I had stepped out onto the deck of a ship. Thunder rumbled continuously. The rain fell in such torrents that each time the lightning flashed, it looked like grey waves breaking against the house.

I ran through the dining room, into the hallway and up the stairs. My brothers slept in the big room upstairs, but there was no sign of the cat on their empty, unmade beds. The spread was smooth and neat on Joe's bed in the corner, and I remembered with a little shock that he was gone. I lifted the edge of the spread and looked underneath the bed, then ran into the girls' room. It still smelled of the bottle of Lily of the Valley cologne that one of my sisters had spilled last month. Tennis shoes and loafers were scattered across the floor, and blouses and shorts hung from doorknobs and bedposts. In a bright flash of lightning, I saw a hairbrush on the dresser, with a few strands of hair caught in the bristles, as if some-one had just been brushing her hair a moment ago.

I shivered. Suddenly I felt lonely and far away from everyone.

"Here kitty, kitty, kitty," I called. I felt the rumpled covers on the top bunk and looked in the closet.

A huge clap of thunder made me jump. I ran downstairs, my heart pounding. I stood at the door of my parents' bedroom, and called the cat again. Then I got down on my hands and knees, and lifted the heavy, fringed chenille spread. I touched something cold which made me draw back my hand in fright. Then I realized that it was my father's leather slipper.

The wind had begun to blow fiercely. It howled along the side of the house, and I could hear it whipping the branches of the mock orange against a window in my own room. I ran down the hall. The lightning flashed. I saw the clipboard on which I was writing a story called "The Robber Bridegroom" still waiting on my bed, and I remembered the last sentence I had written before I had been called to set the table for supper: "The old woman felt the arteries straining in her chest."

I put my hand against my own chest. "Kitty, kitty," I called, but my voice was choked somewhere in the back of my throat. I had never heard wind this loud before, and I remembered the descriptions I had read of approaching tornados: they always sounded like speeding trains.

The wind sounded like that. I heard a large branch crack and fall.

"Oh, my God," I said out loud. "Oh, my God!"

It seemed an immense distance back to the basement. I would have to pass too many windows. I got down on my hands and knees and crawled to the bathroom. I heard a sound in the tub, and when I pushed back the shower curtain, I discovered the cat.

I got into the tub, picked up the cat who was cowering in terror, and stood with my back pressed against the tile wall. The cat struggled, but I kept her against my shoulder until she quieted. During a flash of lightning I saw myself in the mirror across from the tub, my mouth open, my hair fallen around my face. The roar of the wind was so deafening that it seemed as if the house had already been picked up off its foundations, and was spinning through space.

The wind reached a whistling pitch, and then I heard a sharp, explosive crack. Somewhere in the house glass fell and shattered. I closed my eyes in terror. I held the cat so tightly that she cried and jumped out of my arms.

After a while, I grew conscious of the sound of the rain. The wind had died down a little. I stepped cautiously out of the tub and went down the hall. I stopped in amazement at the door of the dining room. The windows had been blown out and rain was being swept in gusts across the room. The faraway lightning kept the sky continuously lit. Broken glass gleamed on the dining room table and on the carpet.

I put my hand on the back of a chair to steady myself. The dining room and beyond the living room, where the windows were also blown out, was strewn with leaves and flowers. Twigs and small branches covered the floor. Mock orange blossoms had been ripped off the bushes outside, and white petals were mixed in with shards of glass. A long runner from a climbing rose bush, with a cluster of red roses still growing along it, hung from the buffet.

I ran through the living room, stumbling over elm branches. On the coffee table I saw a dead sparrow which must have been hurled in and knocked senseless against the wall. I hurried past it. The windows on the front porch, facing another direction, were still intact. I looked out over my neighborhood. The street was impassable. Trees and branches had fallen across it in both directions. Shingles had been lifted from the roof of the house across the street. A big poplar had fallen across a parked car in a driveway, crushing the hood.

I felt dizzy, as if I had been spinning and spinning. This must be like the future, I thought. Your past did not blow away. It was you who blew away. You looked out the window and everything was different.

I spun around. The living room smelled of mud and greenery. I ran breathlessly toward the basement, telling myself that my family was all down there, all of them, every one.

GERALD STERN

Born in Pittsburgh in 1925, Gerald
Stern is the author of *Lucky Life*,
which won the Lamont Prize, *The
Red Coal*, which received the Mel-
ville Cane Award, *Paradise Poems*,
Selected Poems, and other books of
poetry. He teaches at the Univer-
sity of Iowa.

SOULS FROM EMERSON

for Myrna Smith

This is a kind of sunflower,
only smaller and less demanding,
on a side street in Phillipsburg
faced away from the truck fumes and the air horns.

It replaces the dead beehives and tobacco leaves,
bowed over from exhaustion,
and crawls over the side of the bird house and the wire fence
like a morning glory or daisy.

427

I come back here twice,
once to climb the hill
and once to touch the old head
and break a leaf off at the stem.

And I come back to see if I can find
the whitewashed wall
and hear the wild dog again
and see his fenced-in garden, the souls outside

going up and down like souls from Emerson,
trying to find a home on Marshall Street
beside the clothes pins and the oil drum,
near the slush and the pink mimosa—

left on the Parkway just before Jacob's Auto Parts,
across from the green island separating
the cars rushing west to Cleveland and Ypsilanti
and the cars rushing east to Whitehouse and Coney Island.

WEEPING AND WAILING

I love the way my little harp makes trees
leap, how putting the metal between my teeth
makes half the animals in my back yard quiver,
how plucking the sweet tongue makes the stars
live together in love and ecstasy.

I bend my face and cock my head. My eyes
are open wide listening to the sound.
My hand goes up and down like a hummingbird.
My mouth is opening and closing, I am singing
in harmony, I am weeping and wailing.

LEON STOKESBURY

Leon Stokesbury is the author of
Often in Different Landscapes and
The Drifting Away and the editor
of *The Made Thing: An Anthology
of Contemporary Southern Poetry*.
Born in Oklahoma City in 1945, he
lives in Atlanta, where he directs
the creative writing program at
Georgia State University.

LAUDS

Even in Texas there's a rose on the air
for that quick half-hour during summer dawn.
And we, *new meat*, the summer "college boys,"
began our first good look at things
that thirty minutes before time
when the *permanents* came in
to the Texas State Highway Department barn
to sip the liquor of a cup of coffee—
and then go.

Rysinger would not shut up.
No one could shut him up.
Rysinger was our fathers' age,
and every day brought his constant routine,
each morning commencing as a string of jokes
dirtier than the day before. Each day:
if he could gargle forth some image, some
froth,
so strange to the *new meat*
that it could make us turn our eyes away—
then that would make him grin and giggle.
Each day.

But now when I think of Rysinger,
I do not think first of that morning
Plaunty came back from his honeymoon
and Rysinger followed him around asking:
Plaunty?
Why is Plaunty's mouth all puckered up?
What you been eating Plaunty
to cause your mouth to pucker so? Lemons?
Lemons, Plaunty?
And neither do I think of Rysinger's story
of getting two milkshakes down at Dick's Drive-In, nor
of his particularly energetic rendition of The Tale
of Grandpa's French Ticklers, which
brought old Grandma back to life, which
made her go "Whoa!" and then
"Oh!" and then
"Soooooieeeee!"

What I always remember about Rysinger
is the two or three times that summer
along about three or four in the afternoon
when the heat on some country road was killing us,
and the hot asphalt would steam up in our faces,

would billow and speckle our clothes and faces,
and there was nothing but heat,
the world being endless waves of heat—
and I would look over and see Rysinger
trying to hide his red eyes,
making gestures that tried to imply
it was the steam, or the wind,
or the sweat in his eyes,
that made them burn,
there,
by the side of the road.

BARTON SUTTER

Barton Sutter was born in Minne-
apolis in 1949 and raised in small
towns in Minnesota and Iowa. He
is the author of two books of poems,
most recently *Pine Creek Parish
Hall and Other Poems,* which re-
ceived the Bassine Citation from
the Academy of American Poets.

TELLING TIME IN THE MIDDLE OF NOWHERE

Again the sun drops down the sky
into the water beside the moon.

How many days ago
did I drag my canoe up on this rock
and build a fire to eat in the dark?

I go down to the lake with a cup.

JEANIE THOMPSON

The founding editor of *Black War-
rior Review*, Jeanie Thompson is
the author of two books of poems,
Lotus and Psalm and *How to En-
ter the River*. She was born in An-
niston, Alabama, in 1952 and is
currently the assistant director of
the Office of Marketing and Com-
munication in the College of Con
tinuing Studies at the University of
Alabama.

THINKING OF KAY IN GRASMERE

On an afternoon like this
    you taught me afternoon tea
        but I never knew why you poured milk
over the back of a spoon into your cup.
    Something British, a habit I witnessed,
        but never understood.

Kay, it's spring here, green everywhere.
    The fig tree abloom in her gauzy leaves

as if life were all green infusion.
I am afraid of not saying what I mean:
   You are dying;
      I won't see you again.

After school, I boil water, warm the pot,
   exhausted, thinking how today I saw words
      skip and dodge just out of my grasp.
Children's faces, skin taut and clear.
   Tentative, one handed me a poem,
      pressed his small body against mine.

Remember our talks about children?
   The children I'll never know,
      your daughter's you'll never see.
Who are these people? Thoughts we conjure?
   I want to ask hard if they're real,
      or have any meaning, because today I know

you near that place where all
   unborn children are. I could
      imagine mine, blond and fair,
or dark in their secret habits, but what
   use is that? I've done with them, living apart,
      lost in their own world.

Last night I dreamed of England,
   the country where I'd hoped to see you
      delighting in the bright cardinals you love.
Today, my hands gesture as if to touch your face—
   I would pour strong tea in a china cup,
      I would define the exact angle of yellow-

skirted daffodils in sunlight. Pitilessly, the world
   shines on into spring, in New Orleans, where
      one living child dreams the image for *sunrise*.
He picks his words eagerly, breathing them
   in and out, the simple choice
      all that is necessary, friend, for speech.

JOHN UPDIKE

John Updike was born in Shilling-
ton, Pennsylvania, in 1932. His
many books include five collec-
tions of poetry, the most recent of
which are *Tossing and Turning*
and *Facing Nature*, and numerous
novels, including *The Centaur*,
which received the National Book
Award, and *Rabbit Is Rich*, which
earned the Pulitzer Prize, the
American Book Award, and the
National Book Critics Circle
Award.

ALL THE WHILE
(from *Living with a Wife*)

Upstairs to my downstairs
echo to my silence
you walk through my veins shopping
and spin food from my sleep

I hear your small noises
you hide in closets without handles
and surprise me from the cellar
your foot-soles bright black

You slip in and out of beauty
and imply that nothing is wrong
Who sent you?
What is your assignment?

Though years sneak by like children
it stays as unaccountable
as the underpants set to soak
in the bowl
where I would scour my teeth

DAVID WAGONER

Born in Massillon, Ohio, in 1926,
David Wagoner grew up in Whiting, Indiana. He has published fifteen volumes of poetry, including
Through the Forest: New and Selected Poems, and ten novels. The
editor of *Poetry Northwest* and a
chancellor of the Academy of American Poets, he teaches at the University of Washington.

THE SINGING LESSON

You must stand erect but at your ease, a posture
Demanding a compromise
Between your spine and your head, your best face forward,
Your willful hands
Not beckoning or clenching or sweeping upward
But drawn in close:
A man with his arms spread wide is asking for it,
A martyred beggar,
A flightless bird on the nest dreaming of flying.

For your full resonance
You must keep your inspiring and expiring moments
Divided but equal,
Not locked like antagonists from breast to throat,
Choking toward silence.

If you have learned, with labor and luck, the measures
You were meant to complete,
You may find yourself before an audience
Singing into the light,
Transforming the air you breathe—that malleable wreckage,
That graveyard of shouts,
That inexhaustible pool of chatter and whimpers—
Into deathless music.
But remember, with your mouth wide open, eyes shut,
Some men will wonder,
When they look at you without listening, whether
You're singing or dying.
Take care to be heard. But even singing alone,
Singing for nothing,
Singing to empty space in no one's honor,
Keep time: it will tell
When you must give the final end-stopped movement
Your tacit approval.

MICHAEL WATERS

Michael Waters is the author of
*Anniversary of the Air, The Bur-
den Lifters,* and other books of po-
etry. Born in New York in 1949,
he teaches at Salisbury State Uni-
versity in Maryland.

BONWIT TELLER

Who says the light doesn't breathe
or press its thumbprint of snow
upon this rouged cheek
mirrored in the store window?

We stare—
        this reflection and I—
as she brushes her frosted hair
with her fingers, without regard
for little winds that tease the ends.

Above the roofs, the roof of snow
slowly collapses, but never touches
this landscape, so tropical,
where three mannequins,
    almost nude
in the luminous, sand-strewn solitude,
    model bright bikinis—
stars wished above polished knees.

These familiar women also stare
into the fierce and artifical glare
of the yellow, foil sun—
while I pause among them, plump
ghost in a wet, woolen coat,
foolishly brushing my dampening hair.

Couldn't these sisters have prophesied
from their boiling cauldron of sun
what the future stores for flesh?—
how the various lights stress
each withering imperfection?

As a schoolgirl I stopped before this window,
closed my eyes, and rocked upon my flats
until the sidewalk seemed to undulate
and I grew dizzy with despair.
Will the change come? I sighed,
wanting to blossom into the sleek
skins, glossy thighs, impossible waists,
    bracelets and silver fox capes
that pronounced each flake of light.

Even their lashes were lovely, spidering
eyes opened forever in the stunned,
violet gaze of the paralyzed.
Will the change come soon?
Theirs was a perfect, breathless world.
The city could not touch them.

And I?—I stamp my galoshes for warmth,
embarrassed for the woman of snow
embarrassed now among them.
Their world remains, and remains
more eloquent than mine.

I realize the lateness of the hour, realize . . .
the buses will not run on time.

Only the glittering, gypsy taxis
like scarabs along the avenue,
the rows of traffic lights
shuttering—yellow,
        now red, now green—
a universe of diminishing suns,
and the million, heaving snowflakes
    light my skin
as if transforming me
                        Will the change come?
into a speechless mannequin.

MARY JANE WHITE

Mary Jane White was born in 1953
in Charlotte, North Carolina. She
has published two books, *The
Work of the Icon Painter* and *Starry
Sky to Starry Sky*, and has re-
ceived National Endowment for
the Arts fellowships for both her
poetry and her translations of Rus-
sian poetry. She practices law at
her home near Decorah, Iowa.

JANE AUSTEN, PRIVATELY, ON READING

It's encouraging.
It makes one believe
in one's own life
that much of what "passes"
may yet be got
at a calm
and wonderful distance.
My first suitor,
black as he was,

447

appears in this book
in the best light—
blacker than then.
That is the way
I love him.
Sometimes, as I read
I am taken closer—
not often—and
as the image becomes
clear, it becomes
double, like you
in my ordinary myopia
when the moustaches
cross over. *Ah!*
Here you are—
wandered in, my love.
Though this is not
what happens
I would have it so
written, to be able
to read it. This
is fierce. I'm sorry,
this is fierce.

C. K. WILLIAMS

Born in Newark, New Jersey, in
1936, C. K. Williams teaches at
George Mason University. The
most recent of his seven books are
Flesh & Blood, which received the
National Book Critics Circle Award,
and *Poems, 1963–1983*.

STILL LIFE

All we do—how old are we? I must be twelve, she a little older,
    thirteen, fourteen—is hold hands
and wander out behind a barn, past a rusty hay-rake, a half-collapsed old
    Model T,
then down across a barbed-wire gated pasture—early emerald ryegrass,
    sumac in the dip—
to where a brook, high with run-off from a morning storm, broadened
    and spilled over—
turgid, muddy viscous, snagged here and there with shattered branches
    —in a bottom meadow.

I don't know then that the place, a mile from anywhere, or day, brilliant,
    sultry, balmy,
is intensifying everything I feel, but I know now that what made simply
    touching her
almost a consummation was as much the light, the sullen surge of water
    through the grass,
the coils of scent, half hers—the unfamiliar perspiration, talc, something
    else I'll never place—
and half the air's: mown hay somewhere, crushed clover underfoot, the
    brook, the breeze.

I breathe it still, that breeze, and, not knowing how I know for certain
    that it's that,
although it is, I know, exactly that, I drag it in and drive it—rich, delicious,
as biting as wet tin—down, my mind casting up flickers to fit it—another
    field, a hollow—
and now her face, even it, frail and fine, comes momentarily to focus,
    and her hand,
intricate and slim, the surprising firmness of her clasp, how judiciously
    it meshes mine.

All we do—how long does it last? an hour or two, not even one whole
    afternoon:
I'll never see her after that, and, strangely, (strange even now), not mind,
    as though,
in that afternoon the revelations weren't only of the promises of flesh,
    but of resignation—
all we do is trail along beside the stream until it narrows, find the one-
    log bridge
and cross into the forest on the other side: silent footfalls, hills, a crest,
    a lip.

I don't know then how much someday—today—I'll need it all, how
    much want to hold it,
and, not knowing why, not knowing still how time can tempt us so
    emphatically and yet elude us,

not have it, not the way I would, not the way I'd want to have *that* day,
that light,

the motes that would have risen from the stack of straw we leaned on for
a moment,

the tempered warmth of air which so precisely seemed the coefficient of
my fearful ardor,

not, after all, even the objective place, those shifting paths I can't really
follow now

but only can compile from how many other ambles into other woods,
other stoppings in a glade—

(for a while we were lost; we were frightened; night was just beyond the
hills; we circled back)—

even, too, her gaze, so darkly penetrating, then lifting idly past, is so
much imagination,

a portion of that figured veil we cast against oblivion, then try, with little
hope, to tear away.

MILLER WILLIAMS

Miller Williams was born in Hoxie,
Arkansas, in 1930. His many books
include *Distractions, The Boys
on Their Bony Mules, Imperfect
Love, Living on the Surface*, and
Sonnets of Giuseppe Belli, transla-
tions from the Romanesco. The
recipient of the Prix de Rome and
other awards, he has lived and
taught in Chile, Mexico, and Italy
and currently teaches at the Uni-
versity of Arkansas and directs the
University of Arkansas Press.

FOR VICTOR JARA

*Mutilated and Murdered
The Soccer Stadium
Santiago, Chile*

This is to say we remember. Not that remembering saves us.
Not that remembering brings anything usable back.

This is to say that we never have understood how to say this.
Out of our long unbelief what do we say to belief?

Nobody wants you to be there asking the question you ask us.
There had been others before, people who stayed to the end:

Utah and Boston and Memphis, Newgate, Geneva, Morelos—
Changing the sound of those names, they have embarrassed us, too.

What shall we do with the stillness, do with the hate and the pity?
What shall we do with the love? What shall we do with the grief?

Such are the things that we think of, far from the thought that you hung
    there,
Silver inside of our heads, golden inside of our heads:

Would we have stayed to an end or would we have folded our faces?
Awful and awful. Good friend. You have embarrassed our hearts.

DAVID WOJAHN

David Wojahn, born in St. Paul,
Minnesota, in 1953, is the author
of *Icehouse Lights*, which won the
Yale Younger Poets Prize and the
William Carlos Williams Award,
Glassworks, and *Mystery Train*.
He teaches at Indiana University
and in the M.F.A. program at Ver-
mont College, and he edits poetry
for *Crazyhorse*.

PARTICULAR WORDS

for Richard Hugo

Only once we spoke, this long distance about
the hyperbolic foreword to a book.
You wrote of someone almost me, but better.
Today, your death's a year and continent
away. Rain in torrents lathers the Cape,
the beaches shining out from mist until
you'd think we stood on Puget gazing West,

guessing the sunset's color. Now you're the past,
that's all. Now you're what we leave behind,

the way the sea leaves indiscriminate stones.
A fireplace and stairway waver above
the charred foundation of a lighthouse
and Coast Guard barracks. The stairway creaks
and feels drunk. On top you can bellow

your name to the salt spray until it echoes
back, or until your lungs get tired
and you stroll off to some house a mile
up the beach, a big man fumbling in
his raincoat for the key. So let's say
you come in drenched. Let's say I'm here
to meet you, a fifth of Jack, the fire going.

So now, at last, there's time for talk.
Naturally, there's some silence at first,
discomfort of strangers who've only met
in poems. But also my story of an honest
Minnesota ghost town called Hugo,
where I drove when someone phoned with the news.
Embarrassing, the photos I took:

the water tower flounders above lapsed
meadows with your name. The Gold Medal
grain mill glowers over a few sick elms.
It's wind, not drunks, that weaves the streets,
having traveled all night from Billings
and Bozeman, like distant cousins you'd rather
avoid. But you know the story: all towns

die the same, but come back different as lies
we tell to make each town more whole when lost.
Particular words get repeated for
effect: *Humiliation, Don't Come Back,*
Remission, Death. They write them in
to each town charter, honest lies we tell,
to soothe us, Dick, to give these sorrows form.

SONG OF THE BURNING

—Jim Morrison

I wanted the heart to scream.
I wanted the sound of chalk on a blackboard,
shrillness and pain
still echoing from childhood, another way

to talk around love.
I wanted it steady, pulsing of light
from a distant star, the Bo Diddley *thunk*
of drum and bass, the organ
crescendoing. *Who do you love? Who
do you love?* I wanted song without story,
only the cruelest metaphor. But who
finally gives a shit?
The body runs down.
Love turns to habit, and some nights you wail
or meth yourself past forgetting.
This is why you think some nights
you're Satan's poor facsimile, and why

you'll wake up dead one morning.
Talk around love: I mean that,
until love's all spell and incantation,
a name like GLORIA, and you sound
each letter out like need,
or show your cock to half the wasted
little punks of Miami, the strobes
all over you like hands.
In my dream, someone makes a movie

beginning with my song: first you see a jungle
resurrect to yellow flame, rise up
like outstretched arms. On
and on it burns until you'd think
the leaves themselves were howling.
This is the end, I'm singing,

beautiful friend, my only friend,
the flames want to wrap us
all in their hands, and that's
when I know what love is,
perfectly. Then maybe the band
gets projected on the screen, playing tighter
than they've ever been, and we've all
got those bleeding
flaming hearts of Mexican Christs.
We all understand where we're going.
And you all know, you poor dumb fuckers,

what you have to do to follow me.
It's the fifth of July, 1971, and I wake
in the best *pension* in Paris. 4:00 A.M.
I start the day with speedball,
spoon a puddle of flame. Seven floors
below my window, a dwarf on crutches sells
the first edition of *Le Figaro*.

A couple walks arm in arm toward him,
a black guy, Algerian maybe,
the girl with straight blonde hair.
The black guy strokes
her ass as she buys the paper.
She points at something
in the air above them, as all the neon lights
in the city flicker off.

At hours like this you understand
there were songs you were never
able to write, Song Of The Burning,
Song Of Revelation, Song
That Is Past Forgetting.
At hours like this you rise
to address the ages, history,
the universe. You poor dumb bastards,

I swear you'll never hear my voice again.

SUSAN WOOD

Susan Wood is the author of *Ba-
zaar*. The recipient of Bread Loaf
and National Endowment for the
Arts fellowships, she was born in
Commerce, Texas, in 1946 and
currently teaches at Rice
University.

WITNESS

It would be summer, Saturday—the only day
a man can relax, my father said—
and in less than ten minutes
everybody's shirt would be stuck to the upholstery.
Wedged between grown-ups in the Buick, bored,
I tested my father's temper or watched
for Burma Shave signs. They never changed.
It seemed to me then that nothing would.
Not the bleached-blond haze of summer nor the car
turning off the highway, dust spun from its wheels
slurring everything behind us. Not slaps,
nor looks exchanged between parents,
nor an only child, too fat, who talked too much
and wanted too soon to be grown.

459

Freed from the backseat, I followed the men
down to the green pond, bream-stocked and scummed
with growth, and begged to go in the boat.
They teased they would pay me a penny
each minute I was quiet and could I keep my word?
My father threw out his line, waited
for its tug and pull. A snake sunned itself
at the pond's edge. Water moccasin, he said,
soft and quiet as an Indian's shoe.
He looked at us, each one, and smiled
as if surprised to be there and who he was.
This is some life, he said. Some life.
We caught fish after fish while the light lasted,
until it seeped into the pond like ink
spilled on a rug and the women called,
Time to come in, come in now.

Supper over, summer dark, they sat at the table
laughing at somebody's joke,
the women hoarse with cigarettes, Doc's giggle.
Brad, handsome as Ernest Hemingway, bellowed
when he laughed. My father wiped his eyes.
Half my life, or more, has disappeared like theirs.
I think I know now that everything changes
and nothing does, that someone is left
who remembers and then there is no one.

I know as little as the hot breath of a summer night
without a breeze when it is late and a child hopes
no one will notice and send her off to bed.
Ours were the only lights for miles.
We are here, *this place*, I thought, and no one
can see us. This is a question asked in a book:
If a tree falls in a forest and no one hears . . .
And if someone had happened by that night,
what would they have seen?
A child lifted in her father's arms,
slowly giving in to sleep.

CHARLES WRIGHT

Charles Wright was born in 1935
in Pickwick Dam, Tennessee, and
grew up in Tennessee and North
Carolina. Among his books are
*Country Music: Selected Early
Poems,* for which he received the
American Book Award, *The Other
Side of the River,* and *Zone Jour-
nals.* He teaches at the University
of Virginia.

GRACE

Its hair is a fine weed,
Matted, where something has lain,
Or fallen repeatedly:

Its arms are rivers that sink
Suddenly under the earth,
Elbow and wristbone: cold sleeve:

Its face is a long soliloquy,
A language of numerals,
Impossible to erase.

CHILDHOOD'S BODY

This is a rope of stars tied to my wrist.
This is a train, pulling the feckless palmprints of the dead.

It isn't enough to sing and begin again.
It isn't enough to dissemble the alphabet

And listen for
The one heartbeat I listen for,
                    as it comes as it goes,
Keeping the world alive,

My poems in a language now
                 I finally understand,
Little tablets of salt rubbed smooth by the wind.

It isn't enough to transform the curlicues.

(Deep water is what the albums will manifest,
                 the light jagged then not jagged,
The moon dragging her hooks
Through the lakes and the river beds,
              grappling for what comes next.)

This is a lip of snow and a lip of blood.

JAMES WRIGHT

James Wright was born in Martin's
Ferry, Ohio, in 1927. His books
include *The Green Wall*, which
won the Yale Younger Poets Prize,
Collected Poems, which won the
Pulitzer Prize, *To a Blossoming
Pear Tree*, *This Journey*, and *Col-
lected Prose*. He died in 1980.

A FINCH SITTING OUT
A WINDSTORM

Solemnly irritated by the turn
The cold air steals,
He puffs out his most fragile feathers,
His breast down,
And refuses to move.
If I were he,
I would not clamp my claws so stubbornly around
The skinny branch.
I would not keep my tiny glitter
Fixed over my beak, or return

The glare of the wind.
Too many Maytime snowfalls have taught me
The wisdom of hopelessness.

But the damned fool
Squats there as if he owned
The earth, bought and paid for.
Oh, I could advise him plenty
About his wings. Give up, drift,
Get out.

But his face is as battered
As Carmen Basilio's.
He never listens
To me.

CAPRICE

Whenever I get tired
Of human faces,
I look for trees.
I know there must be something
Wrong, either with me or Italy,
The south of the angels.
Nevertheless, I get away
Among good trees, there are
So many. The trouble is
They keep turning faces toward me
That I recognize:

Just north of Rome
An ilex and an olive tangled
Their roots together and stood one afternoon,
Caught in a ring of judas
And double cherry.
They glared at me, so bitter
With something they knew,
I shivered. They knew
What I knew:
One of those brilliant skeletons
Was going to shed her garlands
One of these days and turn back
Into a girl
Again.

Then we were all going to be
Sorry together.

ON HAVING MY POCKET
PICKED IN ROME

   These hands are desperate for me to stay alive. They do not want to lose me to the crowd. They know the slightest nudge on the wrong bone will cause me to look around and cry aloud. Therefore the hands grow cool and touch me lightly, lightly and accurately as a gypsy moth laying her larvae down in that foregone place where the tree is naked. It is only when the hands are gone, I will step out of this crowd and walk down the street, dimly aware of the dark infant strangers I carry in my body. They spin their nests and live on me in their sleep.

DEAN YOUNG

Born in Columbia, Pennsylvania,
in 1955, Dean Young is the author
of *Design with X*. He teaches at
Loyola University of Chicago and
edits poetry for *Crazyhorse*.

THANK YOU, TEACHERS

My teacher is lovely
prying away skin and fascia;
the abdominal obliques
that bend us all to the side and down
rippling under her
transparent gloves. When we're lost
in the imbroglio of flexors and extensors,
she lays her hand against the cheek
like you might someone you love
but would like to smack some sense into.
We've already learned that by five months
the fetal heart has tied itself into a knot.

Once during something classical coming
just barely from the radio in the corner,
I looked at a trachea slide,
the glassy blue hyaline cartilage,
the small squiggles of elastin,
the pseudostratified columnar epithelium
ciliated to keep throats clear enough to sing.
I don't know a thing about music
but it was good to hear something welling,
almost man-made and pure.

Off and on for three days—rain
and until the cold snap that's behind it
this is the air we'll have, fetid
as breathing through an old damp quilt,
narcotic. Today when I get home,
my wife will gently avoid me
as long as I smell like this.
I'll put my clothes in a plastic garbage sack,
clothes only to be washed with each other
and old running shoes. Soon
the air will sweeten with the smell
of rotting cornstalks that surround
this town. In sweaters musty from a summer
packed away, we'll watch the iridescent necks
of pigeons as they bend and forage,
taking the ground apart, looking for what
they somehow know is there.